MathePathics

Copyright © 2021

All right reserved. MathePathics is protected by copyright. The content of this publication may not be reproduced, stored, nor shared or transmitted by any means such as electronically or mechanically, photocopying, recording, or scanning without the consent of the author. Only the creator of this content has the exclusive right to reproduce the work.

MathePathics is not affiliated with any official organization, and just provides unofficial information to prepare for a variety of tests.

Paperback
ISBN 13: 978-1-954590-01-4
ISBN 10: 1-954590-01-6

Introduction

My good friend whom I have never met; Hello!

Dear students, you are going to make the future of your country. We authored this book to guide you towards more success; Success and achievements which first make you a prominent student and then a great person in society.

What we want to tell you is: Never despair. You should know that nothing is impossible and if you try, you can do anything. In the path of everyone's professional and personal life, there are always people who try to deflect you from the path of success; But if you just stay focused on your goal and try, you will achieve it. You should know that you have the right to show them they are wrong.
It is a failure for your enemies when they see you trying to reach your goals and a greater failure for them is when you succeed.

Every day is like a battle in the battlefield and your enemies throw bricks at you to stop you from going towards your goals; But you should not give up. Keep pushing and trying and make a magnificent palace for yourself by those bricks.
It is problems which make us thrive in life. Rather than problems overcome us, we should overcome them. Problems are like stairs; By climbing one at a time, we get one step closer to success.

Dear students, we appreciate you for choosing us to be your guide in this beautiful journey. We hope you finish this journey successfully and by doing so defeat your enemies and prove them wrong and know that it is our greatest wish and honor if you succeed.

Thank you for the purchase of this educational material. Having taken the initiative to acquire this book shows your desire for improvement and commitment to yourself when learning. You have taken a step further than others and we are very happy to have you here now and to be able to equip you with all the necessary tools for you to succeed in your TSI exam.

Contents

Chapter 1: Fraction and Decimals ---- 1
   Simplifying Fraction ---- 2
   Adding and Subtracting Fractions ---- 3
   Multiplying and Dividing Fractions ---- 6
   Adding Mixed Numbers ---- 7
   Subtract Mixed Numbers ---- 8
   Dividing Mixed Numbers ---- 9
   Rounding Decimals ---- 10
   Adding and Subtracting Decimals ---- 13
   Multiplying and Dividing Decimals ---- 14
   Converting Between Fractions, Decimals and Mixed Numbers ---- 16
   Greatest Common Factor ---- 17
   Least Common Multiple ---- 18
   Answers of Worksheets – Chapter 1 ---- 20

Chapter 2: Real Numbers and Integers ---- 28
   Adding and Subtracting Integers ---- 29
   Multiplying and Dividing Integers ---- 31
   Ordering Integers and Numbers ---- 33
   Mixed Integers Computations ---- 36
   Integers and Absolute Value ---- 38
   Answers of Worksheets – Chapter 2 ---- 40

Chapter 3: Proportions and Ratios ---- 47
   Writing Ratios ---- 48

Simplifying Ratios	49
Create a Proportion	50
Similar Figure	51
Simple Interest	52
Ratio and Rates Word Problem	54
Answers of Worksheets – Chapter 3	56
Chapter 4: Percent	60
Percentage Calculations	61
Converting Between Percent, Fractions, and Decimals	62
Percent Problems	63
Markup, Discount, and Tax	64
Answers of Worksheets – Chapter 4	66
Chapter 5: Algebraic Expressions	69
Expressions and Variables	70
Simplifying Variables and Expressions	70
Simplifying Polynomial Expressions	71
Translate Phrases into an Algebraic Statement	72
The Distributive Property	74
Evaluating one Variables	76
Evaluating Two Variables	77
Combining Like Terms	78
Answers of Worksheets – Chapter 5	79
Chapter 6: Equations	84
One – Step Equations	85
Two – Step Equations	87
Multi – Step Equations	88

Answers of Worksheets – Chapter 6 90

Chapter 7: Inequalities 95
   Graphing Single – Variable inequalities 96
   One – Step Inequalities 97
   Two – Step Inequalities 98
   Multi – Step Inequalities 99
   Answers of Worksheets – Chapter7 101

Chapter 8: Linear Functions 106
   Finding Slope 107
   Graphing Lines Using Slope – Intercept form 109
   Graphing Lines Using Standard Form 114
   Writing Linear Equations 116
   Graphing Linear Inequalities 117
   Finding Midpoint 118
   Finding Distance of Two Points 119
   Answers of Worksheets – Chapter 8 121

Chapter 9: Polynomials 128
   Classifying Polynomials 129
   Writing polynomials in Standard Form 130
   Simplifying Polynomials 131
   Adding and subtracting Polynomials 132
   Multiplying Monomials 135
   Multiplying and Dividing Monomials 136
   Multiplying Binomials 137
   Factoring Trinomials 139
   Operations with Polynomials 140

Answers Worksheets – Chapter 9 -- 142

Chapter 10: Quadratic and System of Equations -------------------------- 150

    Solve a Quadratic Equation -- 151

    Solving Systems of equations by Elimination ------------------------------- 153

    Systems of Equations Word Problems --- 154

    Answers of Worksheets – Chapter 10 -------------------------------------- 156

Chapter 11: Quadratic Functions --- 159

    Graphing Quadratic Functions -- 160

    Solving Quadratic Equations --- 164

    Use the Quadratic Formula and the Discriminate ------------------------ 166

    Solve quadratic Inequalities --- 169

    Answers of Worksheets – Chapter 11 -- 171

Chapter 12: Complex Numbers --- 180

    Adding and Subtracting Complex Numbers --------------------------------- 181

    Multiplying and Dividing Complex Numbers -------------------------------- 182

    Graphing Complex Numbers -- 184

    Rationalizing Imaginary Denominators -------------------------------------- 187

    Answers of Worksheets – Chapter 12 --------------------------------------- 188

Chapter 13: Exponents and Radicals --- 194

    Multiplications Property of Exponents --- 195

    Division Property of Exponents --- 197

    Power of Products and Quotients --- 199

    Zero and Negative Exponents --- 201

    Negative Exponents and Negative Bases --------------------------------- 202

    Writing Scientific Notation -- 203

    Square Roots --- 204

Answers of Worksheets – Chapter 13 — 205

Chapter 14: statistics — 212

Mean, Median, Mode, and Range of the Given Data — 213

Box and whisker — 215

Bar Graph — 217

Stem – And – Leaf Plot — 219

The Pie Graph or Circle Graph — 221

Scatter Plots — 223

Probability Problems — 225

Answers of Worksheets – Chapter 14 — 227

Chapter 15: Geometry — 234

The Pythagorean Theorem — 235

Area of Triangles — 237

Perimeter of Polygons — 238

Area and Circumferences of Circles — 239

Area of Squares, Rectangles, and Parallelograms — 240

Area of Trapezoids — 242

Answers of Worksheets – Chapter 15 — 243

Chapter 16: Solid Figures — 246

Volume of Cubes — 247

Volume of Rectangle Prisms — 248

Surface Area of Cubes — 252

Surface of a Rectangle prisms — 252

Volume of Cylinder — 254

Surface Area of Cylinder — 256

Answers of Worksheets – Chapter 16 — 258

Chapter 17: Logarithms — 263
- Rewriting Logarithms — 264
- Evaluating Logarithms — 266
- Properties of Logarithms — 267
- Natural Logarithms — 268
- Solving Exponential Equations Requiring Logarithms — 269
- Solving Logarithmic Equations — 270
- Answers of Worksheets – Chapter 17 — 271

Chapter 18: Matrices — 275
- Adding and subtracting Matrices — 276
- Matrix Multiplication — 278
- Finding Determinants of a Matrix — 280
- Matrix Equations — 282
- Answers of Worksheets – Chapter 18 — 284

Chapter19: Functions Operations — 289
- Function Notation — 290
- Adding and Subtracting Functions — 291
- Multiplying and Dividing Functions — 293
- Composition of Functions — 295
- Answers of Worksheets – chapter 19 — 296

Chapter 20: Trigonometric Functions — 300
- Trig ratios of General Angles — 301
- Sketch Each Angle in standard Position — 303
- Finding Co-terminal Angles and References Angles — 305
- Writing Each Measure in Radians — 307
- Writing Each Measure in Degrees — 308

Evaluating Each Trigonometric Function --- 309

Missing Sides and Angles of a Right Triangle --- 311

Arc Length and Sector Area --- 313

Answers of Worksheets – Chapter 20 --- 315

Chapter 21: Sequences and Series --- 323

Arithmetic Sequences --- 324

Geometric Sequences --- 326

Comparing Arithmetic and Geometric sequences --- 328

Finite Geometric Series --- 329

Infinite Geometric Series --- 329

Answers of worksheets – Chapter 21 --- 332

***Samples: Review & Check** --- 337

Sample Number One --- 338

Sample Number Two --- 351

Sample Number Three --- 363

Sample Number Four --- 377

Chapter 1: Fraction and Decimals

Simplifying Fraction

Adding and Subtracting Fractions

Multiplying and Dividing Fractions

Adding Mixed Numbers

Subtract Mixed Numbers

Dividing Mixed Numbers

Rounding Decimals

Adding and Subtracting Decimals

Multiplying and Dividing Decimals

Converting Between Fractions, Decimals and Mixed Numbers

Greatest Common Factor

Least Common Multiple

Answers of Worksheets – Chapter 1

Simplifying Fraction

Follow the steps:

1. Find the factors of both the numerator and the denominator

2. Find the common factor which is greatest

3. Divide both the numerator and denominator by the greatest factor

📎 A fraction with no common factor or with one as a numerator is in

1. Reduce each fraction to its lowest term.

1. $\dfrac{2}{4} =$

2. $\dfrac{18}{20} =$

3. $\dfrac{3}{10} =$

4. $\dfrac{5}{15} =$

5. $\dfrac{45}{50} =$

6. $\dfrac{2}{6} =$

7. $\dfrac{12}{28} =$

8. $\dfrac{28}{40} =$

9. $\dfrac{14}{18} =$

10. $\dfrac{30}{35} =$

11. $\dfrac{2}{10} =$

12. $\dfrac{25}{60} =$

13. $\dfrac{4}{32} =$

14. $\dfrac{8}{36} =$

15. $\dfrac{35}{40} =$

16. $\dfrac{9}{6} =$

17. $\dfrac{11}{77} =$

18. $\dfrac{27}{18} =$

19. $\dfrac{12}{24} =$

20. $\dfrac{64}{16} =$

2. Find the equivalent fraction for each of the following.

1. $\dfrac{1}{3} = \dfrac{}{9}$

2. $\dfrac{10}{15} = \dfrac{}{3}$

3. $\dfrac{2}{5} = \dfrac{4}{}$

4. $\dfrac{1}{12} = \dfrac{2}{}$

Adding and Subtracting Fractions

 Follow the steps for Addition:

Addition with like denominators

1. Add the numerators

2. Keep the denominator the same

3. simplify (reduce)

Addition with unlike denominators

1. Find the least common denominator of the fractions (LSD)

2. Add the numerators

3. Keep denominator same

Follow the steps for subtraction.

Subtraction with like denominators

1. Subtract the numerators

2. Keep the denominator the same

3. simplify (reduce)

Subtraction with unlike denominators

1. Find the LCD and make equivalent fractions

2. Subtract the numerators

3. Keep denominators same

4. Simplify

3. All the fractions have the same denominator. Add or subtract them and keep the denominator the same!

1. $\dfrac{7}{5} - \dfrac{3}{5} =$

2. $\dfrac{13}{7} + \dfrac{4}{7} =$

3. $\dfrac{15}{12} - \dfrac{8}{12} =$

4. $\dfrac{10}{15} + \dfrac{5}{15} =$

5. $\dfrac{16}{5} - \dfrac{4}{5} =$

6. $\dfrac{10}{4} + \dfrac{2}{4} =$

7. $\dfrac{15}{3} - \dfrac{9}{3} =$

8. $\dfrac{17}{20} + \dfrac{13}{20} =$

9. $\dfrac{9}{3} - \dfrac{6}{3} =$

10. $\dfrac{1}{45} + \dfrac{4}{45} =$

4. Solve the following fractions and finally simplify all the results:

1. $\dfrac{4}{12} + \dfrac{3}{4} =$

2. $\dfrac{9}{3} + \dfrac{3}{8} =$

3. $\dfrac{3}{6} - \dfrac{4}{10} =$

4. $\dfrac{11}{3} - \dfrac{5}{5} =$

5. Convert the two fractions to fractions with the same denominator, then add them up. If one denominator is a multiple of other, then you only need to convert one of the fractions to the denominator of the other.

1. $\dfrac{2}{5} + \dfrac{1}{7} = \dfrac{}{35} + \dfrac{}{35} = \dfrac{}{35}$

2. $\dfrac{5}{6} - \dfrac{1}{2} = \dfrac{}{6} - \dfrac{}{6} = \dfrac{}{6}$

3. $\dfrac{5}{9} + \dfrac{1}{2} = \dfrac{}{} + \dfrac{}{} = \dfrac{}{}$

4. $\dfrac{8}{9} - \dfrac{3}{4} = \dfrac{}{} - \dfrac{}{} = \dfrac{}{}$

5. $\dfrac{5}{6} + \dfrac{7}{12} = \dfrac{}{} + \dfrac{}{} = \dfrac{}{}$

6. $\dfrac{4}{5} - \dfrac{5}{8} = \dfrac{}{} - \dfrac{}{} = \dfrac{}{}$

7. $\dfrac{3}{4} + \dfrac{7}{10} = \dfrac{\ }{\ } + \dfrac{\ }{\ } = \dfrac{\ }{\ }$

8. $\dfrac{4}{7} + \dfrac{1}{6} = \dfrac{\ }{\ } + \dfrac{\ }{\ } = \dfrac{\ }{\ }$

9. $\dfrac{7}{8} - \dfrac{3}{10} = \dfrac{\ }{\ } - \dfrac{\ }{\ } = \dfrac{\ }{\ }$

10. $\dfrac{5}{4} - \dfrac{3}{8} = \dfrac{\ }{\ } - \dfrac{\ }{\ } = \dfrac{\ }{\ }$

6. Find the missing numbers and then add or subtract the following fractions:

1. $\dfrac{\ }{4} + \dfrac{5}{3} = \dfrac{\ }{12} + \dfrac{\ }{12} = \dfrac{29}{12}$

2. $\dfrac{5}{6} - \dfrac{\ }{5} = \dfrac{\ }{30} - \dfrac{\ }{30} = \dfrac{19}{30}$

3. $\dfrac{\ }{3} + \dfrac{4}{7} = \dfrac{\ }{\ } + \dfrac{\ }{\ } = \dfrac{26}{21}$

4. $\dfrac{\ }{\ } + \dfrac{3}{10} = \dfrac{\ }{\ } + \dfrac{\ }{\ } = \dfrac{42}{40}$

Multiplying and Dividing Fractions

 Follow the steps for multiplying:

1. Multiply numerator

2. Multiply Denominator

3. Simplify

 Follow the steps for dividing:

1. Find the reciprocal of the 2nd number

2. Replace ÷ with ×

2. Multiply across

4. Simplify

7. Multiply the fractions then simplify the result if it is possible and circle the results.

1. $\dfrac{11}{11} \times \dfrac{1}{3} =$ 3. $\dfrac{3}{6} \times \dfrac{2}{10} =$

2. $\dfrac{2}{12} \times \dfrac{3}{6} =$ 4. $\dfrac{8}{10} \times \dfrac{7}{12} =$

8. Divide the fractions, simplify the answer if possible.

1. $\dfrac{3}{6} \div \dfrac{4}{10} =$ 3. $\dfrac{11}{3} \div \dfrac{5}{5} =$

2. $\dfrac{10}{12} \div \dfrac{3}{4} =$ 4. $\dfrac{2}{5} \div \dfrac{4}{12} =$

Adding Mixed Numbers

📚 **Follow the steps for adding mixed numbers with same denominator:**

1. Add the whole numbers

2. Add the numerator

3. Keep the denominator the same

📚 **Follow the steps for adding mixed numbers with different denominator:**

1. Find the LCD and convert the fraction

2. Follow all the steps for adding fractions with the same denominator

1. $5\frac{1}{10} + \frac{1}{10} =$

2. $7\frac{7}{9} + \frac{1}{9} =$

3. $2\frac{6}{11} + \frac{6}{11} =$

4. $6\frac{44}{50} + \frac{35}{50} =$

5. $2\frac{2}{6} + \frac{4}{6} =$

6. $8\frac{2}{4} + \frac{3}{4} =$

10. For each problem below, find the missing factor by computing the inverse equation.

1. $\underline{} + 1\frac{1}{2} = 2\frac{7}{8}$

2. $\underline{} + 8\frac{7}{8} = 13\frac{3}{16}$

Subtract Mixed Numbers

> 📚 **Follow the steps for subtracting mixed numbers with same denominator:**
>
> 1. subtract the whole numbers
>
> 2. Subtract the numerator
>
> 3. Keep the denominator the same
>
> 📚 **Follow the steps for subtracting mixed numbers with different denominator:**
>
> 1. Find the LCD and convert the fraction
>
> 2. Follow all the steps for adding fractions with the same

11. Subtract the following problems.

1. $5\frac{10}{21} - 4\frac{5}{7} =$

3. $9\frac{4}{5} - 3\frac{8}{4} =$

2. $\quad 4\dfrac{7}{27} - 3\dfrac{5}{9} =$ 　　　　　4. $\quad 9\dfrac{8}{20} - 4\dfrac{2}{5} =$

12. For each problem below, find the missing factor by computing the inverse equation.

1. $\quad 4\dfrac{1}{2} - \underline{} = 2\dfrac{7}{8}$ 　　　　　2. $\quad 7\dfrac{5}{8} - \underline{} = 5\dfrac{3}{8}$

Dividing Mixed Numbers

 Follow the steps for dividing mixed numbers:

Rule 1:

1. Convert the mixed number to an improper fraction and change the whole number to a fraction.

2. Take the reciprocal of the divider and change the operation from division to multiplication.

3. Simplify (if possible) by across cancelling

4. Multiply

Rule 2: To divide the fraction by the whole number

1. Place the whole number over 1

2. Convert the mixed number to an improper fraction

3. Get the reciprocal of the second fraction

4. Change the division sign to a multiplication sign

5. Multiply the fractions and reduce

13. Solve each expression and then write the answers as a decimal.

1. $8\dfrac{2}{4} \div 6\dfrac{2}{7} =$
2. $6\dfrac{7}{2} \div 2\dfrac{2}{3} =$
3. $7\dfrac{7}{9} \div 6\dfrac{4}{7} =$
4. $6\dfrac{1}{3} \div 4\dfrac{2}{4} =$
5. $4\dfrac{3}{5} \div 8\dfrac{6}{11} =$
6. $4\dfrac{1}{5} \div 5\dfrac{1}{5} =$
7. $7\dfrac{1}{3} \div 6\dfrac{5}{6} =$
8. $9\dfrac{1}{2} \div 2\dfrac{3}{7} =$
9. $4\dfrac{1}{2} \div 3\dfrac{3}{7} =$
10. $6\dfrac{1}{5} \div 3\dfrac{2}{7} =$

Rounding Decimals

 Follow the steps for rounding decimals:

1. Underline the place being rounded

2. Lok at the number to the right

3. five or higher raise the underlined number

4. Four or lower keep the underlined number same

5. change all the numbers to the right of the underlined number to zero.

14. Round each number to the nearest whole number:

1. 56.89 _____
2. 38.25 _____
3. 50.67 _____
4. 49.49 _____
5. 91.10 _____
6. 98.10 _____
7. 71.12 _____
8. 29.84 _____
9. 63.22 _____
10. 72.32 _____

15. Round each number to the nearest tenth (Decimal places).

1. 55.67 _____
2. 48.20 _____
3. 32.88 _____
4. 10.55 _____
5. 88.5 _____

6. 62.81 _____
7. 40.30 _____
8. 3.30 _____
9. 69.90 _____
10. 92.34 _____

16. Use the number line to answer the questions.

A. 2.26

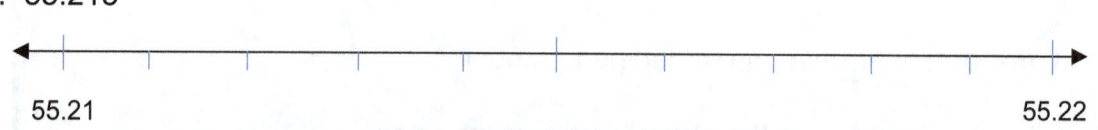

2.2   2.3

    I.   Which decimal is closer to 2.26?   a) 2.3   b) 2.2
    II. Round 2.26 to nearest tenth. _____
    III. Did you round up or round down? _____

B. 55.213

55.21   55.22

    I.   Which decimal is closer to 55.213?   a) 55.21   b) 55.22
    II. Round 55.213 to the nearest hundredth. _____
    III. Did you round up or round down? _____

17. Circle the decimal that round up to 2.

2.54   2.9   1.97   1.6   1.42

2.2   2.76   1.7   1.86   1.5

18. Circle the decimal that round down to 31.12 (Two decimals).

| 31.124 | 29.547 | 31.122 | 30.0567 | 29.214 |
| 31.121 | 30.172 | 30.549 | 31.115 | 31.123 |

19. Round each decimal number to the nearest indicated.

1. 6.552 _____
   Tenth

2. 0.072 _____
   Whole number

3. 6.815 _____
   Hundredth

4. 1.810 _____
   Whole number

5. 6.899 _____
   Tenth

6. 3.410 _____
   Hundredth

7. 6.760 _____
   Whole number

8. 6.626 _____
   Whole number

9. 4.379 _____
   Tenth

10. 5.472 _____
    Whole number

Adding and Subtracting Decimals

 Follow the steps for adding and subtracting decimals:

Adding:

1. Write down the numbers, one under other, with the decimal points lined up

2. Put zeros so the numbers have the same length

3. Then add using column addition, remembering to put the decimal point in the answer

Subtracting:

To subtract, follow the same method: line up the decimals, then subtract.

20. Calculate each sum or differences.

   1. 800.54 – 90.52 =
   2. 94.9 – 41.871 =
   3. 803.309 – 133.36 =
   4. 24.69 – 12.01 =
   5. 67.1 – 1.19 =
   6. 686.4 – 199.61 =
   7. 6.356 +5.8 =
   8. 921.74 + 2.7 =
   9. 343.4 + 5.607 =
   10. 89.88 + 17.5 =
   11. 24.9 + 15.69 =
   12. 46.37 + 21.63 =

21. Calculate the following parts then round the results to Whole number and circle the result.

   1. 22.59
      + 40.19
      _____

   4. 95.58
      - 91.14
      _____

2. 22.33
  + 16.99
  _____

3. 47.33
  + 95.98
  _____

5. 80.74
  - 66.77
  _____

6. 89.52
  - 33.10
  _____

Multiplying and Dividing Decimals

 Follow the steps for multiplying and dividing decimals:

Multiplying:

1. round your numbers and find the product for a reasonable estimate

2. Multiply your numbers without the decimal points

3. Check your estimate. put your comma in a reasonable place

4. Double check the placement of the decimal point

Dividing:

1. Move the decimal to the right (as many times as necessary) to make the divisor a whole number

2. Move the decimal in the dividend the same number of times you moved in the divisor.

3. Place the decimal into the quotient directly above the moved decimal point in the dividend

4. divide

22. Multiply these decimals.

1. 95.98
    x   17
    _____

2. 202.03
    ×   11
    _____

3. 27.332
    x   28
    _____

4. 905.56
    x   29
    _____

5. 30.78
    x   7
    _____

6. 300.52
    -   9
    _____

23. Solve the equations and fill in the blanks with correct numbers.

1. 5.25 ×……. = 52.5
2. 54.1 ×……. = 5410
3. 15.026 × ……. = 150.26
4. 40.04 × ……. = 400.4
5. 0.99 ×…… = 99
6. 7.803 × …… = 78.03
7. 0.1 × …… = 10
8. 0.08 × …… = 8

24. Simplify each following expression.

1. $8 \overline{)5.16}$ =
2. $9 \overline{)63.27}$ =
3. $7 \overline{)63.049}$ =
4. $5 \overline{)4.80}$ =
5. $3 \overline{)1.72}$ =
6. $7 \overline{)3.02}$ =

Converting Between Fractions, Decimals and Mixed Numbers

 Follow the steps for Converting each group

- **Fraction to decimal** →

Divide numerator by denominator

- **Decimal to fraction** →

1. write down the decimal divided by 1

2. Multiply both top and bottom by 10 for every number after the decimal point

3. Simplify or reduce the fraction

- **Fraction to mixed numbers** →

1. Divide the numerator by denominator
2. quotient is the whole number, denominator stays same, numerator is the remain.

- **Mixed number to fraction** →

1. Multiply denominator and whole number

2. Add product to the numerator

3. Put new numerator over the original denominator

- **Decimal to mixed** →

1. Whole number does not change

2. Write decimal over last place value

- **Mixed to decimal** →

Convert the fractional part only then add it to the whole number

25. Convert improper fractions to mixed numbers.

1. $\dfrac{29}{4} =$
2. $\dfrac{17}{2} =$
3. $\dfrac{37}{6} =$
4. $\dfrac{91}{10} =$
5. $\dfrac{5}{2} =$
6. $\dfrac{73}{9} =$
7. $\dfrac{19}{3} =$
8. $\dfrac{25}{4} =$
9. $\dfrac{13}{6} =$

26. In the following table convert the improper fractions to mixed numbers and decimals to fractions.

A. $\dfrac{21}{10}$ Mixed number

B. $\dfrac{55}{36}$ Mixed number

C. $\dfrac{16}{9}$ Mixed number

D. 8.09 Fractions

F. 0.394 Fractions

G. 14.09 Fractions

Greatest Common Factor

 Identify the largest factor numbers have in common

27. Find the greatest common factor for each pair of numbers.

    A. 4, 8

    Factors of 4 =

    Factors of 8 =

    GCF (4,8) =

    B. 12, 20

    Factors of 12 =

    Factors of 20 =

    GCM (12, 20) =

C. 14, 16

   Factors of 14 =

   Factors of 16 =

   GCM (14 ,16) =

D. 24 ,6

   Factors of 24 =

   Factors of 6 =

   GCM (24 ,6) =

28. Find the GCF of below numbers by using factor trees.

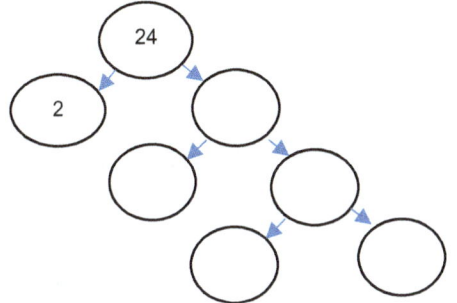 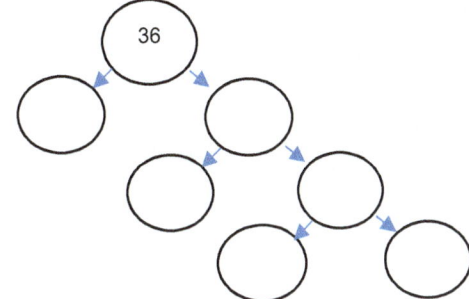

Least Common Multiple

 Identify the first number that numbers have in common

29. What are the least common multiples of the following number sets?

   A. 8, 12 , 20

   B. 5, 10, 25

   C. 9, 15, 18

D. 9, 12, 28

E. 3, 20, 25

F. 5, 14, 16

30. Find the greatest common factor and the least common multiple of each pair of integers.

	GCF	LCM
A. 60, 66		
B. 44, 14		
C. 7, 56		
D. 20, 22		
E. 13, 31		
F. 16, 60		

Answers of Worksheets – Chapter 1

Simplifying Fraction

1.

1. $\frac{1}{2}$ 6. $\frac{1}{3}$ 11. $\frac{1}{5}$ 16. $\frac{3}{2}$

2. $\frac{9}{10}$ 7. $\frac{3}{7}$ 12. $\frac{5}{12}$ 17. $\frac{1}{7}$

3. $\frac{3}{10}$ 8. $\frac{7}{10}$ 13. $\frac{1}{8}$ 18. $\frac{3}{2}$

4. $\frac{1}{3}$ 9. $\frac{7}{9}$ 14. $\frac{2}{9}$ 19. $\frac{1}{2}$

5. $\frac{9}{10}$ 10. $\frac{6}{7}$ 15. $\frac{7}{8}$ 20. 4

2.

1. 3   2. 2   3. 10   4. 24

Adding and Subtracting Fractions

3.

1. $\frac{4}{5}$ 6. $\frac{12}{4}$

2. $\frac{17}{7}$ 7. $\frac{6}{3}$

3. $\frac{7}{12}$ 8. $\frac{30}{20}$

4. $\frac{15}{15}$ 9. $\frac{3}{3}$

5. $\frac{12}{5}$ 10. $\frac{5}{45}$

4.

1. $\frac{13}{12}$ 3. $\frac{1}{10}$

2. $\frac{29}{12}$ 4. $\frac{8}{3}$

5.

1. $\frac{19}{35}$
2. $\frac{2}{6}$
3. $\frac{19}{18}$
4. $\frac{5}{36}$
5. $\frac{17}{12}$

6. $\frac{7}{40}$
7. $\frac{58}{40}$
8. $\frac{31}{42}$
9. $\frac{46}{80}$
10. $\frac{7}{8}$

6.

1. $\frac{3}{4} + \frac{5}{3} = \frac{9}{12} + \frac{12}{12} = \frac{29}{12}$
2. $\frac{5}{6} - \frac{1}{5} = \frac{25}{30} - \frac{6}{30} = \frac{19}{30}$
3. $\frac{2}{3} + \frac{4}{7} = \frac{14}{21} + \frac{12}{21} = \frac{26}{21}$
4. $\frac{3}{4} + \frac{3}{10} = \frac{30}{40} + \frac{12}{40} = \frac{42}{40}$

Multiplying and Dividing Fractions

7.

1. $\frac{1}{3}$
2. $\frac{1}{12}$
3. $\frac{1}{10}$
4. $\frac{27}{60}$

8.

1. $\frac{5}{4}$
2. $\frac{10}{9}$
3. $\frac{11}{3}$
4. $\frac{6}{5}$

Adding Mixed Numbers

9.

1. $\frac{52}{10}$
2. $\frac{79}{9}$
3. $\frac{34}{11}$
4. $\frac{379}{50}$
5. $\frac{18}{6}$
6. $\frac{37}{4}$

10.

    1. $\frac{11}{8}$ 2. $\frac{85}{16}$

Subtract Mixed Numbers

11.

    1. $\frac{16}{21}$ 3. $\frac{96}{20}$

    2. $\frac{19}{27}$ 4. $\frac{100}{20}$

12.

    1. $\frac{13}{8}$ 2. $\frac{9}{4}$

Dividing Mixed numbers

13.

    1. 1.352   6. 0.808

    2. 3.562   7. 1.073

    3. 1.184   8. 3.912

    4. 1.407   9. 1.312

    5. 0.538   10. 1.887

Round Decimals

14.

1. 57	3. 51	5. 91	7. 71	9. 63
2. 38	4. 49	6. 98	8. 30	10. 72

MathePathics

15.

| 1. 55.7 | 3. 32.9 | 5. 88.5 | 7. 40.3 | 9. 69.9 |
| 2. 48.2 | 4. 10.6 | 6. 62.8 | 8. 3.3 | 10. 92.3 |

16.

A.   I. a

       II. 2.3

       III. Round up

B.   I. a

       II. 55.21

       III. Round down

17.

1.97 - 1.6 - 1.5 - 1.7 - 1.86

18.

31.115 - 31.121 - 31.122 - 31.123 - 31.124

19.

| 1. 6.6 | 3. 6.82 | 5. 6.9 | 7. 7 | 9. 4.4 |
| 2. 0 | 4. 2 | 6. 3.41 | 8. 7 | 10. 5 |

Adding and Subtracting Decimals

20.

1. 710.02
2. 53.029
3. 669.949
4. 12.68
5. 65.91
6. 486.79
7. 12.156
8. 924.44
9. 349.007
10. 107.38
11. 40.59
12. 68

MathePathics

21.
- 1. 62.78 → 63
- 2. 39.32 → 39
- 3. 143.31 → 143
- 4. 4.44 → 4
- 5. 13.97 → 14
- 6. 56.42 → 56

Multiplying and Dividing Decimals

22.
- 1. 1,631.66
- 2. 2,22.33
- 3. 765.296
- 4. 26,261.24
- 5. 215.46
- 6. 2,704.68

23.
- 1. 10
- 2. 100
- 3. 10
- 4. 10
- 5. 100
- 6. 10
- 7. 100
- 8. 100

24.
- 1. 1.55
- 2. 0.14
- 3. 0.11
- 4. 1.04
- 5. 1.74
- 6. 2.31

Converting Between Fractions, Decimals and Mixed Numbers

25.
- 1. $7\frac{1}{4}$
- 2. $8\frac{1}{2}$
- 3. $6\frac{1}{6}$
- 4. $9\frac{1}{10}$
- 5. $2\frac{1}{2}$
- 6. $8\frac{1}{9}$
- 7. $6\frac{1}{3}$
- 8. $6\frac{1}{4}$
- 9. $2\frac{1}{6}$

26.

A. $2\frac{1}{10}$ C. $1\frac{7}{9}$ E. $\frac{394}{100}$

B. $1\frac{19}{36}$ D. $8\frac{9}{100}$ F. $14\frac{9}{100}$

Greatest Common Factor

27.

  A. Factors of 4 = 1, 2, 4

  Factors of 8 = 1, 2, 4, 8

  GCF (4,8) = 4

  B. Factors of 12 = 1, 2, 3, 4, 6, 12

  Factors of 20 = 1, 2, 4, 5, 10, 20

  GCM (12 ,20) = 4

  C. Factors of 14 = 1, 2, 7, 14

  Factors of 16 = 1, 2, 4, 8, 16

  GCM (14 ,16) = 2

  D. Factors of 24 = 1, 2, 3, 4, 6, 8, 12, 24

  Factors of 6 = 1, 2, 3, 6

  GCM (24 ,6) = 6

28.

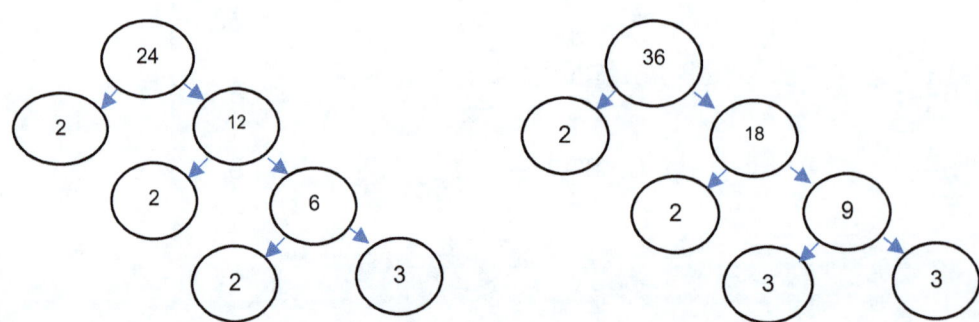

24
    → 12
36

Least Common Factor

29.
- A. 8, 12, 20 → 120
- B. 5, 10, 25 → 50
- C. 9, 15, 18 → 90
- D. 9, 12, 28 → 252
- E. 3, 20, 25 → 300
- F. 5, 14, 16 → 560

30.

	GCF	LCM
A. 60, 66	6	660
B. 44, 14	2	308
C. 7, 56	7	56
D. 20, 22	2	220
E. 13, 31	1	403
F. 16, 60	4	240

Extra Note for Chapter 1:

//MathePathics

Chapter 2:
Real Numbers and Integers

Adding and Subtracting Integers

Multiplying and Dividing Integers

Ordering Integers and Numbers

Mixed Integers Computations

Integers and Absolute Value

Answers of Worksheets – Chapter 2

Adding and Subtracting Integers

For adding or subtracting integers, follow these rules:

- If two numbers have the same signs, (both have positive or negative sign) add numbers with sign of the numbers.

  Example: 4 + 5 = 9, -4 – 5 = -9

- If two numbers have different signs, (one of them positive and other negative) subtract them with sign of the bigger number.

  Example: -5 + 9 = 4   5 – 9 = -4

If a number does not have a sign, it means that it is a positive number.
4 = +4

1. Use an integer strategy to find each answer.

1.	(-3) + (+12) =	11.	(-15) + (-10) =	21.	(+15) + (-10) =
2.	(-15) + (-3) =	12.	(+6) + (+5) =	22.	(-7) + (-5) =
3.	(+9) + (+4) =	13.	(+9) + (+11) =	23.	(+10) + (+11) =
4.	(-15) + (+15) =	14.	(-7) + (+5) =	24.	(-2) + (+11) =
5.	(+11) + (-3) =	15.	(-9) + (-14) =	25.	(+14) + (+11) =
6.	(-5) + (-7) =	16.	(-10) + (+2) =	26.	(+4) + (+13) =
7.	(+11) + (+13) =	17.	(-7) + (-12) =	27.	(-4) + (-7) =
8.	(-14) + (+5) =	18.	(-1) + (+10) =	28.	(-5) + (-11) =
9.	(+5) + (-14) =	19.	(-3) + (-10) =	29.	(-8) + (-50) =
10.	(+8) + (-12) =	20.	(-10) + (-9) =	30.	(-1) + (+3) =

2. Use the Number lines to solve.

   A. 4 + (-5) =

   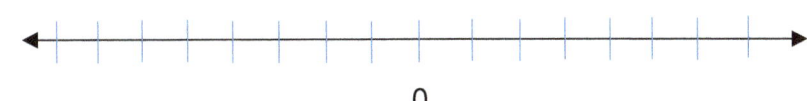
   0

   B. -2 + 2 =

   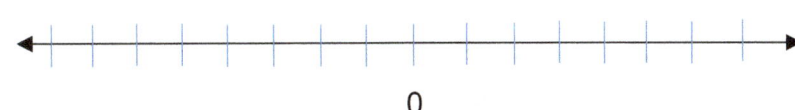
   0

   C. -3 +7 =

   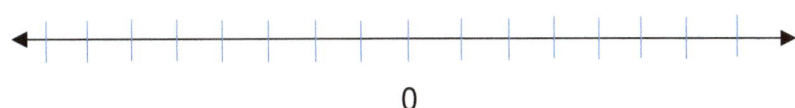
   0

   D. -1 + (-2) =

   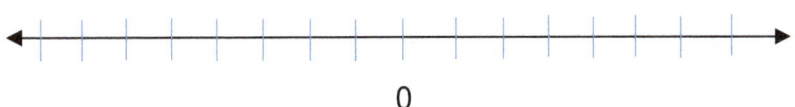
   0

   E. 6 + (-4) =

   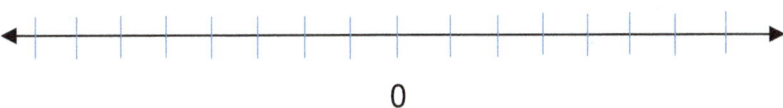
   0

   F. -6 + 12 =

   0

3. Fill in the blanks to the right with integer equations that match with the story. Solve all equations to see how much Carl is left with at the end of the week.
   A. Carl owed his mom $27.   ---------------------

   B. So, he decided to get a job to pay her back. On his way to the   ---------------------
      pet store to apply for a job as a dog groomer, he found a dollar
      bill.

C. It was his lucky day because also he got the job. The manager   --------------------
    told him that he would have to buy an apron with the store's
    name on it. It cost $12.

D. On the first day of work, Carl got a $4 tip for chipping Fifi's nail.   --------------------

E. However, Fifi left a sizeable, deep scratch in Carl's arm that   --------------------
    needed to be stitched by doctor for $10.

F. A couple days later, Carl's friend came by and returned the   --------------------
    $10 that he owed Carl.

G. Carl's grandma forgot his birthday last month and sent him a   --------------------
    check today for $50.

H. In the middle of the week, Carl forgot to bring his lunch and   --------------------
    had to buy it. Lunch costs $5.

I. Late in the week, Cal was not paying attention and stepped on   --------------------
    his brother's CD. He had to buy a new one for $13.

J. Finally, Carl received his first paycheck for $56. "Yippee,"   --------------------
    thought Carl, "I'm Finally out of debt and even have some cash
    in my wallet."

k. Then, he dropped his wallet. The wallet fell into the sewer and   --------------------
    disappeared, along with the $12 he had in there.

L. How much did /carl end his week with?   --------------------

Multiplying and Dividing Integers

Multiplying and dividing integers are like other numbers. But there are three rules about sign of numbers.

- Positive number (+)   ×   Positive number (+) = Positive number (+)

    Example: $(+2) \times (+6) = +12 \quad \dfrac{12}{6} = 2$

- Negative number (−)   ×   Negative number (−) = Negative number (−)

    Example: $(-2) \times (-6) = +12 \quad \dfrac{-12}{-6} = +2$

- Positive number (+) × Negative number (−) = Negative number (−)

Example: $(-2) \times (+6) = -12 \quad \dfrac{-12}{6} = -2$

4. Find each product.

1. 6 x 8 =
2. 1 x 8 =
3. 0 x (-6) =
4. +1 x (-3) =
5. (-9) x (-9) =
6. (-5) x 9 =
7. (-8) x 2 =
8. (-4) x 11 =
9. 10 x (-10) =
10. (-7) x (-8) =
11. (-5) x (-1) =
12. (-1) x (-1) =
13. (-90) x 0 =
14. (-30) x (-5) =
15. 8 x 0 =
16. (-5) x (-3) =
17. 100 x (-2) =
18. 21 x (-14) =
19. (-7) x (-5) =
20. (-2) x 0 =
21. (-11) x (-1) =
22. (-60) x 1 =
23. 10 x (-100) =
24. 30 x (-4) =
25. 22 x (-2) =
26. (-12) x 0 =
27. (-3) x (-6) =
28. 100 x 0 =
29. (-9) x (-8) =
30. 61 x 22 =
31. 21 x (-5) =
32. 1 x (-6) =
33. 6 x (-9) =
34. 31 x (-7) =
35. 3 x (-6) =
36. (-70) x (-2) =
37. (-96) x (-1) =
38. (-3) x (20) =
39. 7 x 40 =
40. (-6) x 2 =

5. Fill the missing integer(s).

    a. ------ ÷ (-12) = 6
    b. (-2) x ------ = (-10)
    c. 121 ÷ ------ = (-11)
    d. ------ x (-1) = 9
    e. ------ ÷ 10 = 14
    f. 7 x ------ = (-91)
    g. ------ ÷ 8 = (-7)
    h. 6 x ------ = 24
    i. ------ ÷ 12 = -7
    j. 100 ÷ (-5) = ------
    k. 25 x ------ = (-125)
    l. 3 x ------ = (-18)
    m. ------ ÷ 7 = 15
    n. ------ x (-2) = 30
    o. 48 ÷ ------ = (-12)
    p. (-5) x ------ = (-75)
    q. ------ ÷ (-10) = 3
    r. 12 x ------ = 108
    s. ------ ÷ 14 = (-2)
    t. ------ x 11 = 132
    u. 88 ÷ ------ = (-11)
    v. 60 ÷ ------ = (-10)

Ordering Integers and Numbers

On a number line, integers on the right side are always greater than integers on the left side.

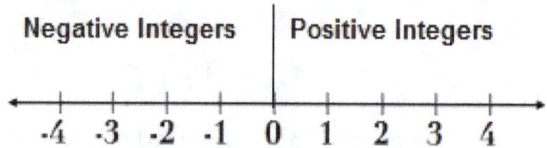

9 > 8   -1 > -4

Arrange, Order, and Comparing Integers

Operation means adding, subtraction, multiplication, division, etc.

To solve a mathematic expression, perform following steps in the order below.

1- Powers and roots
2- Multiply and divide
3- Add and subtract

 If there is parenthesis, first you must solve parenthesis.

Example: $2 + (3^2 \times 5) - (5 \times 8) = 2 + (9 \times 5) - 40 = 2 + 45 - 40 = 7$

There are two states for arranging integers. It may be **increasing** or **decreasing**.

Example: Arrange set of number. -9, 4, 3, -10, 1, 0

Increasing: -10, -9, 0, 1, 3, 4

Decreasing: 4, 3, 1, 0, -9, -10

Comparing
There are three rules.

1. Positive integers are bigger than negative numbers.   5 > -5   9 > -6
2. When positive integers increase, they become bigger.   9 > 8 > 7
3. When negative integers increase, they become smaller.   -9 < -8 < -7

6. Write each set of integers in the order shown.

a.
```
         Least
-76      ____
-14      ____
+56      ____
+30      ____
-18      ____
         Greatest
```

b.
```
         Least
-63      ____
-40      ____
-3       ____
+26      ____
+95      ____
         Greatest
```

c.
```
         Least
-12      ____
-25      ____
 0       ____
+1       ____
 89      ____
         Greatest
```

d.
```
         Least
-88      ____
-15      ____
+12      ____
+5       ____
-6       ____
         Greatest
```

e.
```
         Least
+47      ____
+58      ____
-32      ____
-1       ____
-41      ____
         Greatest
```

f.
```
         Least
+33      ____
+40      ____
-2       ____
 0       ____
+1       ____
         Greatest
```

7. Compare the pairs of integers using <, >, or =.

-10		9		66		-50		12		-6
76		67		99		-1		32		-52
-69		-11		28		32		88		-16
-79		-9		-27		68		-31		-79
18		-27		-56		38		-74		-63
-12		-81		-1		-98		-3		-7
-61		57		30		-46		-58		-58
-44		-98		88		-41		-91		0
-5		-68		-77		-2		-37		-37
-14		-21		-32		-1		12		0
-1		-1		-56		63		30		-31
0		-4		66		23		70		51
12		-60		69		-1		-14		-14
-90		-50		-100		+100		-3		-9

Mixed Integers Computations

For computation mixed integers, you should follow order of operations.

Example:

$(+2) \times (-10) = -20$

$(-6) + (+3) = -6 + 3 = -3$

$(-7) + (-15) = -22$

8. Solve the following expressions.

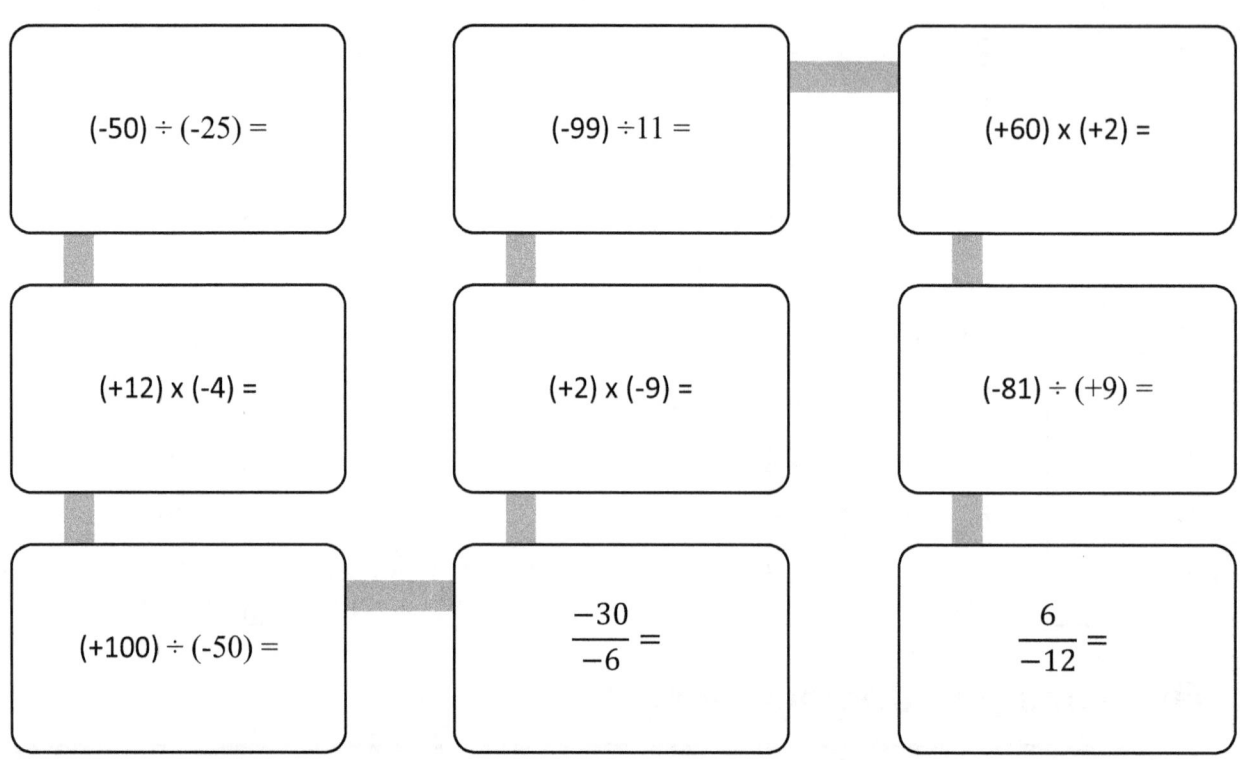

Finish

9. Compute the following expressions.
   A. (+47 − 2 + 5) ÷ (16 +20) =
   B. (+60 − 40 +3) ÷ (+3 − 6) =
   C. 6 x (3 +5 -10) =

Integers and Absolute Value

Numbers on opposite sides of zero and the same distance from zero have the same absolute value.

The symbol for absolute value is | |.

The absolute value of the positive integers is positive.

Example: | 7 | = 7

The absolute value of the negative integers is positive.

Example: | -7| = 7

10. Write the absolute value of each number below.

1. |−2| =
2. |−8| =
3. |−22| =
4. |12| =
5. |30| =
6. |9|
7. |−0.356| =
8. |5| =
9. |9.23| =
10. |200| =
11. |−6.30| =
12. |111| =
13. |−91| =
14. |20| =
15. |−865| =
16. |−76| =
17. |32| =
18. |32.14| =
19. |−4.03| =
20. |97| =

11. Find the absolute value and then compare the pair of integers.

A.	$|-1|$		$|2|$	I.	$|23|$		$|-6|$
B.	$|-0.23|$		$|0.23|$	J.	$|-89|$		$|-98|$
C.	$|5.6|$		$|5.4|$	K.	$|2.98|$		$|-2.98|$
D.	$|5|$		$|-12|$	L.	$|61|$		$|-61.1|$
E.	$|13|$		$|-14|$	M.	$|-18|$		$|18|$
F.	$|-6|$		$|-6.1|$	N.	$|100.2|$		$|-100.6|$
G.	$|32|$		$|-1|$	O.	$|3|$		$|-9.2|$
H.	$|-80|$		$|-81|$	P.	$|-99|$		$|-98|$

Answers of Worksheets – Chapter 2

Adding and Subtracting Integers

1.

1. (+9)		11. (-25)		21. (+5)
2. (-18)		12. (+11)		22. (-12)
3. (+13)		13. (+20)		23. (+21)
4. (0)		14. (-2)		24. (+9)
5. (+8)		15. (-23)		25. (+25)
6. (-12)		16. (-8)		26. (+17)
7. (+24)		17. (-19)		27. (-11)
8. (-9)		18. (+9)		28. (-16)
9. (-9)		19. (-13)		29. (-13)
10. (-4)		20. (-19)		30. (+2)

2.

A

B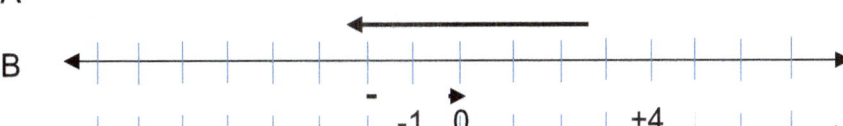

C

D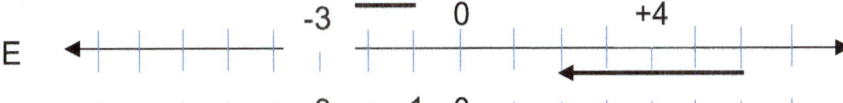

E

F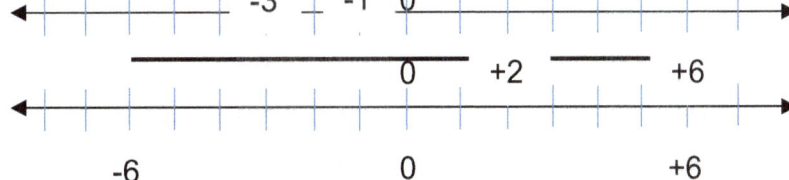

-6　　　　　　0　　　　　　+6

40

3.

A. -27
B. +1+ (-27) = -26
C. -26 + (-12) = -38
D. -38 +4 = -34
E. -34 + (-50) = -84
F. -84 + 10 = -74
G. -74 + 50 = -24
H. -24 + (-5) = -29
I. -29 + (-13) = -42
J. -42 + 56= +14
L. +14 + (-12) = +2
L. +2

Multiplying and Dividing Integers

4.

1. 48
2. 8
3. 0
4. (-3)
5. +81
6. (-45)
7. (-16)
8. (-44)
9. (-100)
10. +56
11. +5
12. +1
13. 0
14. +150
15. 0
16. +15
17. (-20)
18. (-294)
19. +35
20. 0
21. +11
22. (-60)
23. (-1000)
24. (-120)
25. (-44)
26. 0
27. +18
28. 0
29. +72
30. 1,342
31. (-105)
32. (-6)
33. (-54)
34. (-217)
35. (-18)
36. +140
37. +96
38. (-60)
39. 280
40. (-12)

5.

a. -72
b. +5
c. -11
d. -9
e. 140
f. -13
g. -56
l. -6
m. +105
n. -60
o. -4
p. +15
q. -300
r. +9

MathePathics

    h. +4
    i. -84
    j. -20
    k. -5

    s. -28
    t. 12
    u. -8
    v. -6

Ordering Integers and Numbers

6.

a. Least
-76
-18
-14
+30
+56
Greatest

d. Least
-63
-40
-3
+26
+95
Greatest

b. Least
-25
-12
0
+1
+89
Greatest

e. Least
-88
-15
-6
+5
+12
Greatest

c. Least
-41
-32
-1

f. Least
-2
0
+1

+47   +33

+58   +40

Greatest   Greatest

7.

-10	<	9	66	>	-50	12	>	-6
76	>	67	99	>	-1	32	>	-52
-69	<	-11	28	<	32	88	>	-16
-79	<	-9	-27	<	68	-31	>	-79
18	>	-27	-56	<	38	-74	<	-63
-12	>	-81	-1	>	-98	-3	>	-7
-61	<	57	30	>	-46	-58	=	-58
-44	>	-98	88	>	-41	-91	<	0
-5	>	-68	-77	<	-2	-37	=	-37
-14	>	-21	-32	<	-1	12	>	0
-1	=	-1	-56	<	63	30	>	-31
0	>	-4	66	>	23	70	>	51
12	>	-60	69	>	-1	-14	=	-14
-90	<	-50	-100	<	+100	-3	>	-9

Mixed Integers Computations

8.

+2	-9	+120
-48	-18	-9
-2	+6	$-\frac{1}{2}$

9.
- A. $\frac{25}{18}$
- B. $-\frac{23}{3}$
- C. -12

Integers and Absolute Value

10.

1. +2
2. +8
3. +22
4. +12
5. +30
6. +9
7. +0.356
8. +5
9. +9.23
10. +200
11. +6.30
12. +111
13. +91
14. +20
15. +865
16. +76
17. +32
18. +32.14
19. +4.03
20. +97

11.

A.	1	<	2	I.	23	>	6
B.	0.23	=	0.23	J.	89	<	98
C.	5.6	>	5.4	K.	2.98	=	2.98
D.	5	<	12	L.	61	<	61.1
E.	13	<	14	M.	18	=	18
F.	6	<	6.1	N.	100.2	<	100.6
G.	32	>	1	O.	3	<	9.2
H.	80	<	81	P.	99	>	98

Extra Note for Chapter 2:

Chapter 3: Proportions and Ratios

Writing Ratios

Simplifying Ratios

Create a Proportion

Similar Figure

Simple Interest

Ratio and Rates Word Problem

Answers of Worksheets – Chapter 3

MathePathics

Writing Ratios

A ratio is used to compare between two things.

Thera are different ways for writing ratio.

- Fraction
- Use the word "to".
- Colon ":".

Example:

Ratio of squares to circles is $\frac{6}{4}$ or **6 to 4** or **6:4**.

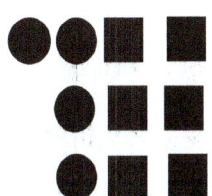

1. Solve. If the problem asks for a ratio, give it in simplified form.

   A. A math club has 25 members, of which 11 are males and the rest are females. What is the ratio of males to all club members?

   B. A group of preschoolers has 16 boys and 24 girls. What is the ratio of girls to all children?

   C. A pattern has 4 green triangles to every 12 yellow triangles. What is the ratio of green triangles to all triangles?

   D. Sarah drew 1 heart, 2 stars, and 12 circles. What is the ratio of circles to hearts?

2. On a shelf there are 8 math books, 12 science books, and 20 history workouts the ratios of:
   A. Math books to science books:
   B. Science books to history books:
   C. History books to math books:

3. Express each ratio as a fraction in the simplest form.

1. 18 pounds to 22 pounds   --------   11. 12 pints to 36 pints   --------
2. 16 feet out of 18 feet   --------   12. 25 red bikes out of 60 bikes   --------
3. 12 pennies to 24 pennies   --------   13. 32 quarts to 48 quarts   --------
4. 12 blue cars out of 48 cars   --------   14. 30 beetles out of 35 insects   --------
5. 6 gallons to 42 gallons   --------   15. 21 dimes to 24 dimes   --------
6. 12 cups to 21 cups   --------   16. 22 cakes out of 24 cakes   --------
7. 10 dimes out of 35 coins   --------   17. 21 inches to 28 inches   --------
8. 10 nickels to 18 nickels   --------   18. 7 footballs to 56 footballs   --------
9. 20 points out of 45 points   --------   19. 60 miles out of 72 miles   --------
10. 18 rainy days out of 24 days   --------   20. 9 snow days out of 30 days   --------

Simplifying Ratios

To simplify ratio:

- First find GCF (Greatest Common Factor) for two numbers.
- Divide both number values by the GCF.

For finding GCF, find all the factors of each number then circle the greatest factor.

 Example:

18 : 12

Factors of 18: 1, 2, 3, 6, 9   Factors of 12: 1, 2, 3, 4, 6

GCF (greatest common factor): 6   3 : 2

4. Fill in the blank to make an equivalent ratio.

1. ----:9 = 10:45		11. ----: 3 = 12: 18
2. ----:3 = 40:15		12. 9: 3 = 32: ----
3. 9: ---- = 18:14		13. 28: 24 = ----: 6
4. 6: 4 = ----: 12		14. 40: ---- = 8: 2
5. 6: 8 = ----: 16		15. 45: 35 = ----: 7
6. 3: 9 = ----: 36		16. 18: 10 = ----: 5
7. 9: 3 = ----: 15		17. ----: 8 = 16: 32
8. 4: ---- = 20: 25		18. 3: ---- = 9: 6
9. 6: 9 = ----: 3		19. 3: 2 = 9: ----
10. 6: ---- = 30: 30		20. 6: 8 = ----: 8

Create a proportion

To state two equal ratios, use proportion.

A proportion can be written in two ways.

$\dfrac{a}{b} = \dfrac{c}{d}$ $a : b = c : d$

We use proportion to solve percent and triangles.

5. Create proportion for from the given set of numbers.

1. 2, 4, 3, 6, 5, 10, 11, 22
2. 2, 6, 3, 9, 10, 30, 11, 33
3. 2, 8, 3, 12, 14, 21
4. 3, 12, 4, 16, 5, 20
5. 8, 7, 24, 21
6. 16, 18, 24, 27, 32, 36
7. 5, 9, 10, 18, 25, 45
8. 4, 7, 8, 14, 20, 35
9. 1, 7, 3, 21, 8, 56
10. 5, 6, 10, 12, 35, 42

6. You can buy six cans of root beer for $ 2.50. How many cans of root beer can you buy with $20?

7. When juggling a ball travels in a complete circle every 2 seconds. How many circles does it make in 2 minutes?

Similar Figure

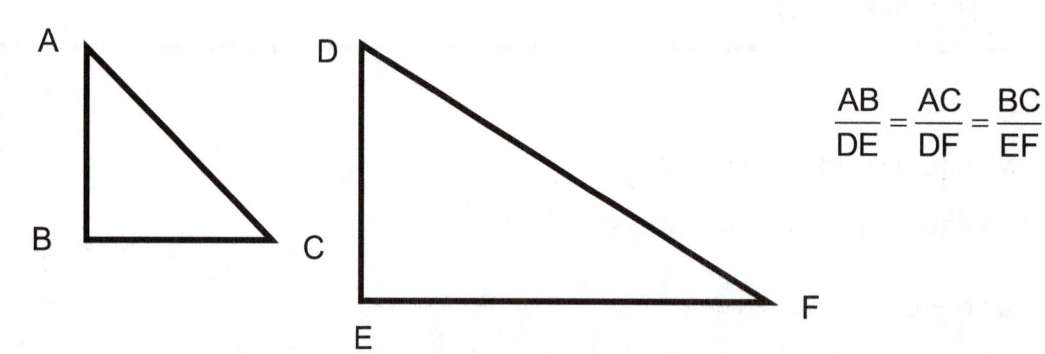

If two figures have same shape, they are similar.

In this state, the ratios of the lengths of their corresponding sides are equal.

$$\frac{AB}{DE} = \frac{AC}{DF} = \frac{BC}{EF}$$

8. Find the missing side of similar figures.

   A.

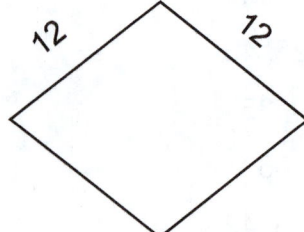
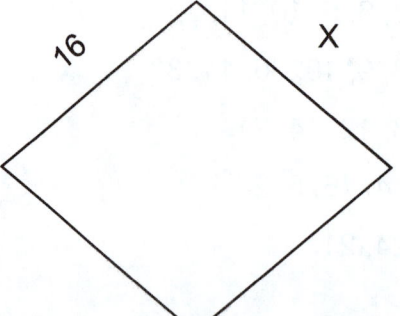

B.

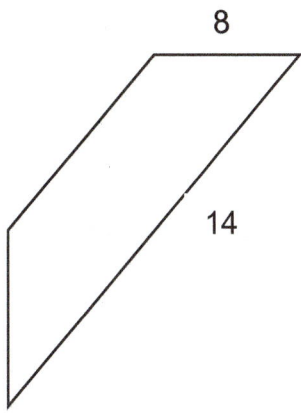

C.

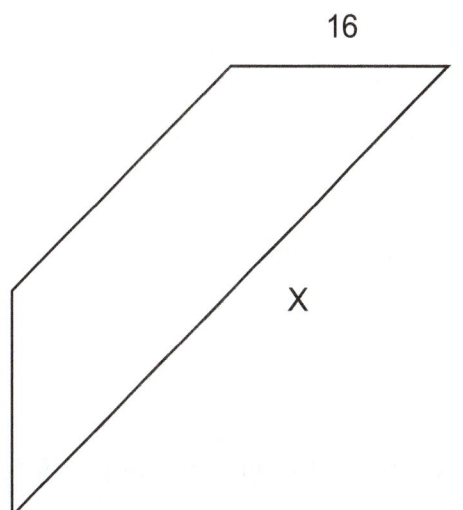

Simple Interest

The money that you can earn by initially investing some money is called simple interest. Use below formula for calculating interest.

I = P r t (I: Interest, P: Principal (amount borrowed), t: interest rate)

Example:

Tim borrows $2000 for 6 years. At %7 simple interest:

I=Prt=$2000×%7×6 Years=$840+2000=$2840

The money that Alex needs to pay after 6 years → 840+2000=$2840

9. Calculate the simple interest for the word problems.

   A. How much interest does a $ 9.66 investment earn at 10% over eight years?

   B. How much interest is earned on a principal of $ 2.58 invested at an interest rate of 5% for four years?

   C. If you borrow $ 5.93 for nine years at an interest rate of 6%, how much interest will you pay?

   D. How much interest is earned on $ 5.43 at 5% for five years?

   E. How much interest is earned on a principal of $9.02 invested at an interest rate of 8% for three years?

   F. If the balance at the end of eight years on an investment of $7.97 that has been invested at a rate of 9% is $ 13.71, how much was the interest?

Ratio and Rates Word Problem

Follow these steps:

- Identify knowns and unknown
- Plug values in proportion
- Solve proportion

Example: Kate can make 3 cakes in 7 hours. Assuming all of the cake that she makes have the same shape and size, how many hours would it take her to make 24 cakes?

Cake	Hour
3	7
24	x

$$\frac{3}{24} = \frac{7}{x} \longrightarrow 3x = 7 \times 24 \longrightarrow x = \frac{7 \times 24}{3} = 56$$

10. If a student solves 120 questions in 100 minutes, in how many minutes will he solve 90 questions?

11. 5 workers weave a carpet of 10 m^2 in 24 days. In how many days do 4 workers weave a carpet of 8 m^2 ?

12. A car travels 150 kilometers in 3 hours. How many kilometers will it travel in 7 hours?

13. Joe earn $18 per week. He saves $5 per week. What is the ratio of his saving to his earning?

14. If 16 men can build 3 cabinets in one day. How many men are needed to build 9 cabinets in one day?

15. Larry answered 8 out of every 10 questions on a test correctly. The test had 70 questions. How many correct answers did Larry give?

16. There are 15 quarters and 10 dimes in the jar. What is the ratio of quarters to dimes?

17. In a managed forest, three different trees are planted. The trees are beech, holly and maple. For every beech tree planted, there are 2 holly trees planted and 5 maple trees planted.

   A. Write down the ratio of trees.
   B. If 6 beech trees were planted, how many holly trees would be planted?
   C. If 40 maple trees were planted, how many beech trees would be planted?

Answers of Worksheets – Chapter 3

Writing Ratios

1.

   A. Total member = 25
   Males = 11
   Females = 25 – 11 = 14
   Ratio of males to all club member = $\frac{11}{25}$

   B. All children = 14 + 26 = 40
   Ratio of girls to all children = $\frac{24}{40} = \frac{6}{10} = \frac{3}{5}$

   C. All triangles = 4 + 12 = 16
   Ratio of green triangles to all triangles = $\frac{4}{16} = \frac{1}{4}$

   D. Heart = 1
   Circles = 12
   Ratio of circles to heart = $\frac{12}{1} = 12$

2.

   A. 8:12   B. 12:20   C. 20:8

3.

1.	18:22	= 9:11	11.	12:36	= 1:3
2.	16:18	= 8:9	12.	25:60	= 5:12
3.	12:24	= 1:2	13.	32:48	= 2:3
4.	12:48	= 1:4	14.	30:35	= 6:7
5.	6:42	= 1:7	15.	21:24	= 7:8
6.	12:21	= 4:7	16.	22:24	= 11:12
7.	10:35	= 2:7	17.	21:28	= 7:9
8.	10:18	= 5:9	18.	7:56	= 1:8
9.	20:45	= 4:9	19.	60:72	= 5:6
10.	18:24	= 3:4	20.	9:30	= 3:10

Simplifying Ratios

4.
1. 2	11. 2
2. 8	12. 12
3. 7	13. 7
4. 18	14. 10
5. 12	15. 9
6. 12	16. 9
7. 45	17. 2
8. 5	18. 2
9. 18	19. 6
10. 6	20. 6

Create a proportion

5.

1. $\frac{2}{4} = \frac{3}{6} = \frac{5}{10} = \frac{11}{22}$

2. $\frac{2}{6} = \frac{3}{9} = \frac{10}{30} = \frac{11}{33}$

3. $\frac{2}{8} = \frac{3}{12} = \frac{14}{21}$

4. $\frac{3}{10} = \frac{4}{16} = \frac{5}{20}$

5. $\frac{8}{7} = \frac{24}{21}$

6. $\frac{16}{18} = \frac{24}{27} = \frac{32}{36}$

7. $\frac{5}{9} = \frac{10}{18} = \frac{24}{45}$

8. $\frac{4}{7} = \frac{8}{14} = \frac{20}{35}$

9. $\frac{1}{7} = \frac{3}{21} = \frac{8}{56}$

10. $\frac{5}{6} = \frac{10}{12} = \frac{35}{42}$

6. 48 cans of root beer

7. 60 circles in 2 minutes

Similar Figure

8. A. X = 16   B. X = 10   C. X = 28

Simple Interest

9. A. I = 7.728
   B. I = 0.516
   C. I = 3.2022

   D. I = 1.3575
   E. I = 2.1648
   F. I = 5.6088

Ratio and Rates Word Problem

10. 75 Minutes
11. 19.2 Days
12. 64.28 Kilometers
13. 0.62
14. 48 Men
15. 56
16. 1.5
17. A. 1 beech: 2 holly: 5 maple tree   B. 12   C. 8

Extra Note for Chapter 3:

Chapter 4:

Percent

Percentage Calculations

Converting Between Percent, Fractions, and Decimals

Percent Problems

Markup, Discount, and Tax

Answers of Worksheets – Chapter 4

MathePathics

Percentage Calculations

The numbers are used to state percentage have two formats, decimal and fraction.

Decimal: 0.5   Fraction: $\frac{5}{10}$

The symbol of percent is %.

Example:

It rained 12 times in the last 100 days.

It means 12 percent of the time. 12%

1. Round your answer to two decimal points if required.

    1. 44 ÷ 65 = ---- %
    2. 31 ÷ 54 = ---- %
    3. 53 % x 19 = -----
    4. 64 % x 52 = ----
    5. 19 ÷ 28 = ---- %
    6. 31 ÷ 82 % = ----
    7. 40 % x 45 = ----
    8. 42 ÷ 61 = ---- %
    9. 38 ÷ 40% = ----
    10. 1 % x 89 = ----

2. Answer the following questions:
    1. What is the 100 percent of 67.1?
    2. What is 1 percent of 94.8?
    3. What is 1000 percent of 25.6?
    4. What is 0.1 percent of 95.6?
    5. What is 0.1 percent of 39.1?
    6. What is 1000 percent of 66.5?
    7. What is 1 percent of 41.6?
    8. What is 100 percent of 98.3?
    9. What is 10 percent of 43.2?
    10. What is 100 of 23.1?

3. Calculate the percentage.

   1. 150% 0f 50   ----------------------
   2. 100% of 60   ----------------------
   3. 350% of 50   ----------------------
   4. 450% of 100   ----------------------
   5. 250% of 50   ----------------------
   6. 350% of 80   ----------------------
   7. 400% of 80   ----------------------
   8. 200% of 20   ----------------------
   9. 15% of 45   ----------------------
   10. 25% of 50   ----------------------
   11. 150% of 15   ----------------------
   12. 14% of 300   ----------------------
   13. 60% of 800   ----------------------
   14. 356% of 145 ----------------------
   15. 30% of 89   ----------------------
   16. 10% of 95   ----------------------

Converting Between Percent, Fractions, and Decimals

- Convert decimal to percent → 5 × 100 = 0.05 %

- Convert decimal to fraction → 5 × 100 = 0.05 → $\frac{5}{100} = \frac{1}{4}$

- Convert fraction to decimal → $\frac{7}{2} = 3.5$

- Convert fraction to percent → $\frac{2}{10} = \frac{1}{5} = 0.2$ → 0.2 × 100 = 20%

- Convert percentage to fraction → 46% = $\frac{46}{100} = \frac{23}{50}$

4. Fill the missing gaps.

A.
Decimal	0.1	0.2	0.61				
Percentage				90%	41%	92%	86%

B.
Percentage		7%			11%		8%
Decimal	0.03		0.06	0.09		0.02	

C.	Fraction	$\frac{1}{2}$	$\frac{1}{4}$	$\frac{47}{100}$				
	Percentage				10%	23%	75%	1%

D.	Fraction				$\frac{1}{2}$	$\frac{1}{4}$	$\frac{67}{100}$	$\frac{3}{4}$
	Decimal	0.7	0.3	0.07				

5. Convert Decimal to percent.
   1. 1.55 =
   2. 0.86 =
   3. 0.3 =
   4. 1.89 =
   5. 0.963 =
   6. 0.541

6. Convert percent to decimal.
   1. 184% =
   2. 83% =
   3. 35% =
   4. 342% =
   5. 92.2% =
   6. 144% =

7. Convert Decimal to fraction.
   1. 0.91 =
   2. 1.35 =
   3. 1.87 =
   4. 0.44 =
   5. 0.723 =
   6. 0.61 =

Percent Problems

If we want to solve A% of B:

Write A% as a fraction → $A\% = \frac{A}{100}$

Multiply $\frac{A}{100}$ to B. → $\frac{A}{100} \times B$

Example: 25% of 30.

$25\% = \frac{25}{100} \times 30 = \frac{75}{10} = 7.5$

8. Sarah and Jonathan made a total of $125 at work today. If Sarah has $50, what percent of money is Jonathan's?

9. Michael took a test with 200 questions on it and answered 165 of them correctly. What percentage of questions did Michael get right?

10. If Daniel ordered a pizza with 12 slices and ate 5 of them, what percentage of the pizza did he eat?

11. Franklin bought a book with 220 pages. If he read 40% of the pages on the first night, how many pages does he have left to read?

12. You paid $ 32.30 for a sweater that originally cost $ 90.60. What percentage of the original price was the sweater on sale for?

Markup, Discount, and Tax

Markup

Imagine a bookstore is selling a famous novel for $12. If the bookstore had to pay $9 for the book, the percent of markup is calculated according to example below.

$$\frac{12}{9} = \frac{x}{100} \quad x = \text{percent of markup} \rightarrow x = \frac{100 \times 12}{9} = 133.3\%$$

Discount

Adam is offering 30% off all clothes. If you want to buy $150 clothes, your final price is

$$\frac{30}{100} = \frac{x}{150} \longrightarrow x = \frac{150 \times 30}{100} = 45 \longrightarrow 150 - 45 = 105$$

Tax

A blue car costs $200 and the sale's tax is 6%. What is the total cost?

$$100\% + 6\% = 106\% \qquad \frac{x}{200} = \frac{106}{100} \longrightarrow x = \frac{200 \times 106}{100} = 212\$$$

13. A clothing store is selling one sweater for $60. The store only had to pay $54 for the sweater. What is the percentage of markup?

14. Marshall's is offering 40% off all shoes. If you want to buy a boot which its price is $120, what would be the final price after the discount?

15. Do the math and calculate the answer.

    iPad mini = $ 269.04

    Scoter = $ 110.17

    Zoomer Dino = $ 28.33

    Gaming Chair = $ 107.60

    Lego Friends = $ 58.63

1. What is the total cost of Lego Friends and Scoter?

2. What is the total cost of an iPad Mini and a Gaming chair if the sale tax is five percent?

3. What is the total cost of a Zoomer Dino if there is a five percent sale tax?

Answers of Worksheets – Chapter 4

Percentage Calculations

1.

1. 67 %
2. 57 %
3. 10.07 → 10.10
4. 32.28 → 32.30
5. 67 %
6. 37.80 → 37.80
7. 18
8. 68 %
9. 95
10. 0.89 → 0.90

2.

1. 67.1	3. 256	5. 0.0391	7. 0.416	9. 4.32
2. 0.948	4. 0.0956	6. 665	8. 98.3	10. 23.1

3.

1. 75
2. 60
3. 175
4. 450
5. 12.5
6. 280
7. 320
8. 40
9. 6.75
10. 12.5
11. 22.5
12. 42
13. 480
14. 516.2
15. 26.7
16. 9.5

Converting Between Percent, Fractions, and Decimals

4.

B.							
Decimal	0.1	0.2	0.61	0.90	0.41	0.92	0.86
Percentage	10%	20%	61%	90%	41%	92%	86%

B.

Percentage	3%	7%	6%	9%	11%	2%	8%
Decimal	0.03	0.07	0.06	0.09	0.11	0.02	0.08

C.

Fraction	$\frac{1}{2}$	$\frac{1}{4}$	$\frac{47}{100}$	$\frac{10}{100}$	$\frac{23}{100}$	$\frac{75}{100}$	$\frac{1}{100}$
Percentage	50%	25%	47%	10%	23%	75%	1%

D.

Fraction	$\frac{7}{10}$	$\frac{3}{10}$	$\frac{7}{100}$	$\frac{1}{2}$	$\frac{1}{4}$	$\frac{67}{100}$	$\frac{3}{4}$
Decimal	0.7	0.3	0.07	0.5	0.25	0.67	0.75

5.
1. 155%
2. 86%
3. 30%
4. 189%
5. 96.3%
6. 54.1%

6.
1. 1.84
2. 0.83
3. 0.35
4. 3.42
5. 0.922
6. 1.44

7.
1. $\frac{91}{100}$
2. $\frac{135}{100} = 1\frac{7}{20}$
3. $1\frac{87}{100}$
4. $\frac{44}{100} = \frac{11}{20}$
5. $\frac{723}{1000}$
6. $\frac{61}{100}$

8. 60%   9. 82.5%   10. 41.66%   11. 132 pages   12. 35.65%

Markup, Discount, and Tax

13. 11.1% markup
14. $72
15. 1. 168.8   2. 395.47   3. 29.75

Extra Note for Chapter 4:

Chapter 5: Algebraic Expressions

Expressions and Variables

Simplifying Variables and Expressions

Simplifying Polynomial Expressions

Translate Phrases into an Algebraic Statement

The Distributive Property

Evaluating one Variables

Evaluating Two Variables

Combining Like Terms

Answers of Worksheets – Chapter5

Expressions and Variables

Variable

It's a symbol that represents a changeable quantity. We use alphabet as a symbol for a variable. Like "x", "y".

Expression

It is a mathematical phrase. It makes up of a sequence of mathematical symbols.

Example: $\frac{1}{2}a.b$

1. Solve the following equations.

   1. $x - 3 = 6$
   2. $x - 12 = 14$
   3. $n - 8 = 12$
   4. $a - 9 = 15$
   5. $n - 9 = 13$
   6. $b - 8 = 9$
   7. $x - 5 = 16$
   8. $n - 6 = 17$

Simplifying Variables and Expressions

For simplifying variable expressions follow steps below:

- Find like terms
- Rewrite like terms
- Combine (add or subtract) like terms

We want to simplify $2x + 5y - 7x + 2y$.

Step1: $\underline{2x} + \underline{5y} - \underline{7x} + \underline{2y}$

Step2: $2x - 7x + 5y + 2y$

Step3: $-5x + 7y$

2. Simplify the following expressions.

1. $5a + 6a =$
2. $10a - 2a =$
3. $4b + 3b =$
4. $3a + a =$
5. $9a + 4a =$
6. $12b - 6b =$
7. $4a - 3a =$
8. $11a - 7a =$
9. $5b + 9b =$

3. Solve for each variable.

1. $3z + 4 = 34$
2. $2u + 22 = 10$
3. $2y + 1 = 17$
4. $3c + 8 = 14$
5. $2c + 7 = 17$
6. $3x + 2 = 5$
7. $2a + 4 = 14$
8. $2c + 10 = 20$
9. $2u + 4 = 10$
10. $2u + 4 = 16$
11. $2c + 7 = 21$
12. $2x + 5 = 15$
13. $2c + 4 = 20$
14. $3z + 4 = 22$
15. $2x + 8 = 22$

4. Solve the equations to find x.

1. $\dfrac{x}{3} = 4$
2. $\dfrac{x}{2} = 8$
3. $\dfrac{x}{5} = 7$
4. $\dfrac{x}{8} = 4$
5. $\dfrac{x}{7} = 3$
6. $\dfrac{x}{5} = 4$
7. $\dfrac{x}{2} = 9$
8. $\dfrac{x}{7} = 6$
9. $\dfrac{x}{12} = 6$
10. $\dfrac{x}{14} = 2$
11. $\dfrac{x}{30} = 300$
12. $\dfrac{x}{5} = 10$

Simplifying Polynomial Expressions

To simplify polynomial expressions, there are three steps to be followed.

1- Find like terms.
2- Rewrite like terms next to each other.
3- Combine them

Example: Simplify $2x^2 + 3x - 4 + 7x - 5x^2 + 8$.

Step 1: $2x^2 + 3x - 4 + 7x - 5x^2 + 8$

Step 2: $2x^2 - 5x^2 + 3x + 7x - 4 + 8$

Step 3: $-3x^2 + 10x + 4$

5. Simplifying each expression.

1. $(q^2 - 8q^5 - 7) + (3q^2 + 4 - 5q^5) - (9q^2 - q - 2) =$
2. $6c^2 + 5 - 6c + 9c + 5c^2 + 10 =$
3. $8q^2 - 4 + q^2 - 12q + 5q^2 =$
4. $-(14x - 5 + 10x^2 + 2x^4 - 14) =$
5. $(-5y + y^3 + y - 90y^3 + 10 =$
6. $-(3x + 14 - 6x^2 - 2) + (-2 + x + 3x^3) - 15 =$
7. $2p - 2p^3 - 13 + 3p - 52p^3 =$
8. $-(-x + 23x^2 - 12) - 10x + 5 =$
9. $+c - 12 - c^2 + 35c^4 - c^4 =$
10. $4x^2 + 50 - x + x^2 =$

Translate Phrases into an Algebraic Statement

For translating phrases into an algebraic statement, you must use symbols and variables.

There are more common phrases that translated into algebraic statements.

A plus B	A+B
A minus B	A-B
A multiply B	A.B
A divided by B	$\frac{A}{B}$

Example: The difference between 9 and 4 equals 5.

Difference means subtraction. (-)

9 – 4 = 5

6. Translate each verbal phrase into an algebraic expression.

1. P decreased by the total of q and r　---------------------------
2. The sum of nine and a number x　---------------------------
3. Fifteen decreased by a number p　---------------------------
4. Fifteen less than a number p　---------------------------
5. Three less than sum of x any y　---------------------------
6. c added to the square of b　---------------------------
7. The sum of m and n　---------------------------
8. 5 times g reduced by the square of h　---------------------------
9. Twice of p minus q　---------------------------
10. Subtract the product of x and y from 58　---------------------------
11. Three multiplied by a number g　---------------------------
12. 10 divided by p　---------------------------
13. The product of nine and a number of y　---------------------------
14. The quotient of nine and x　---------------------------
15. The product of twelve and a number is forty-eight.　---------------------------
16. Twice the difference between 6 times h　---------------------------

7. Translate algebraic expressions

1. One –fourth of the sum of n and 8 minus the product of 6 and b　---------------------------
2. Add one – fourth to 3 times c　---------------------------
3. One – sixth of x is added to 5　---------------------------
4. q cubed minus the product of 6 and k plus 5　---------------------------
5. Take away 4 from 8 times n　---------------------------
6. Add 7 to 8 times g　---------------------------
7. Five – sixths of 6 is added to the product of 6 and c　---------------------------
8. The sum of one – sixth of n and one fifth of g, minus 7　---------------------------
9. One – half of the sum of 5 and s　---------------------------

10. The sum of one – fifth of w, one – fourth of x, and 7   ----------------------------

The Distributive Property

The distributive property tells us if we have an expression like $a(b + c)$, we can multiply a in both terms of parentheses so, $a(b + c) = ab + ac$

Example

$4(x+3)=16$

For solving this equation, we must use the distributive property. $4x+12=16$

$4x = 16-12$

$4x = 4$

$x = 1$

8. Choose the correct choice equivalent to the statement.

1. 5 x (3 + 7) =
   a. 5 +(3 x7)
   b. 5 +3 x 5 + 7
   c. 5 x3 + 5 x 7
   d. 5 x3 x7
   Correct answer →

6. 15 x (3 + 8) =
   a. 15 + 3 x 15 + 8
   b. 15 x 3 x 8
   c. 15 x 3 + 15 x 8
   d. 15 + (3 x 8)
   Correct answer →

2. 8 x (6 +4) =
   a. 8 x 6 x 4
   b. 8 x 6 + 8 x 4
   c. 8 + (6 x 4)
   d. 8 + 6 x 8 x 4
   Correct answer →

7. 13 x (2 + 8) =
   a. 13 x 2 + 13 x8
   b. 13 x 2 x 8
   c. 13 + 2 x 13 + 8
   d. 13 + (2 x 8)
   Correct answer →

3. 11 x (3 + 7) =
    a. 11 x 3 + 11 x 7
    b. 11 x 3 x7
    c. 11 + 3 x 11 x 7
    d. 11+ (3 x 7)
    Correct answer →

4. 4 x (12 + 8) =
    a. 4 x 12 + 8 x 12
    b. 4 x 12 x 8
    c. 4 x 12 + 4 x 5
    d. 4 + (12 x 5)
    Correct answer →

5. 7 x (9 + 6) =
    a. 7 + (9 x 6)
    b. 7 x 9 + 7 x 6
    c. 7 + 9 x 7 + 6
    d. 7 x 9 x6
    Correct answer →

8. 2 x (9 + 5) =
    a. 2 x 9 + 2 x 5
    b. 2 + 9 x 2 +5
    c. 2 x 9 x 5
    d. 2 + (9 x 5)
    Correct answer →

9. 7 x (14 + 2) =
    a. 7 + 14 x 7 + 2
    b. 7 x14 x 2
    c. 7 x 14 + 7 x 2
    d. 7 + (14 x 2)
    Correct answer →

10. 6 x (9 + 3) =
    a. 6 + 9 x 6 + 3
    b. 6 + (9 x 3)
    c. 6 x 9 x 3
    d. 6 x 9 + 6 x 3
    Correct answer →

9. Use the distributive property as shown to find each product.

   1. 97 x 4 =   --- x --- + --- x --- =   ---- + ---- =
   2. 72 x 7=   --- x --- + --- x --- =   ---- + ---- =
   3. 19 x 2 =   --- x --- + --- x --- =   ---- + ---- =
   4. 23 x 9 =   --- x --- + --- x --- =   ---- + ---- =
   5. 46 x 9 =   --- x --- + --- x --- =   ---- + ---- =

6. 15 x 2 =   --- x --- + --- x --- =   ---- + ---- =

7. 95 x 9 =   --- x --- + --- x --- =   ---- + ---- =

8. 55 x 7 =   --- x --- + --- x --- =   ---- + ---- =

9. 64 x 4 =   --- x --- + --- x --- =   ---- + ---- =

10. 43 x 9 = --- x --- + --- x --- =   ---- + ---- =

Evaluating One Variables

To evaluate a mathematical expression that has one variable, find variable and replace a number instead of it.

Example: Evaluate $y = 2x - 8$. ($x=3$)

Variable is x. Now put 3 instead of "x" in the function.

$y = 2(3) - 8 = 6 - 8 = -2$

10. Evaluate each expression using the value given.

1. $c \cdot c \div 4$
$c = 5$

2. $u + 4u$
$u = 4$

3. $u \div u^2$
$u = 2$

4. $2b - b$
$b = 9$

6. $u + 4 + 8$
$u = 2$

7. $7b \div b$
$b = 2$

8. $10 + 2 - x$
$x = 6$

9. $c(6 - 2)$
$c = 4$

5. $8 - c$

    $c = 8$

10. $(10 + y) \div y$

    $y = 9$

Evaluating Two Variables

To evaluate mathematical expressions that has two variables, find variables, and replace numbers instead of them.

Example:

2a + 3b (a = 4, b = 6)

Variables are *a and b.* Replace 4 instead of "*a*" and 6 instead of "*b*".

2 (4) + 3 (6) = 8 + 18 = 26

11. Evaluate each expression using the value given.

    1. $1 \div (z \times y)$

        $z = 1, y = 4$

    2. $10(x - b)$

        $x = 8, b = 3$

    3. $z \times 4 \div x$

        $x = 8, z = 6$

    4. $c - (8 - b)$

        $c = 8, b = 8$

    5. $a \div 10 + b$

        $a = 8, b = 1$

    6. $3x(2y + 1)$

        $x = 1, y = 3$

    7. $2(c + 2x)$

        $c = 3, x = 3$

    8. $3y - (3 + c)$

        $y = 3, c = 1$

    9. $(z \times 3) + 2x$

        $z = 2, x = 5$

    10. $5c + 3y$

        $c = 8, y = 4$

Combining like Terms

Like terms have similar terms. For example, *2x*, *-7x*, and *8x* are like terms. Because their variables are "x".

We can combine like terms. It means we can add or subtract them.

Example:

Find like terms and combine them.

4a + 5x – 3y – 9a + 6y + 2a + 7y – 10x

Like terms: (4a, -9a, 2a), (5x, -10x), (-3y, 6y, 7y)

Now we combine them. 4a – 9a +2a + 5x -10x -3v +6v +7v = -3a -10x +10v

12. Solve the expressions by combining like terms.

1. $x + 2x =$
2. $6x - 3x =$
3. $2x - x =$
4. $4x + 2x =$
5. $5x + x =$
6. $2x + 2x =$
7. $7x - 5x =$
8. $3x - 2x =$
9. $X + x =$
10. $x^2 + 2x^2 =$
11. $4x^2 - 3x^2 =$
12. $3x^2 + 2x^2 =$
13. $2x^2 + 2x + x =$
14. $5x + x^2 - 2x + x^2 =$
15. $3x + 2x - x + 2x^2 =$
16. $6x + 3x^2 - x - x^2 =$
17. $4x + 3 + x^2 + x =$
18. $2x + 3x + 9 + x =$
19. $2x^2 + 3 + 3x - 1 =$
20. $2x + 5 + x^2 =$
21. $x + y + 2y + 5 =$
22. $2x + 3y + x^2 + 6y =$
23. $2x + 2y + x^2 - x + 2x^2 =$
24. $5 + 2x - x^2 + 3x =$
25. $2y + x - x + 3 =$
26. $6y + 2x + y - 2 =$

Answers of Worksheets – Chapter 5

Expressions and Variables

1.
   1. 9
   2. 26
   3. 20
   4. 24
   5. 22
   6. 17
   7. 21
   8. 23

Simplifying Variables and Expressions

2.
   1. $11a$
   2. $8a$
   3. $7b$
   4. $4a$
   5. $13a$
   6. $6b$
   7. $1a$
   8. $4a$
   9. $14b$

3.
   1. $z = 10$
   2. $u = -6$
   3. $y = 8$
   4. $c = 2$
   5. $c = 5$
   6. $x = 1$
   7. $a = 5$
   8. $c = 5$
   9. $u = 3$
   10. $u = 6$
   11. $c = 7$
   12. $x = 5$
   13. $c = 8$
   14. $z = 6$
   15. $x = 8$

4.
   1. $x = 12$
   2. $x = 16$
   3. $x = 35$
   4. $x = 32$
   5. $x = 21$
   6. $x = 2$
   7. $x = 18$
   8. $x = 42$
   9. $x = 72$
   10. $x = 28$
   11. $x = 9000$
   12. $x = 50$

MathePathics

Simplifying Polynomial Expressions

5.

1. $-(13q^5 + 5q^2 + q + 5)$
2. $11c^2 + 3c + 15$
3. $14q^2 - 12q - 4$
4. $-(2x^4 + 10x^2 + 4x - 19)$
5. $-89y^3 - 4y + 10$
6. $3x^3 + 6x^2 + x - 1$
7. $-54p^3 + 5p - 13$
8. $-23x^2 - 9x + 17$
9. $34c^4 - c^2 + c - 12$
10. $5x^2 - x + 50$

Translate Phrases into an Algebraic Statement

6.

1. $p - (q + r)$
2. $9 + x$
3. $15 - p$
4. $p - 15$
5. $(x + y) - 3$
6. $c + b^4$
7. $m + n$
8. $5g - h^4$
9. $2p - q$
10. $xy - 58$
11. $3(g)$
12. $10 \div p$
13. $9y$
14. $9 \div x$
15. $12x = 48$
16. $2(2h)$

7.

1. $\frac{1}{4}(n + 8) - 6b$
2. $\frac{1}{4} + c^3$
3. $\frac{1}{6}x + 5$
4. $q^3 - 6k + 5$
5. $3^n - 4$
6. $7 + g^8$
7. $5 + 6c$
8. $\frac{1}{6}n + \frac{1}{5}g - 7$
9. $\frac{1}{2}(5 + s)$
10. $\frac{1}{5}w + \frac{1}{4}x + 7$

80

MathePathics

The Distributive Property

8.

1. c. 5 x 3 + 5 x 7
2. b. 8 x 6 + 8 x 4
3. a. 11 x 3 + 11 x 7
4. a. 4 x 12 + 8 x 12
5. b. 7 x 9 + 7 x 6
6. c. 15 x 3 + 15 x 8
7. a. 13 x 2 + 13 x 8
8. a. 2 x 9 + 2 x 5
9. a. 7 + 14 x 7 + 2
10. d. 6 x 9 + 6 x 3

9.

1. 97 x 4 =   90 x 4 + 7 x 4 =   360 + 28 = 388
2. 72 x 7=   70 x 7 + 2 x 7 =   490 + 14 = 504
3. 19 x 2 =   10 x 2 + 9 x 2 =   20 + 18 = 38
4. 23 x 9 =   20 x 9 + 3 x 9 =   180 + 27 = 207
5. 46 x 9 =   40 x 9 + 4 x 9 =   360 + 36 = 396
6. 15 x 2 =   10 x 2 + 5 x 2 =   20 + 10 = 30
7. 95 x 9 =   90 x 9 + 5 x 9 =   810 + 45 = 855
8. 55 x 7 =   50 x 7 + 5 x 7 =   350 + 35 = 385
9. 64 x 4 =   60 x 4 + 4 x 4 =   240 + 16 = 256
10. 43 x 9 =   40 x 9 + 3 x 9 =   360 + 27 = 387

Evaluating One Variables

10.

1. 6.25
2. 20
6. 14
7. 7

3. 0.5
4. 9
5. 0

8. 6
9. 16
10. 2.11

Evaluating Two Variables

11.
1. 0.25
2. 50
3. 3
4. 8
5. 0.72

6. 21
7. 18
8. 5
9. 16
10. 52

Combining like Terms

12.
1. $3x$
2. $3x$
3. x
4. $6x$
5. $6x$
6. $4x$
7. $2x$
8. x
9. $2x$
10. $3x^2$
11. x^2
12. $5x^2$
13. $2x^2 + 3x$

14. $3x + 2x^2$
15. $4x + 2x^2$
16. $5x + 2x^2$
17. $x^2 + 5x + 3$
18. $6x + 9$
19. $2x^2 + 4x - 1$
20. $x^2 + 2x + 5$
21. $3y + x + 5$
22. $x^2 + 2x + 9y$
23. $3x^2 + x + 2y$
24. $-x^2 + 5x + 5$
25. $2y + 3 =$
26. $7y + 2x - 2$

Extra Note for Chapter 5:

Chapter 6: Equations

One – Step Equations

Two – Step Equations

Multi – Step Equations

Answers of Worksheets – Chapter 6

One – Step Equations

In this state, by doing one step, you can solve an equation.

Look at the example:

$2 + x = 7$

For finding x, you must just subtract 2 from 7.

$x = 7 - 2 = 5$

1. Solve each one – step equation.

1.	$4.5 = z + 33$		17.	$-12 = -9 + t$
2.	$-156 = x + 5.6$		18.	$+20v = 5$
3.	$21v = 72$		19.	$-5 + n = 32$
4.	$-8 = 67 + m$		20.	$3y = 8 + 2$
5.	$33.6 = 4.8p$		21.	$6 = 9v$
6.	$\dfrac{k}{4} = -22$		22.	$7 - m = 8$
7.	$-6.3 = 3 + p$		23.	$3 - j = 2$
8.	$n + 7 = 14$		24.	$33 = \dfrac{m}{3}$
9.	$-24 = \dfrac{y}{4}$		25.	$-6x = -36$
10.	$5.5k = 60$		26.	$\dfrac{x}{4} = 8$
11.	$-6d = -24$		27.	$\dfrac{-30}{x} = -0.3$
12.	$h + 3 = -4$		28.	$7x = 42$
13.	$-12 = f - 7$		28.	$-2x = -42$
14.	$9 = -4 + c$		30.	$15 + x = 17$
15.	$\dfrac{g}{5} = -13$		31.	$x - 13 = 23$
16.	$4v = -40$		32.	$-6c = 9$

MathePathics

2. Solve each one – step equation. Use your answer to navigate through the maze.

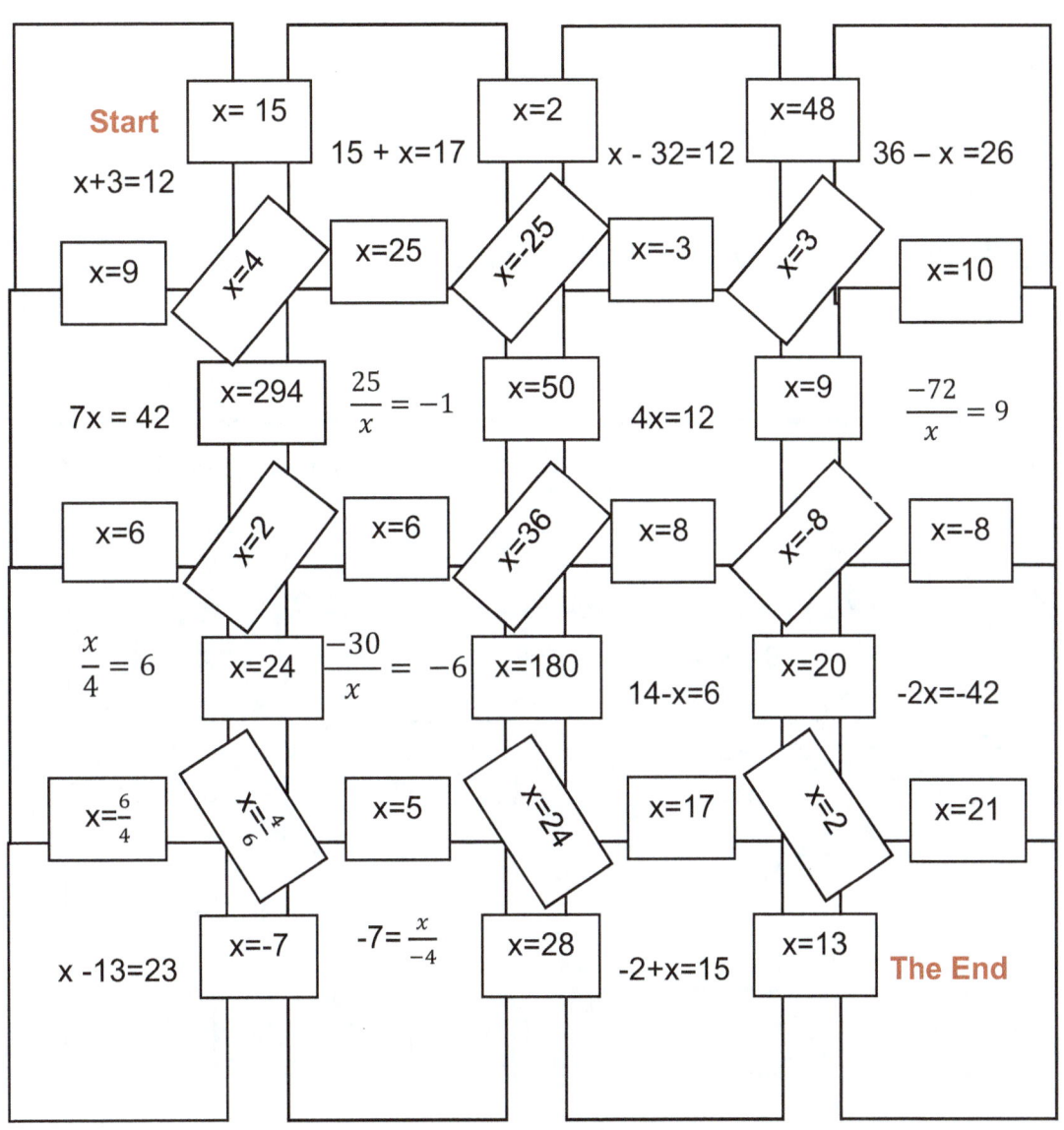

Two – Step Equations

86

MathePathics

In this state, by doing two steps you can solve an equation. It means you need to do two operations among addition, subtraction, multiplication, and division.

Example:

$2x + 3 = 12$

Step 1: Take 3 to the right side and subtract 12 from it.

$2x = 12 - 3 \longrightarrow 2x = 8$

Step 2: Divide both sides by two to leave x alone.

$\dfrac{2x}{2} = \dfrac{8}{2} \rightarrow x = 4$

3. Solve each one – step equation. Use your answer to navigate through the maze.

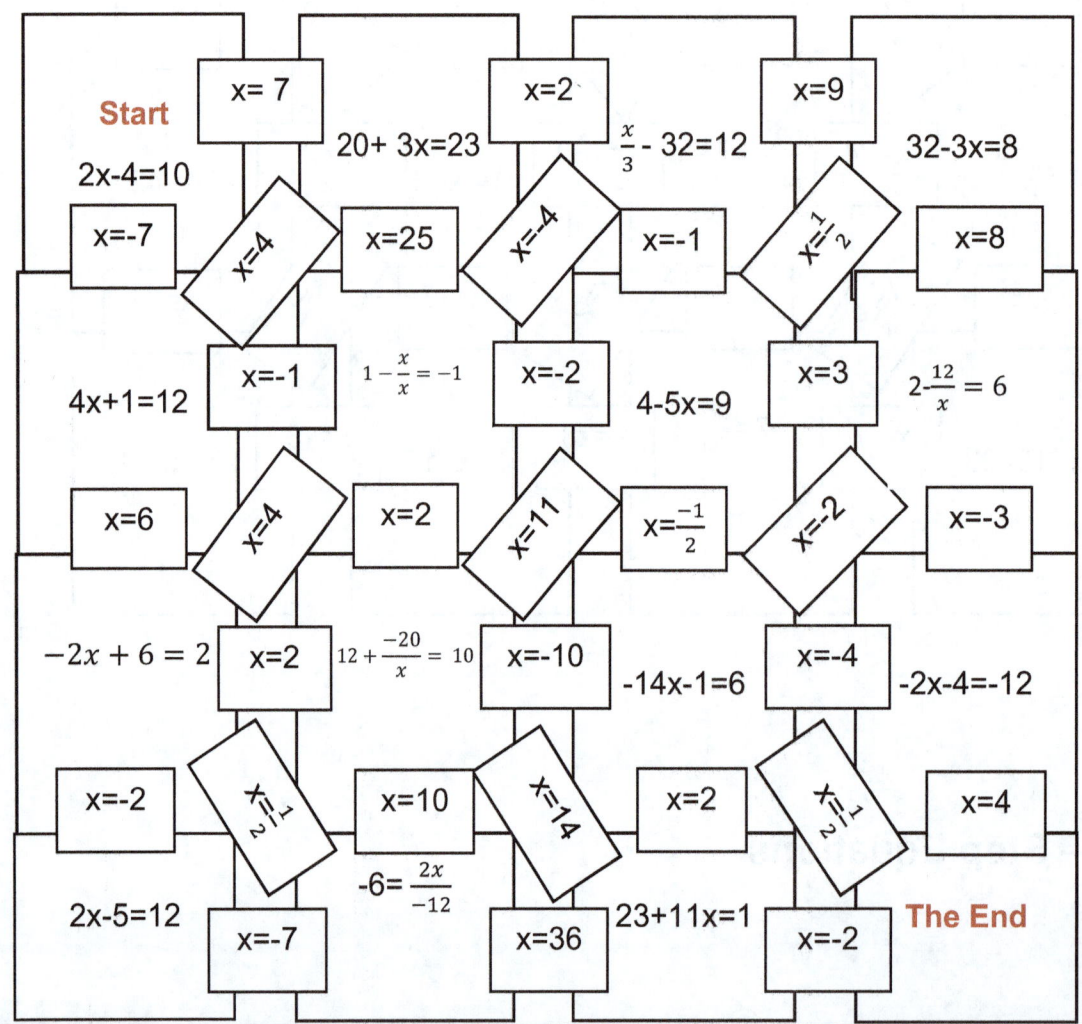

4. Solve each two – step equation.

1. $\dfrac{v}{2} - 9 = -12$
2. $6 - \dfrac{x}{9} = -3$
3. $\dfrac{v}{2} + (-9) = 0$
4. $1 - \dfrac{a}{5} = -3$
5. $-2 + \dfrac{x}{6} = -5$
6. $\dfrac{a}{6} + 10 = 5$
7. $-1 - \dfrac{x}{2} = 2$
8. $\dfrac{v}{4} - (-9) = 15$
9. $-2 + \dfrac{x}{6} = 6$
10. $-1 + \dfrac{y}{3} = 3$
11. $-3 + \dfrac{y}{-6} = -7$
12. $+9 - \dfrac{v}{6} = 2$
13. $\dfrac{y}{2} + (-5) = 12$
14. $\dfrac{x}{5} - (-31) = 1$
15. $-6 - \dfrac{y}{3} = 14$

Multi – Step Equation

There are equations that need to be solved by doing some steps.

We want to solve $\dfrac{2(5+x)}{4} = 3x + 7$. For solving it we need to perform 4 steps.

Step 1: $\dfrac{2(5+x)}{4} = 3x + 7 \longrightarrow \dfrac{5+x}{2} = 3x + 7$

Step 2: Multiply 2 by (3x+7). $5 + x = 6x + 14$

Step 3: Take variables left side and numbers right side.
$x - 6x = 14 - 5 \longrightarrow -5x = 9$

Step 4: Divide both sides by -5 to leave x alone. $\dfrac{-5x}{-5} = \dfrac{9}{-5} \longrightarrow x = -\dfrac{9}{5}$

5. Solve each equation.

1. $-20 = -4x - 6x$
2. $8x - 2 = -9 + 7x$
3. $4m - 4 = 5m$
4. $5p - 14 = 8p + 4$
9. $6 = 1 - 2n + 5$
10. $a + 5 = -5a + 5$
11. $p - 1 = 5p + 3p - 8$
12. $p - 4 = -9 + 6p$

5. $\quad -8 = -(x+4)$
6. $\quad 14 = -(p-8)$
7. $\quad -18 - 6k = 6(1+3k)$
8. $\quad 2(4x-3) - 8 = 4 + 2x$

13. $\quad 12 = -4(-6x-3)$
14. $\quad -(7-4x) = 9$
15. $\quad 5n + 34 = -2(1-7n)$
16. $\quad 3n - 5 = -8(6+5n)$

6. Solve each equation and find x.

1. $\quad 3x + 5 = 9x \quad$ x= ------------------
2. $\quad 4x + 5 = 9 + x \quad$ x= ------------------
3. $\quad 5x + 5 = 3x + 11 \quad$ x= ------------------
4. $\quad 6x + 14 = 7x + 8 \quad$ x= ------------------
5. $\quad 8x = 5x + 7 \quad$ x= ------------------
6. $\quad 12x - 4 = 5x - 25 \quad$ x= ------------------
7. $\quad 6x + 7 = x - 8 \quad$ x= ------------------
8. $\quad 9x + 10 - 5 = -x + 8 \quad$ x= ------------------
9. $\quad 2(x+1) - 3 = x - 2 \quad$ x= ------------------
10. $\quad 5(x+2) = 2x - 4 \quad$ x= ------------------
11. $\quad 3x = 16 - x \quad$ x= ------------------
12. $\quad 5x + 3 - 6 = 9 - x \quad$ x= ------------------
13. $\quad 3(x+1) = 4x + 6 \quad$ x= ------------------
14. $\quad 8x = 5x - 6 \quad$ x= ------------------
15. $\quad 7x - 2 = 15x \quad$ x= ------------------

Answers of Worksheets – Chapter 6

One – Step Equations

1.

1.	$z = -37.5$		17.	$t = -3$
2.	$x = -150.4$		18.	$v = 0.25$
3.	$v = 3.42$		19.	$n = 37$
4.	$-75 = m$		20.	$y = 2.6$
5.	$p = 8$		21.	$v = 0.66$
6.	$k = -88$		22.	$m = -1$
7.	$p = -3.3$		23.	$j = 1$
8.	$n = 7$		24.	$m = 99$
9.	$y = -96$		25.	$x = 6$
10.	$k = 10.90$		26.	$x = 32$
11.	$d = 4$		27.	$x = 100$
12.	$h = -7$		28.	$x = 6$
13.	$f = -5$		28.	$x = 21$
14.	$c = 13$		30.	$x = 2$
15.	$g = -65$		31.	$x = 33$
16.	$v = -10$		32.	$c = 1.5$

MathePathics

2.

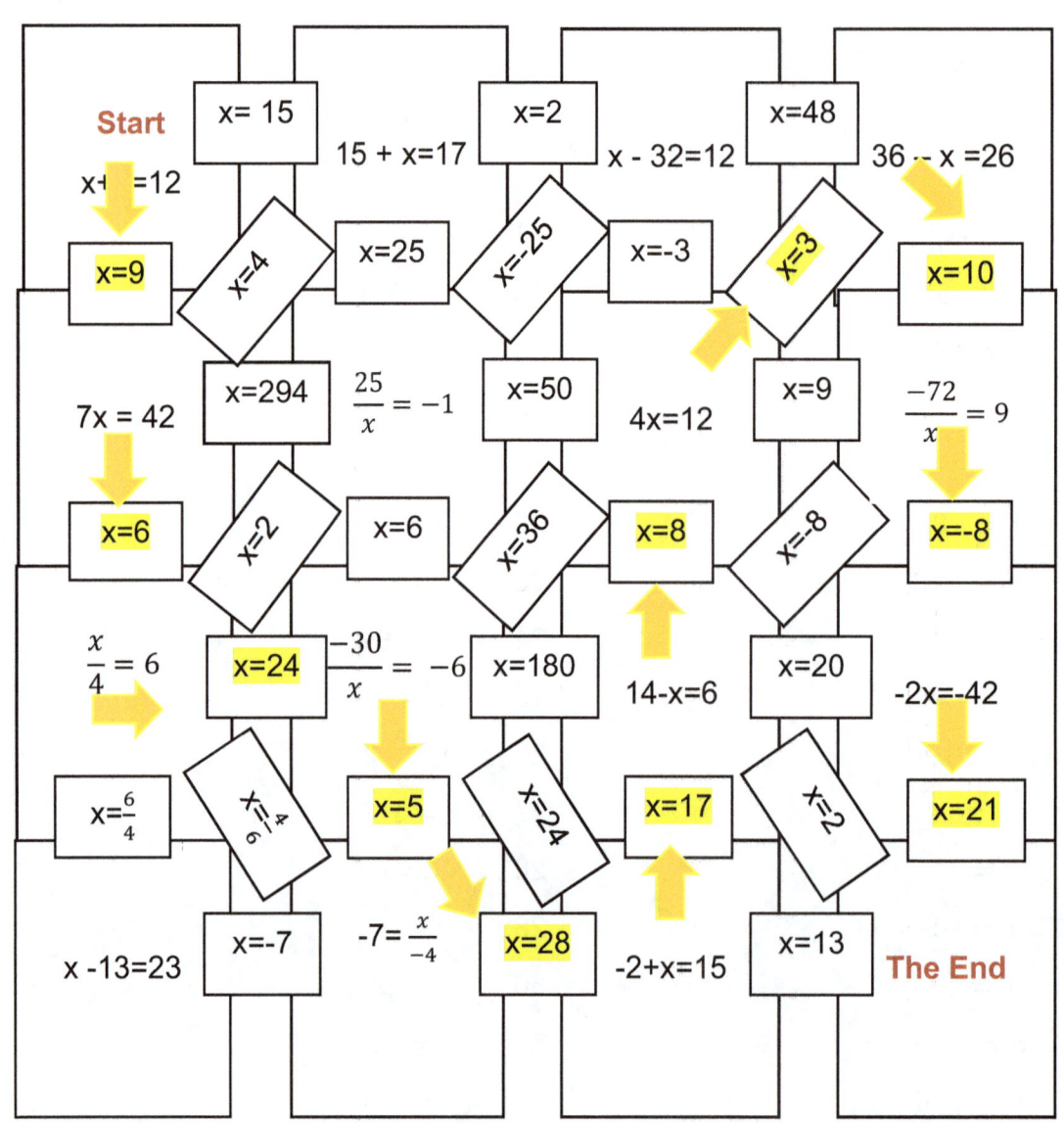

MathePathics

Two – Step Equation

3.

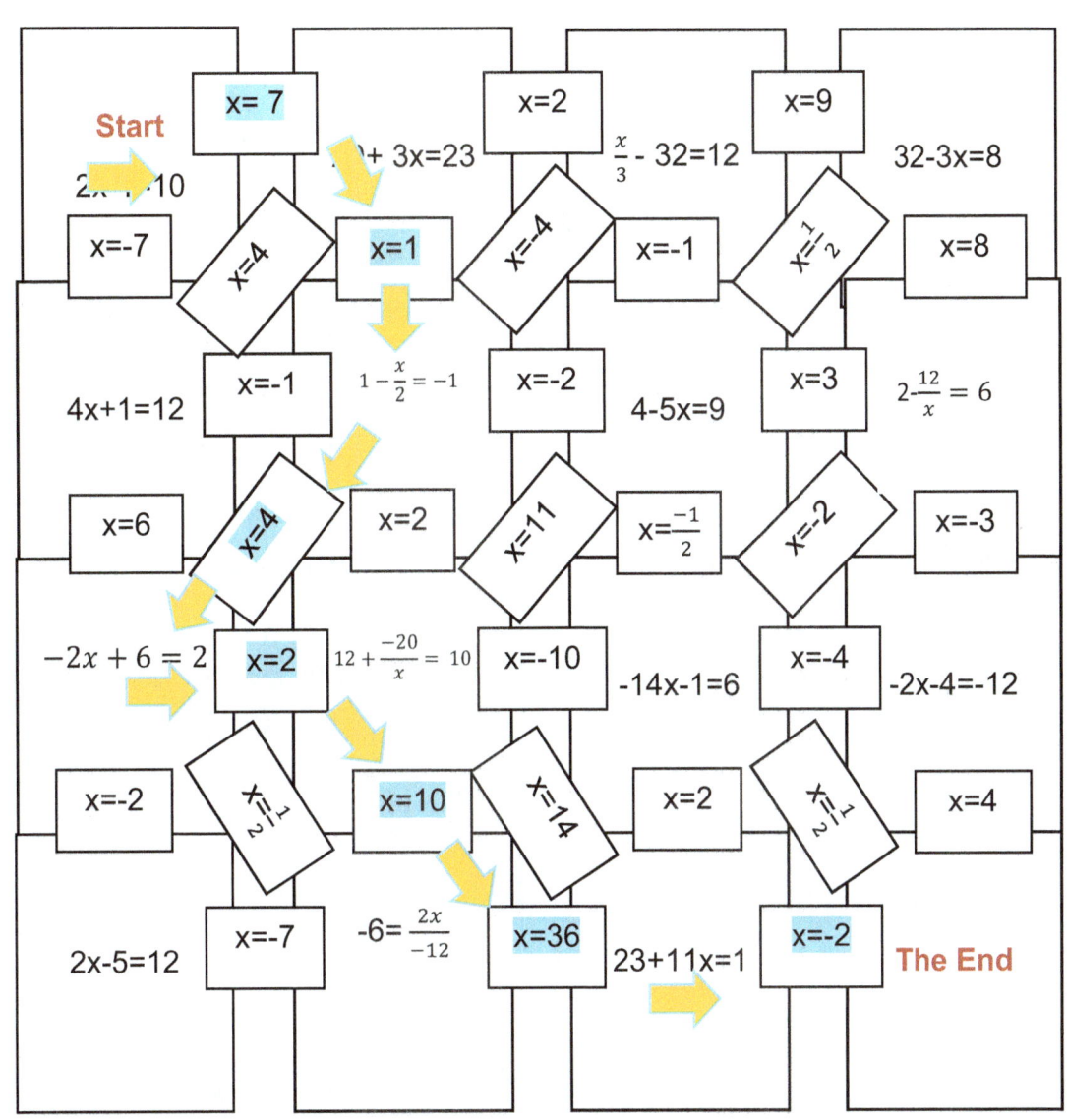

4.

1. $v = -6$
2. $x = 81$
3. $v = 18$
4. $a = 20$
5. $x = -18$
6. $a = -30$
7. $x = -6$
8. $v = 24$
9. $x = 48$
10. $y = 12$
11. $y = 24$
12. $v = 42$
13. $y = 34$
14. $x = -150$
15. $y = -60$

MathePathics

Multi – Step Equations

5.

1. $x = 2$
2. $x = 7$
3. $m = -4$
4. $p = -6$
5. $x = 4$
6. $p = -6$
7. $k = -1$
8. $x = 3$
9. $n = 0$
10. $a = 0$
11. $p = 1$
12. $p = 1$
13. $x = 0$
14. $x = 4$
15. $n = \dfrac{32}{9}$
16. $n = -1$

6.

1. x = 0.83
2. x = 1.33
3. x = 3
4. x = 6
5. x = 2.33
6. x = -3
7. x = -3
8. x = 0.3
9. x = 3
10. x = 4.66
11. x = 4
12. x = 2
13. x = -3
14. x = -2
15. x = -0.25

Extra Note for Chapter 6:

Chapter 7:

Inequalities

Graphing Single – Variable inequalities

One – Step Inequalities

Two – Step Inequalities

Multi – Step Inequalities

Answers of Worksheets – Chapter 7

Graphing Single – Variable inequalities

We can indicate answer of an inequalities on the number lines. We use dot and line for indicating.

For > or <, use open dot.

For ≤ or ≥, use closed dot.

Example:

$x > 2$ $x \leq -3$

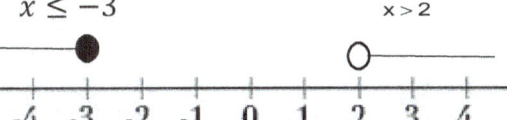

1. Graph each inequality on a number line.

   1. $x < 1$

      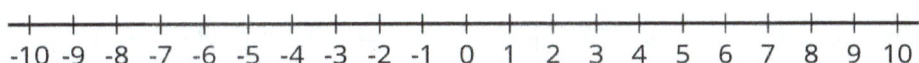

   2. $x \geq -6$

      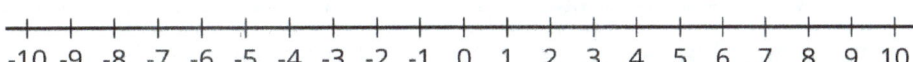

   3. $x \geq 4$

      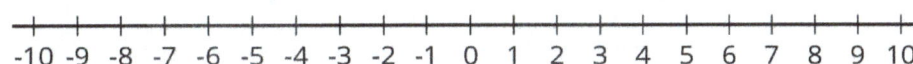

   4. $x \geq 8$

      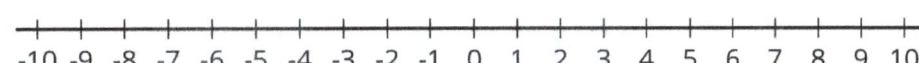

   5. $x \leq 1$

      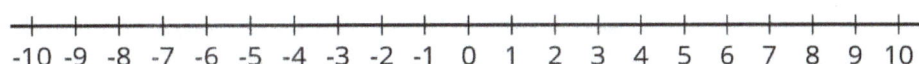

2. Solve the inequalities and find each variable then show them in number line.

1. $\dfrac{x}{3} \geq 5$
2. $\dfrac{1}{2} < x$
3. $x - 6 > 1$
4. $\dfrac{x}{4} < 1$
5. $6 - x \leq 8$
6. $3 + x > \dfrac{2}{3}$
7. $x \geq \dfrac{2}{4}$
8. $12 < x + 8$
9. $2 \leq x < 5$
10. $60 < x + 3$
11. $\dfrac{x}{9} \geq 2 - 1$
12. $2 < \dfrac{x}{3} \leq 1$
13. $-x + 1 < 2$
14. $x + 2 > \dfrac{3}{8}$
15. $12 - 2x < 2$

One – step Inequalities

Some inequalities are simple and for solving them you should perform one step.

Example: We want to solve $x - 3 > 8$.

We just take -3 to the right side of inequalities and add 8 to 3.

-x > 8 + 3 → x > 11

3. Circle the possible values that satisfy each inequality.

1. $2x \geq 8$
   1   3   4   6

2. $\dfrac{x}{2} > 9$
   2   20   6   8

5. $x - 3 < 9$
   16   5   18   10

6. $5x \leq 10$
   5   1   2   4

9. $12 > x + 6$
   2   3   6   5

10. $x + 5 > 9$
    2   1   7   9

97

3. $x + 7 \geq 14$

    3   11   5   7

7. $\dfrac{x}{3} < 5$

    17   12   6   16

11. $16 > x + 7$

    8   10   15   12

4. $5 > \dfrac{x}{5}$

    20   125   5   15

8. $6x \leq 18$

    5   4   3   2

12. $20 \geq 2x$

    13   10   9   8

Two – step Inequalities

For solving some inequalities, you need to perform two steps. Consider following example.

5x – 2 < 23

Step 1: Take 2 to the right side. 5x < 23+2 → 5x < 25

Step 2: Divide both sides of inequality by 5 to leave **x** alone.

$\dfrac{5x}{5} < \dfrac{25}{5}$ → x < 5

4. Solve the following two – step inequalities.

1. $5x - 6 > 1$
2. $36x - 36 \leq 6$
3. $32 + 2x > 5$
4. $6x - 2 < 12$
5. $3x + 8 \geq 1$
6. $1 > 9 + 3x$
9. $1 - 6x > -15$
10. $21x - 7 \leq 3$
11. $30x - 5 \geq 6$
12. $35 - 7x > 6$
13. $12x - 6 > 15$
14. $3 - 6x > 1$

7. $34 - 32x < 1$

8. $50x - 4 \geq 3$

15. $6x + 10 \leq 2$

16. $3x - 2 \leq 12$

Multi – step Inequalities

For solving difficult inequalities follow below steps.
- If there are parentheses, you must do functions in it.
- Write variables on the left side and numbers on the right side.
- Find like term and combine them.

📎 If an inequality gets multiplied or divided by a negative number, unequal direction changes.

Example: Solve $3(5x – 2) < 7x – 8$

Step 1: Use distributive properties to delete parentheses. $15x – 6 < 7x – 8$

Step 2: Write variables left and numbers right. $15x – 7x < -8 + 6$

Step 3: $8x < -2$ → $\dfrac{8x}{8} < \dfrac{-2}{8}$ → $x < -\dfrac{1}{4}$

5. Choose the correct solution that best describes each inequality.

1. $5x - 2 \geq 3$

2. $\dfrac{x-1}{4} \leq 3$

3. $19 + 2x > 5$

4. $5x - 17 \geq 3$

5. $\dfrac{x}{7} + 1 > 5$

6. $6x + 2 < 14$

7. $\dfrac{x}{2} + 4 < 6$

8. $7x + 3x \leq 10$

9. $4x + 9 > 1$

10. $\dfrac{x+9}{3} \geq 6$

MathePathics

6. Solve the Multi – step inequalities and find the variables.

A) $6 > -\dfrac{2}{3}(7x - 2)$

B) $-\dfrac{1}{3}(x - 9) + 4 < -2$

C) $-\dfrac{1}{4}x - 8 < \dfrac{3}{4}$

D) $-\dfrac{2}{7}(1 - 4x) + 8 < 18$

E) $\dfrac{2.6x - 4.8}{-2} + 3.2 > -8.7$

F) $7(2 - x) + 9 > 2$

G) $2 - 3(x + 4) > 17$

H) $-\dfrac{1}{3}(5x - 9) + 4 < -2$

I) $-\dfrac{2}{3}(7x - 2) > 6$

J) $-\dfrac{2}{7}(1 - 4x) + 8 > 18$

K) $-3(4 + 2x) < 18$

L) $-32.9 < 1.2(6 - 4.3x) - 6.44x$

M) $10 < -2x - 5x - 4$

N) $-2 < -\dfrac{1}{3}(x - 9) + 4$

O) $-\dfrac{2}{7}(3 - 4x) < 18$

P) $-\dfrac{1}{3}(5x - 9) + 4 > -2$

Q) $-3x + 4 > 5$

R) $7(2 - x) + 9 < 2$

S) $-2x - 5x - 4 < 10$

T) $-32.9 > 1.2(4.3x) - 6.44x$

U) $2 - 3(x + 4) < 17$

V) $\dfrac{2.6x - 4.8}{-2} + 3.2 < -8.7$

W) $\dfrac{2}{7}(3 - 4x) + 8 > 18$

X) $-3x + 4 < 5$

Y) $-3(4 + 2x) > 18$

Z) $-\dfrac{1}{4}x - 8 > \dfrac{3}{4}$

MathePathics

Answers of Worksheets – Chapter 7

Graphing Single – Variable inequalities

1.

   1.

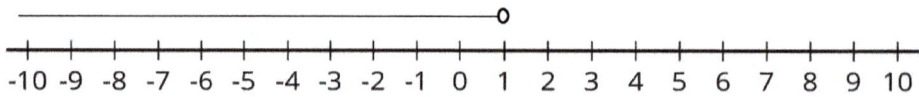

   2.

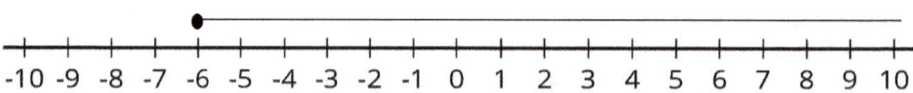

   3.

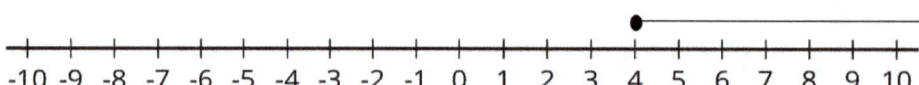

   4.

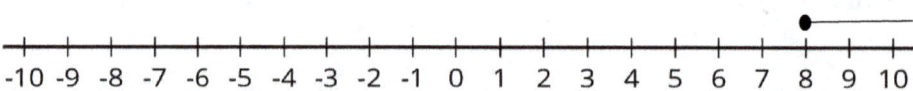

   5.

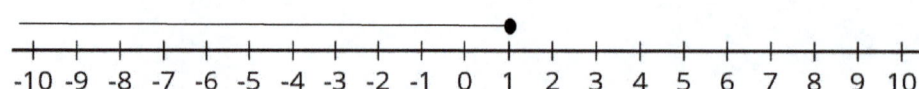

One – step Inequalities

2.

   1. $x \geq 15$ 9. $2 \leq x < 5$

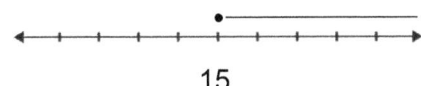

15

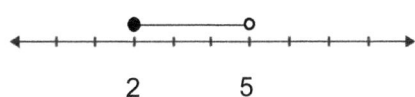

2   5

2. $\frac{1}{2} < x$

10. $57 < x$

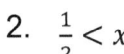

$\frac{1}{2}$

57

3. $x > 7$

11. $x \geq 9$

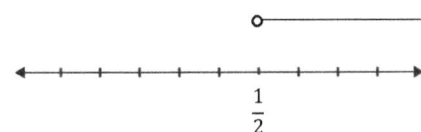

7

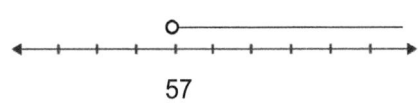

9

4. $\frac{x}{4} < 1$

12. $6 < x \leq 3$

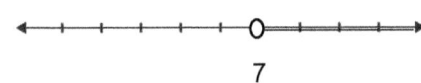

4

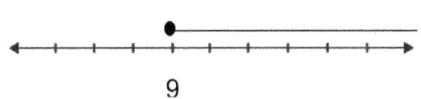

3   6

5. $x \leq 2$

13. $x < -1$

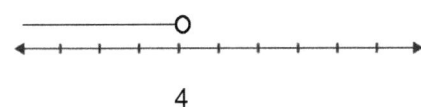

2

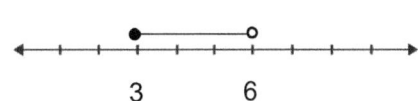

-1

6. $x > -2$

14. $x > \frac{-5}{8}$

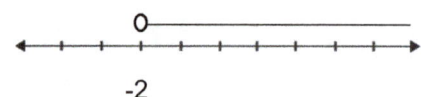
-2

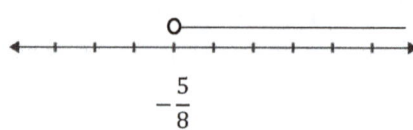
$-\frac{5}{8}$

7. $x \geq \frac{1}{2}$

15. $x < 5$

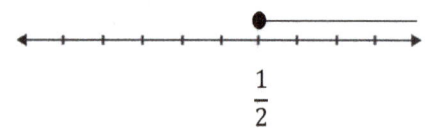
$\frac{1}{2}$

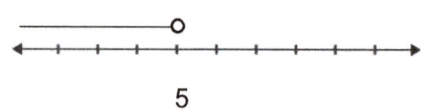
5

8. $4 < x$

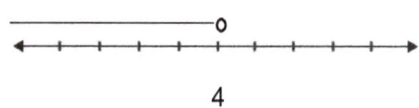
4

3.

1. $x \geq 4$
   1   3   [4]   [6]

2. $x > 18$
   2   [20]   6   8

3. $x \geq 7$
   3   [11]   5   [7]

4. $125 > x$
   [20]   125   [5]   [15]

5. $x < 12$
   16   [5]   18   [10]

6. $x \leq 2$
   5   [1]   [2]   4

7. $x < 15$
   17   [12]   [6]   16

8. $x \leq 3$
   5   4   [3]   [2]

9. $6 > x$
   [2]   [3]   6   [5]

10. $x > 3$
    2   1   [7]   [9]

11. $9 > x$
    [8]   10   15   12

12. $10 \geq x$
    13   [10]   [9]   [8]

MathePathics

Two – step Inequalities

4.

1. $x > \dfrac{7}{5}$
2. $x \leq \dfrac{7}{6}$
3. $x > -\dfrac{27}{2}$
4. $x < \dfrac{7}{3}$
5. $x \geq \dfrac{-7}{3}$
6. $x < \dfrac{-8}{3}$
7. $x > \dfrac{33}{32}$
8. $x \geq \dfrac{7}{50}$
9. $x < \dfrac{8}{3}$
10. $x \leq \dfrac{10}{21}$
11. $x \geq \dfrac{11}{30}$
12. $x < \dfrac{29}{7}$
13. $x > \dfrac{7}{4}$
14. $x < \dfrac{1}{3}$
15. $x \leq -\dfrac{4}{3}$
16. $x \leq \dfrac{14}{3}$

Multi – step Inequalities

5.

1. $x \geq 1$
2. $x \leq 13$
3. $x > -7$
4. $x \geq 4$
5. $x > 28$
6. $x < 2$
7. $x < 4$
8. $x \leq 1$
9. $x > -2$
10. $x \geq 9$

6.

- A $\quad x > -1$
- B $\quad x > 27$
- C $\quad x > -35$
- D $\quad x < 9$
- E $\quad x < 11$
- F $\quad x < 3$
- G $\quad x < -9$
- H $\quad x > \dfrac{27}{5}$
- I $\quad x < -1$
- J $\quad x > 9$
- K $\quad x > -5$
- L $\quad x < \dfrac{401}{116}$
- M $\quad x < -2$
- N $\quad x < 27$
- O $\quad x < \dfrac{33}{2}$
- P $\quad x < \dfrac{27}{5}$
- Q $\quad x < -\dfrac{1}{3}$
- R $\quad x > 3$
- S $\quad x > -2$
- T $\quad x > 22.70$
- U $\quad x > -9$
- V $\quad x > 11$
- W $\quad x < -8$
- X $\quad x > -\dfrac{1}{3}$
- Y $\quad x < -5$
- Z $\quad x < -35$

Extra Note for Chapter 7:

Chapter 8: Linear Functions

Finding Slope

Graphing Lines Using Slope – Intercept form

Graphing Lines Using Standard Form

Writing Linear Equations

Graphing Linear Inequalities

Finding Midpoint

Finding Distance of Two Points

Answers of Worksheets – Chapter 8

Finding Slope

For finding slop of a line, you should find two points on it and calculate slop using the formula below.

$A(x_1, y_1)$ $A(-3, 0)$
$B(x_2, y_2)$ $B(0, 3)$

$m = \dfrac{y_2 - y_1}{x_2 - x_1}$ $m = \dfrac{3 - 0}{0 - (-3)} = 1$

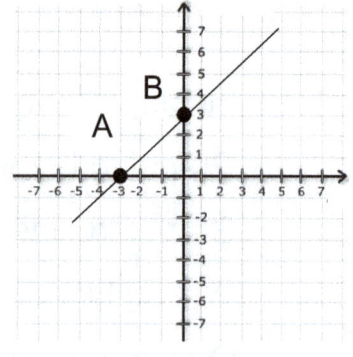

1. Find the slope of the line that goes through the pair of points.

   1.   (2,9) and (-6, -7)   7.   (4, -2) and (-8, -2)   13.   (-9,0) and (-9,7)

   2.   (5,2) and (4, -1)   8.   (0,6) and (5, -4)   14.   (6,1) and (6, -1)

3. (0,2) and (-3,2)

9. (-1, -5) and (2,3)

15. (2,5) and (4,6)

4. (-1,4) and (2,3)

10. (5,0) and (5, -1)

16. (2,5) and (4,6)

5. (10,4) and (5, -6)

11. (-3,0) and (5,0)

17. (0,9) and (-5,7)

6. (3, -4) and (2,0)

12. (0,2) and (3,8)

18. (6,40) and (4,30)

MathePathics

Graphing Line Using slope – Intercept Form

When a liner equation is written in the form of y = mx + b, slope intercept is used.

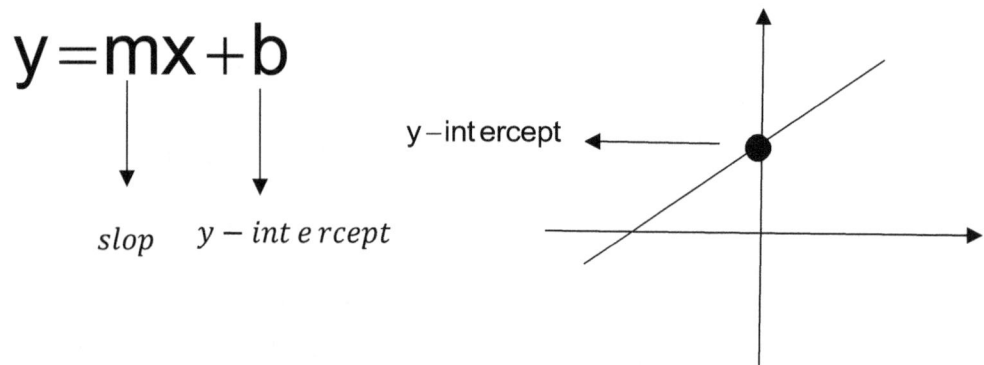

.y- intercept is the point where line crosses the y-axis.

2. Write an equation of the line with the given slope and y–intercept.

1. Slope: 5, y-intercept: -3

2. Slope: -6, y-intercept: -2

3. Slope: 3, y-intercept: 2

4. Slope: 1, y-intercept: -12

5. Slope: -2, y-intercept: 7

6. Slope: 7, y-intercept: 1

7. Slope: -4, y-intercept: -9

8. Slope: 0, y-intercept: 8

3. Find the value of "y" so that the line passing through the two points has the given slope.

1. (2, y); (3, 3); m=2

2. (3, 5); (1, y); m=2/3

109

4. Write an equation of the line shown in each graph.

1.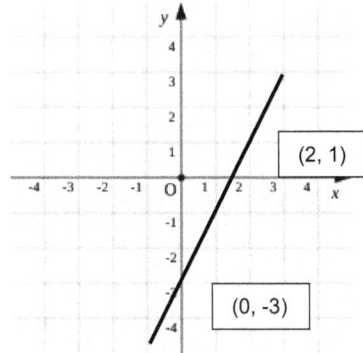

b = _____

m = _____

Equation: _____

2.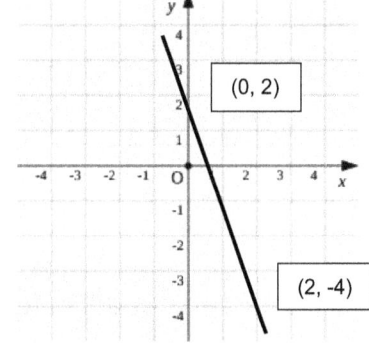

b = _____

m = _____

Equation: _____

3.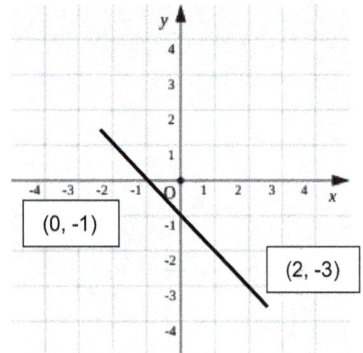

b = _____

m = _____

Equation: _____

4.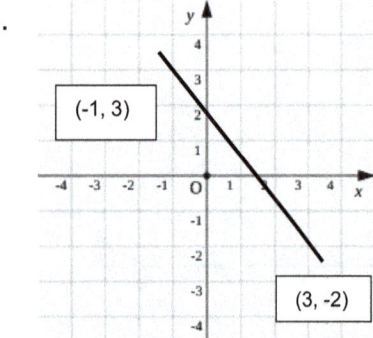

b = _____

m = _____

Equation: _____

5. Write the equation for each graph then find the slope, X – intercept, and Y- intercept of each line.

1.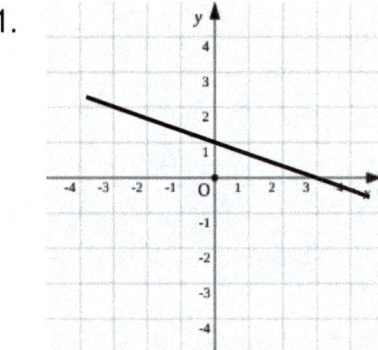

7.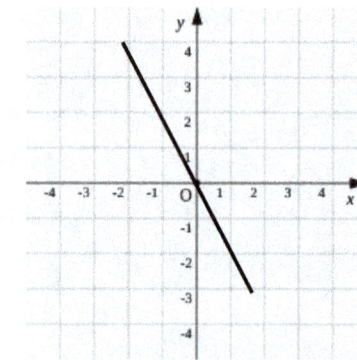

111

Slope =

Y- Intercept =

X- Intercept =

y =

Slope =

Y- Intercept =

X- Intercept =

y=

2.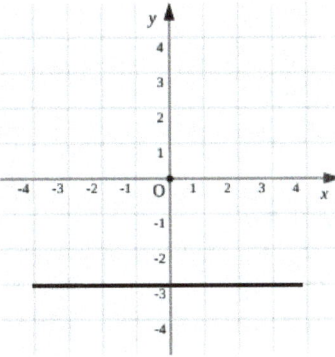

8.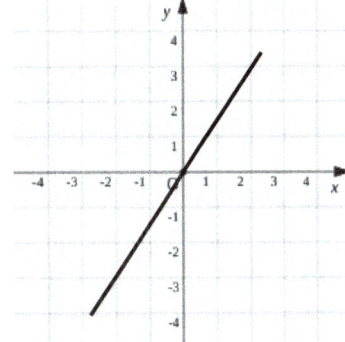

Slope =

Y- Intercept =

X- Intercept =

y =

Slope =

Y- Intercept =

X- Intercept =

y =

3.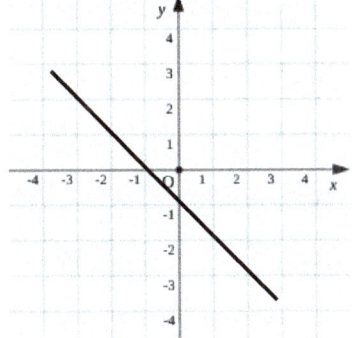

9.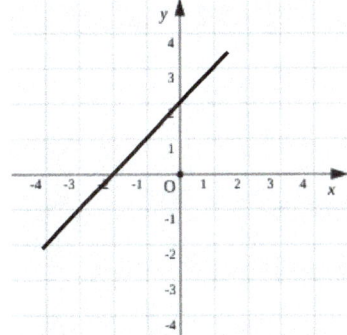

Slope =

Y- Intercept =

X- Intercept =

y =

Slope =

Y- Intercept =

X- Intercept =

y =

4.

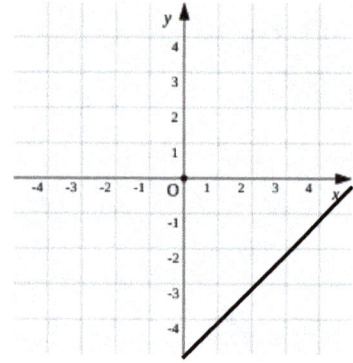

Slope =

Y- Intercept =

X- Intercept =

y =

10.

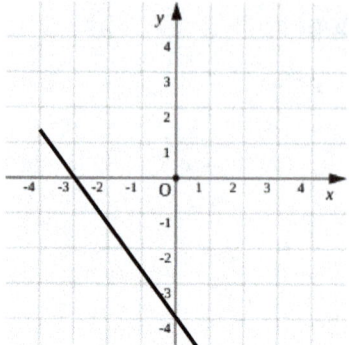

Slope =

Y- Intercept =

X- Intercept =

y =

5.

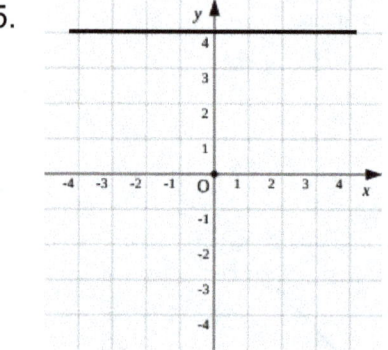

Slope =

Y- Intercept =

X- Intercept =

y =

11.

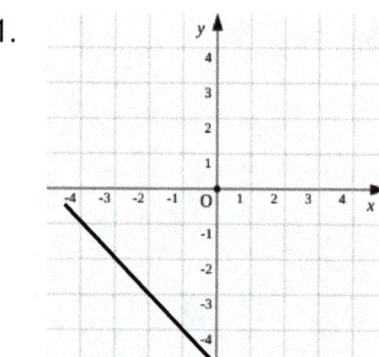

Slope =

Y- Intercept =

X- Intercept =

y =

6.

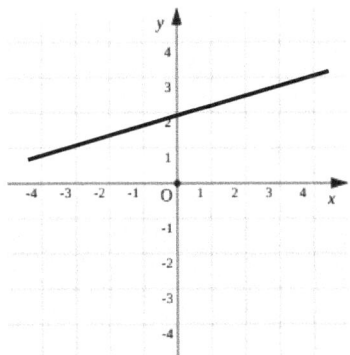

Slope =

Y- Intercept =

X- Intercept =

y =

12.

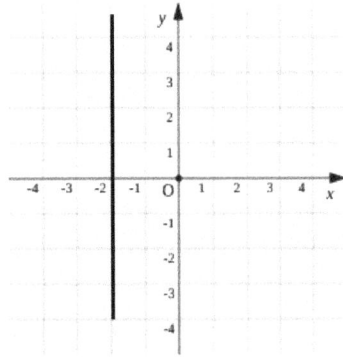

Slope =

Y- Intercept =

X- Intercept =

y =

Graphing Line Using Standard Form

To graph a line in standard form of AX+BY=C:

- You must leave **Y** alone.
- Move the **X** term to the right side.
- $BY = C - AX \longrightarrow Y = \dfrac{C - AX}{B}$
- Find two points for graphing line.

(Put two different values of x in equation and find y.)

A and B → Coefficient

C → Constant

Example:

$3x + 3y = 12 \rightarrow 3y = -3x + 12 \rightarrow y = -x + 4$

$x = 2 \rightarrow y = -(2) + 4 = 2 \rightarrow (2,2)$

$x = 3 \rightarrow y = -(3) + 4 = 1 \rightarrow (3,1)$

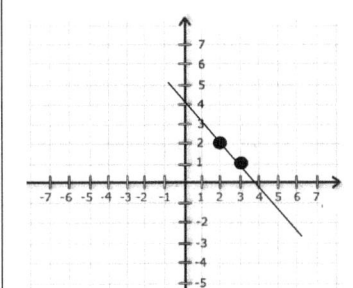

6. Write the equation of the line through the given points in slope–intercept form. Then rewrite the equation in standard form.

1. (8, 2), (14, 1)
5. (-5, 13), (-10, 9)

2. (5, -3), (-2, 0)

6. (-6, 2), (0, 5)

3. (4, 8), (2, 12)

7. (6, 2), (-1, 7)

4. (0, 7), (-5, 12)

8. (100, 90), (80, 120)

7. Convert standard to slope-intercept form.

   1. Standard form: $10x - 7y = -8$
      Slope-intercept form:

   6. Standard form: $8x + y = 9$
      Slope-intercept form:

   2. Standard form: $x + 6y = -2$
      Slope-intercept form:

   7. Standard form: $4x + 3y = 9$
      Slope-intercept form:

   3. Standard form: $3x + 12y = -8$
      Slope-intercept form:

   8. Standard form: $x + 2y = -8$
      Slope-intercept form:

   4. Standard form: $11x - 8y = 3$
      Slope-intercept form:

   9. Standard form: $4x + 5y = 4$
      Slope-intercept form:

5. Standard form: $10x - 12y = -4$

    Slope-intercept form:

10. Standard form: $3x - y = 9$

    Slope-intercept form:

Writing Linear Equation

To write an equation for a line:

- Choose two points on the line. $A(x_1, y_1)$, $B(x_2, y_2)$
- Find slop (m). $m = \dfrac{y_2 - y_1}{x_2 - x_1}$
- Find y-intercept (b).
- Place "m" and "b" in the y = mx + b

Example: Write equation of the line.

$A(-1,-3) \quad B(-2,-2) \Rightarrow m = \dfrac{-2-(-3)}{-2-(-1)} = \dfrac{-2+3}{-2+1} = \dfrac{1}{-1} = -1$

$m = -1, b = -4 \Rightarrow y = -x - 4$

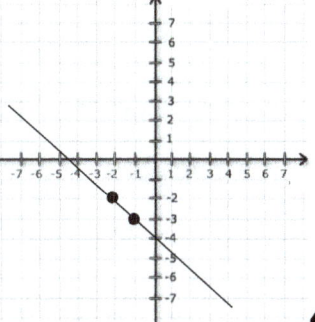

8. Write the linear equation of the line passing through the two given points. Write the answer in slope-intercept form.

1. (1, 2) and (0, 4)   y=_____
2. (-4, 2) and (1, 0)   y=_____
3. (2, -3) and (4, -2)   y=_____
4. (3, 4) and (2, -2)   y=_____
5. (1, 4) and (4, -4)   y=_____
6. (-3, -1) and (4, -3)   y=_____
7. (1, 4) and (-3, 4)   y=_____
8. (1, 2) and (-3, -2)   y=_____
9. (1, 2) and (4, 4)   y=_____
10. (-4, -4) and (4, 4)   y=_____

11. (3, -2) and (3, 4)   y=_____

12. (1, 3) and (-2, -4)   y=_____

Graphing Linear Inequalities

To graph inequalities like $y + mx \geq b$
- You should leave "y" alone on the left side. $y \geq mx + b$
- Change inequality to equation and draw it. $y = mx + b$
- If $y >$ or $y \geq$, shade above the line.
- If $y <$ or $y \leq$, shade below of the line.

For y> or y <, draw dashed line because they do not include equals to.

Example:

$y + x \leq 1 \rightarrow y \leq -x + 1 \rightarrow y = -x + 1$

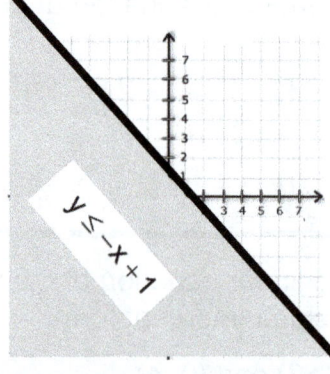

9. Graph the equations and inequalities onto the given coordinate axis.

1. $y = \dfrac{7}{2}x - 4$

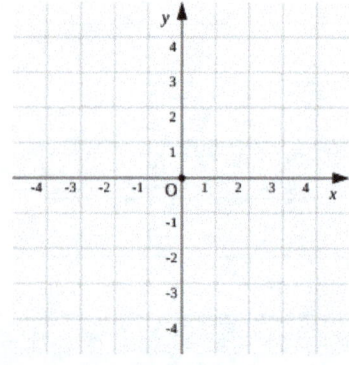

4. $y = -\dfrac{2}{4}x + 2$

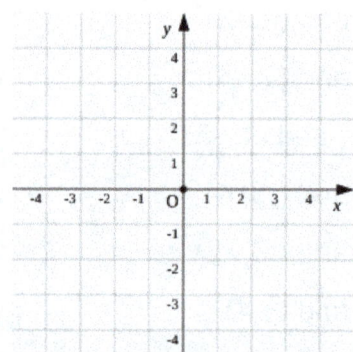

2. $y \geq -\dfrac{10}{3}x + 5$

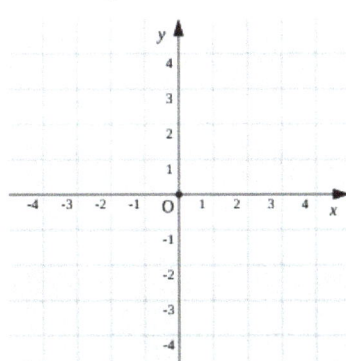

5. $y \leq -\dfrac{5}{2}x - 3$

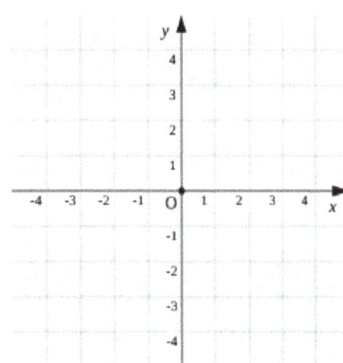

3. $y \leq 3$

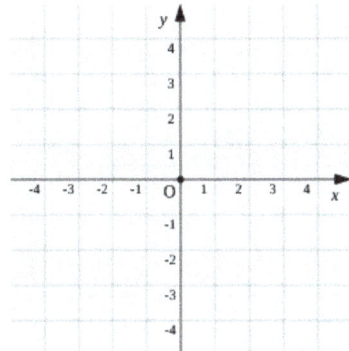

6. $x \geq 4$

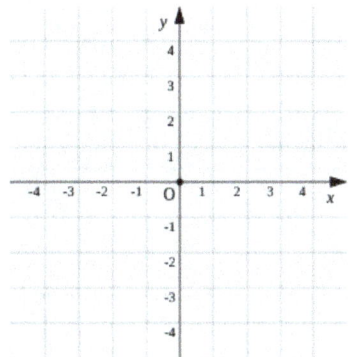

Finding Midpoint

Midpoint is a point at the middle of other two points.

For finding midpoint of $A(x_1, y_1)$ and $B(x_2, y_2)$ use below formula.

$C(\text{midpoint}) = \left(\dfrac{x_1 + x_2}{2}, \dfrac{y_1 + y_2}{2}\right)$

Example: What is the midpoint of $(-9, 5)$ and $(3, 7)$?

$C = \left(\dfrac{-9+3}{2}, \dfrac{5+7}{2}\right) = (-3, 6)$

10. Find the midpoint of the line segment with the given endpoints.

1. (5, 0), (1, 4)

2. (-9, 3), (7, -8)

3. (-2, 9), (-7, 7)

4. (5, 10), (-3, 6)

5. (-1, -6), (-2, -8)

6. (8, 1), (-2, -5)

7. (4, -1), (-5, 9)

8. (4, 1), (2, -5)

9. (-9, -4), (-3, 6)

10. (-13, 10), (-20, -8)

Finding Distance

If $A(x_1, y_1)$ and $B(x_2, y_2)$, the distance between them is:

$C = B - A = B(x_2, y_2) - A(x_1, y_1) = ((x_2 - x_1), (y_2 - y_1))$

Example:

What is distance of (11, -3) and (8, 6)?

$C(x, y) = ((11 - 8), (-3 - 6)) = (3, -9)$

MathePathics

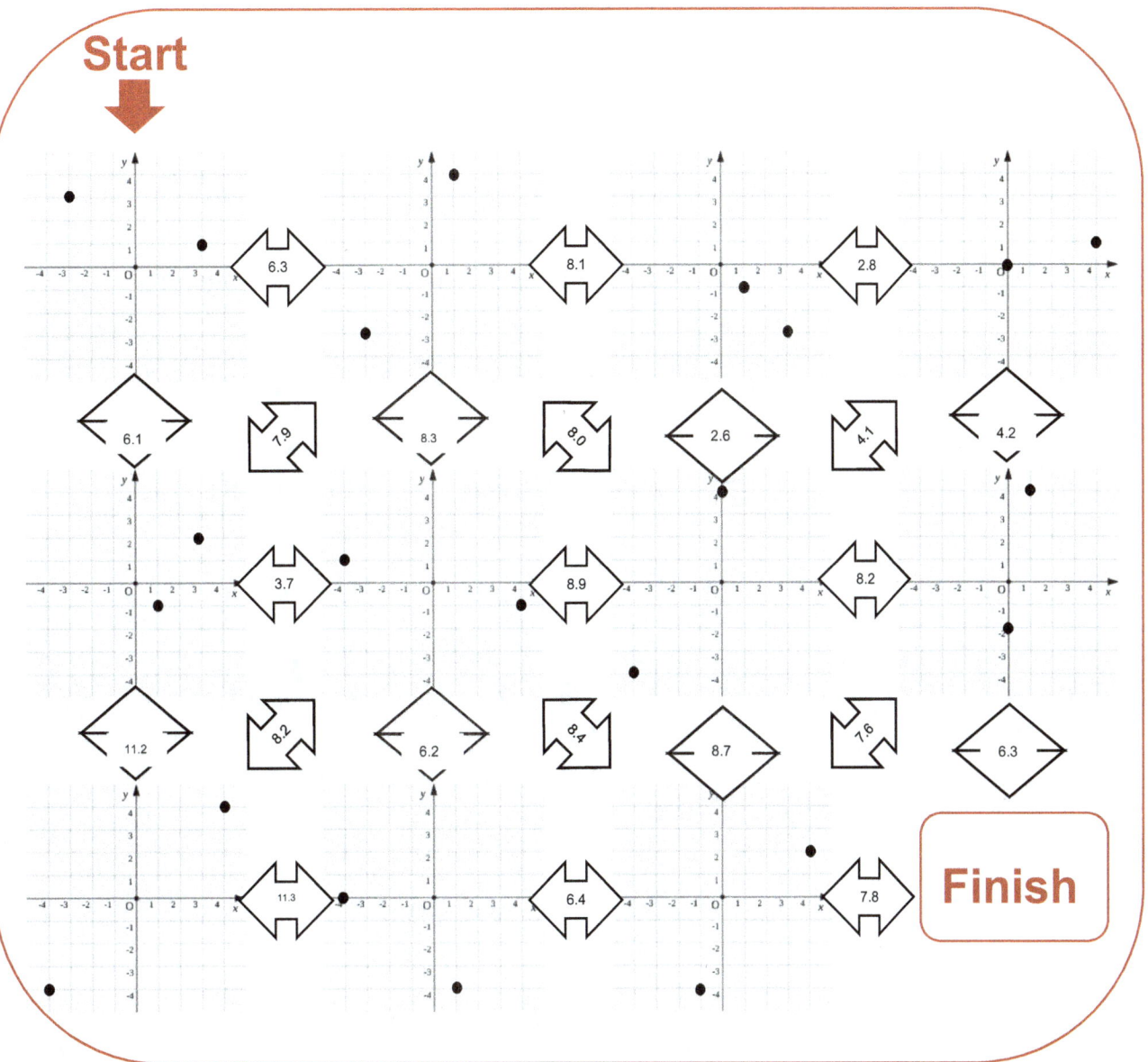

120

MathePathics

Answers of Worksheets – Chapter 8

Find Slope

1.

1. $m = 2$	7. $m = 0$	13. $m \to Undefined$
2. $m = -3$	8. $m = -2$	14. $m \to Undefined$
3. $m = 0$	9. $m = 2.66$	15. $m = 0.5$
4. $m = 0.33$	10. $m \to Undefined$	16. $m = 0.5$
5. $m = 0.5$	11. $m = 0$	17. $m = 0.4$
6. $m = -4$	12. $m = 2$	18. $m = 5$

Graphing Line Using Slope-Intercept Form

2.

1. $y = 5x - 3$
2. $y = -6x - 2$
3. $y = 3x + 2$
4. $y = x - 12$
5. $y = -2x + 7$
6. $y = 7x + 1$
7. $y = -4x - 9$
8. $y = 8$

3.

1. $y = 1$
2. $y = 2.7$

4.

1. $b = -3$

   $m = 2$

3. $b = -2$

   $m = -1$

121

Equation → $y = 2x - 3$ Equation → $y = -1x - 2$

2. b = 2   4. b = 2

   m = -3   m = -1.25

   Equation → $y = -3x + 2$ Equation → $y = -1.25 + 2$

5.

1. Slope = -0.33
   Y- Intercept = 1
   X- Intercept = 3
   $y = -0.33x + 1$

2. Slope = 0
   Y- Intercept = -3
   X- Intercept = -
   $y = -3$

3. Slope = 1
   Y- Intercept = -1
   X- Intercept = -1
   $y = x - 1$

5. Slope = 0
   Y- Intercept = 4
   X- Intercept = -
   $y = 4$

6. Slope = 0.33
   Y- Intercept = 2
   X- Intercept = -5
   $y = 0.33x + 2$

7. Slope = -2
   Y- Intercept = 0
   X- Intercept = 0
   $y = -2x$

9. Slope = 1
   Y- Intercept = 2
   X- Intercept = -2
   $y = x + 2$

10. Slope = -1.33
    Y- Intercept = -4
    X- Intercept = -3
    $y = -1.33x - 4$

11. Slope = -0.75
    Y- Intercept = -5
    X- Intercept = -5
    $y = -0.75x - 5$

MathePathics

4. Slope = 1
   Y- Intercept = 5
   X- Intercept = 5
   $y = x + 5$

8. Slope = 1.5
   Y- Intercept = 0
   X- Intercept = 0
   $y = 1.5x$

12. Slope = Undefined
    Y- Intercept = -
    X- Intercept = -2
    $x = -2$

Graphing Line Using Standard Form

6.

1. $m = -\dfrac{1}{6}$
   $y = -\dfrac{x}{6} + \dfrac{4}{6}$
   $X + 6Y = 4$

2. $m = -\dfrac{3}{7}$
   $y = -\dfrac{3}{7}x - \dfrac{6}{7}$
   $3X + 7Y = -6$

3. $m = -2$
   $y = -2x + 16$
   $2X + Y = +16$

4. $m = -1$
   $y = -x + 7$
   $X + Y = 7$

5. $m = \dfrac{4}{5}$
   $y = \dfrac{4}{5}x + 17$
   $-4X + 5Y = 85$

6. $m = \dfrac{1}{2}$
   $y = \dfrac{1}{2}x + 5$
   $-X + 2Y = 10$

7. $m = -\dfrac{5}{7}$
   $y = -\dfrac{5}{7}x + \dfrac{44}{7}$
   $5X + 7Y = 44$

8. $m = -\dfrac{3}{2}$
   $y = -\dfrac{3}{2}x + 240$
   $3X + 2Y = 480$

7.

1. $y = \dfrac{10}{7}x - \dfrac{8}{7}$

2. $y = -\dfrac{1}{6}x - \dfrac{1}{3}$

3. $y = -\dfrac{x}{4} - \dfrac{2}{3}$

5. $y = \dfrac{5}{6}x + \dfrac{1}{3}$

6. $y = -8x + 9$

7. $y = -\dfrac{4}{3}x + 3$

9. $y = -\dfrac{4}{5}x + \dfrac{4}{5}$

10. $y = 3x - 9$

4. $y = \frac{11}{8}x + \frac{3}{8}$

8. $y = -\frac{x}{2} - 4$

Writing Linear Equations

8.

1. $y = -2x + 4$
2. $y = -\frac{2}{5}x + \frac{2}{5}$
3. $y = \frac{1}{2}x$
4. $y = 6x - 14$
5. $y = -\frac{8}{3}x + \frac{21}{3}$
6. $y = -\frac{2}{7}x - \frac{13}{7}$
7. $y = 4$
8. $y = x + 1$
9. $y = \frac{2}{3}x + \frac{4}{3}$
10. $y = x$
11. $y = 4$
12. $y = \frac{7}{3}x + \frac{2}{3}$

Graphing Linear Inequalities

9.

1.

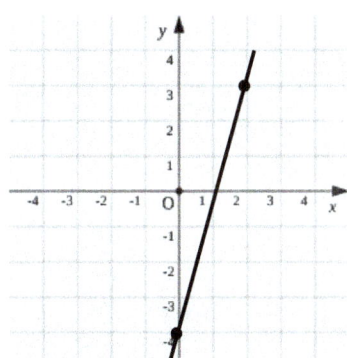

4.

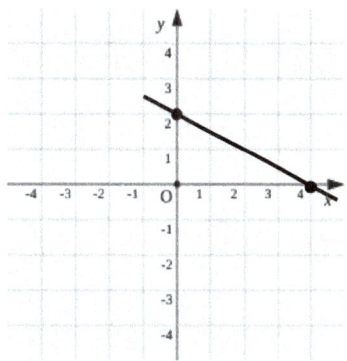

2.

5.

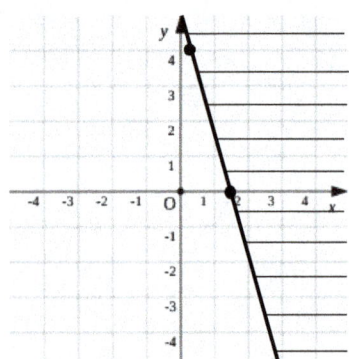
3.

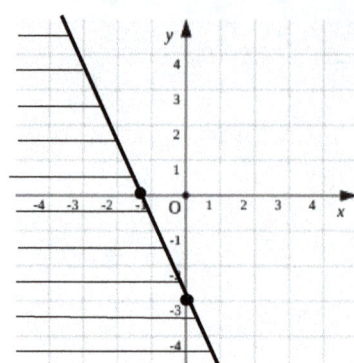
6.

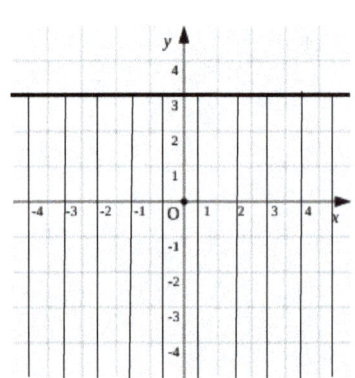

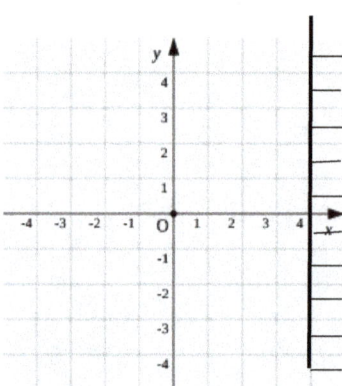

Finding Midpoint

10.

1. M = (3, 2)
2. M = $(1, -\frac{8}{2})$
3. M = $(-\frac{9}{2}, 8)$
4. M = (1, 8)
5. M = $(-\frac{3}{2}, -7)$
6. M = (3, -2)
7. M = $(\frac{1}{2}, 4)$
8. M = (3, -2)
9. M = (-6, 1)
10. M = $(-\frac{33}{2}, 1)$

MathePathics

11.

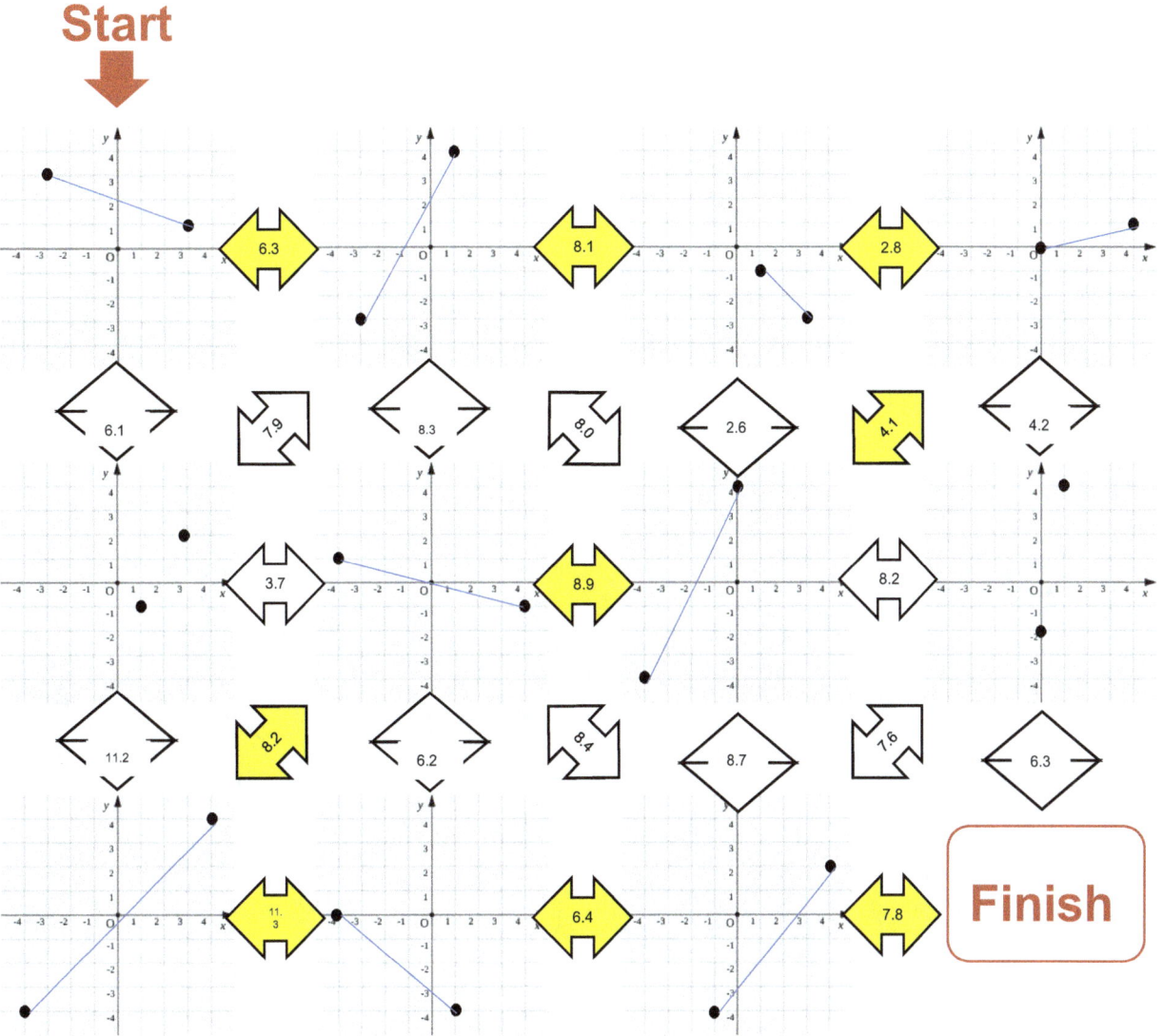

Extra Note for Chapter 8:

Chapter 9: Polynomials

Classifying Polynomials

Writing polynomials in Standard Form

Simplifying Polynomials

Adding and subtracting Polynomials

Multiplying Monomials

Multiplying and Dividing Monomials

Multiplying Binomials

Factoring Trinomials

Operations with Polynomials

Answers Worksheets – Chapter 9

Classifying Polynomials

Polynomials can be classified in two different ways - by the number of terms and by their degree.

Number of terms.

- A **monomial** has just one term. For example: $5x^2$
- A **binomial** has two terms. For example: $5x^2 + x$
- A **trinomial** has three terms. For example: $5x^2 + x + 2$

Degree
The degree of the polynomial is found by looking at the term with the highest exponent on its variable(s).

1. Classify each polynomial based on the number of terms.

    1. $8x + 6y - 9z$

    2. $p + qr$

    3. $r^2s + 7s^2 + r^2 - 2rs + 4s - 3t$

    4. $4a - a^2b - 3b + 14$

    5. m^2n

    6. $u - 6u^2 + 4u^2 - 15 + u^4$

2. Classify each polynomial based on the degree.

    1. $-7a + 5a^2bc + 3ca - 12$

    2. -13

    3. $-11 + 4s + 7t$

    4. $11 - uv - 4v + u^4$

    5. $xy + 6x$

    6. $p + 3q^2 + 4pqr - 9$

3. Classify each polynomial based on degree and the number of terms.

1. $-xy - 7y^2z^3 + 2x^3 - 5xy^2z$

   _____

2. $2m^2 - 9m^5 + 4m^2$

   _____

3. $5uv + uv^2w - 8vw^2 + 2u^2 + v - 7$

   _____

4. $-h - 9$

   _____

5. $\sqrt{5}$

   _____

6. $-a^2 - 2ab + 4a^2 - a + 14ab$

   _____

7. $6u^2 - u^2v$

   _____

8. $-3pq + q - 7r + 2qr - 4$

   _____

9. $9a^4b^2$

   _____

10. $n^2 + 2n - 5n^2 + 8$

    _____

11. $-b + c + d - 3bc - 5cd + 1$

    _____

12. $7rs^2 - t^5 - 6s^2$

    _____

Writing Polynomials in Standard Form

In order to write any polynomial in standard form, follow steps below.

❖ Look at the degree of each term.

❖ Write each term in order of degree, from highest to lowest, left to right.

Example: $-3 + x^2 - 6x$ → $x^2 - 6x - 3$

4. Put the following polynomials in standard form.

1. $3x^2 + 4x^5 - 3x^2 + 5x^2$

    _____

2. $8x + 3x^2 + 1 + 3x^3$

    _____

3. $6x + x^3 - 7x^2 - 5x + 80$

    _____

4. $x^4 - \frac{2}{6}x - 40 + \frac{x}{3} + x^2$

    _____

5. $x^3 - 3x^2 + 2x + 5x^2$

    _____

6. $6x - 7x^5 + 4x^2$

    _____

7. $4x^5 + 3x^6 - 2x^3 + 2x - 10$

    _____

8. $5x^3 - 3x + 60 + 4x^2$

    _____

Simplify Polynomials

To simplify a polynomial expression:

❖ Find like terms (terms with same variables and same powers.)

❖ Then combine them.

Example

$y = 1 + 2x^3 - x + 4x + 5x^3 - 9$

$y = 7x^3 + 3x - 8$

$y = (2x^3 + 5x^3) + (-x + 4x) + (1 - 9)$

5. Simplify the polynomials.

1. $3(2x - 4) + 2(4 - 6x)$

    _____

8. $\frac{8}{5}(-5x^3 - 10x + 25) - 3x^3 - \frac{x^2}{5}$

    _____

131

2. $\frac{1}{2}x(3-4) - 12x + 6$

_____

3. $(2x^2 + 4x + 1) - (\frac{3x^2}{2} - 5x - 7)$

_____

4. $-x^2 + 4x + 6x^2 - 4$

_____

5. $(-4x^3 + x^2 - 1) - (-3x^2 - 61)$

_____

6. $-(4x - 3x^4 + 3) - 4x^4 + 2x^3$

_____

7. $4(3x - 2x^2) - 4x - 12$

_____

9. $3x - 14 + 7x^2 - (x + 4x^2)$

_____

10. $x^3 + 4x^3 - 2(x^2 - x^3 - \frac{4}{6})$

_____

11. $-6(x + 6) - \frac{12}{3}(x - 2)$

_____

12. $-5x + 2x^4 - 12x^2 + x - 12$

_____

13. $-2(3x^2 - 4x) + 2x - 3x^2$

_____

14. $2x - 6 - (5x^2 + 6)$

_____

Adding and Subtracting Polynomials

Adding Polynomials $\qquad (2x - 4x^2 + 6) + (7x - 1)$

❖ Place the like terms together $\quad -4x^2 + (2x + 7x) + (6 - 1)$
  → $-4x^2 + 9x + 5$
❖ Add the like terms

Subtracting Polynomials $\qquad 2x - 4x^2 + 6 - 7x + 1$

❖ Reverse the sign of each term
  $-4x^2 + (2x - 7x) + (6 + 1) \rightarrow -4x^2 + -5x + 7$
❖ Add terms

132

6. Add the polynomials and find the final block.

1.

$(3y^5 + 4y) + 4(3y + 3y^3) + 2$ ➕ $2y^2 + 3y - \frac{y}{3} - 1$

2.

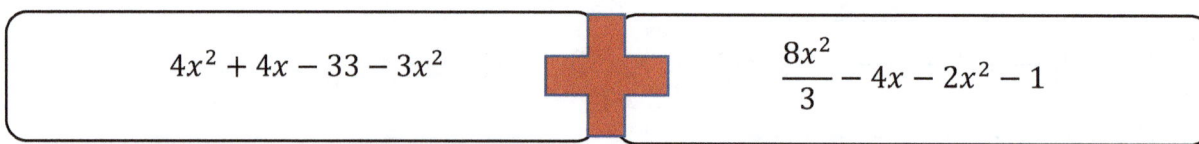

$4x^2 + 4x - 33 - 3x^2$ ➕ $\frac{8x^2}{3} - 4x - 2x^2 - 1$

=

3.

$10xy + x - xy + 6$ ➕ $-(xy + 6x - 18)$

4.

$\frac{x}{2} + 43x - x^2 - 10$ ➕ $6x^3 + \frac{12}{3} - x + 2.5$

MathePathics

7. Subtract the following blocks and find the results.

1.

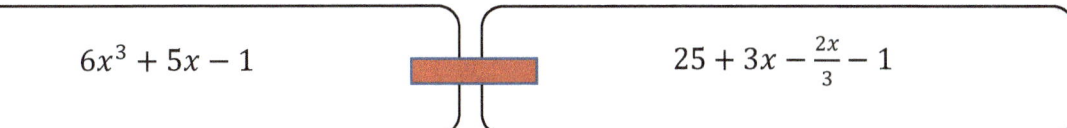

$6x^3 + 5x - 1$ — $25 + 3x - \frac{2x}{3} - 1$

2.

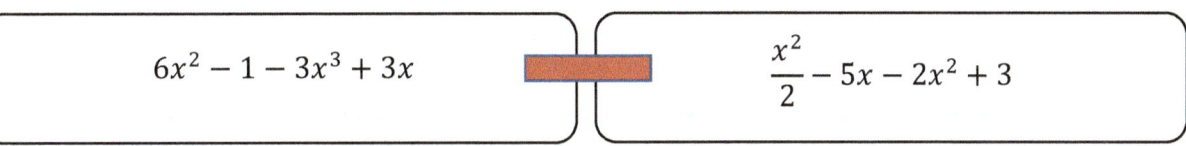

$6x^2 - 1 - 3x^3 + 3x$ — $\frac{x^2}{2} - 5x - 2x^2 + 3$

3.

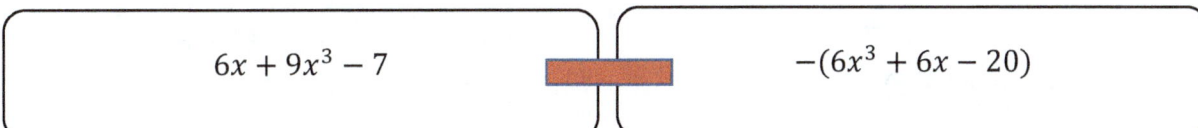

$6x + 9x^3 - 7$ — $-(6x^3 + 6x - 20)$

4.

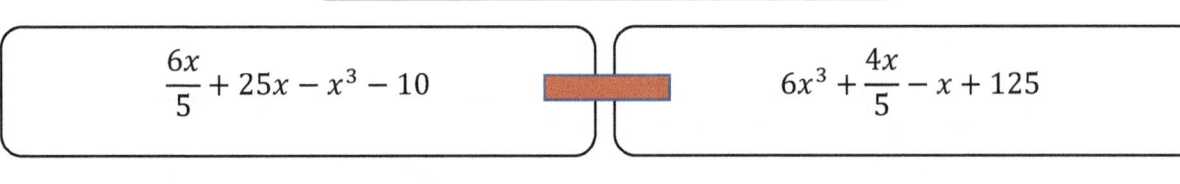

$\frac{6x}{5} + 25x - x^3 - 10$ — $6x^3 + \frac{4x}{5} - x + 125$

Multiply Monomials

For multiplying monomials, follow steps below.

❖ Multiply the coefficients (Numbers)

❖ Multiply the variables. (Use the laws of exponents when necessary)

Example:

$a^2 \cdot a^3 = a^{2+3} = a^5$ $(a^2)^3 = a^6$

8. Multiply the following.

1. $x^3(x^2 + 2x)$

2. $-5(x - x^3 + 6)$

3. $\frac{-xy}{2}(4xy - 12)$

4. $(2x + 6)(x - 2)$

5. $3xy(3x^2y + 6xy^2 + 4)$

11. $10xy(2xy - \frac{xy}{2})$

12. $-\frac{3}{8}(8x^2 + 12x - 1)$

13. $3x^2 - 2(9 - x)$

14. $2x^3(3x + 45y)$

15. $4y(y^3 - 2y + 5)$

6. $y(3x^2 + 6xy - 7y)$

16. $30(x^2 + 2x + 12)$

_____

_____

7. $6(-6 - xy + x - y^2)$

17. $x^2y(23x^2 + 2)$

_____

_____

8. $(6x + 7y - 4x^2 + 5)(-3x)$

18. $(8x + 5)(11x - 12)$

_____

_____

9. $3x - 1(4x^2 + 4x)$

19. $(4x^2)(5x - 1)$

_____

_____

10. $-(3x - 12)(5x - 2)$

20. $4xy(1 - xy)$

_____

_____

Multiply and Dividing Monomials

For multiplying monomial, follow these three steps.
1. Multiply the coefficients.
2. If you have same variables, write one of them and add their powers.
3. If you do not have same variables, multiply them and write.

$(2a^2)(4a) = 8a^3$ $(2a)(3b) = 6ab$

For dividing monomial, follow these two steps.

1. Divide the coefficients
2. Divide variable powers with the same base by subtracting the exponents.

$\dfrac{8a^4}{4a} = 2a^3$

9. Divide the monomials.

1. $\dfrac{6xy^{11}}{2x^3y^{22}} =$

2. $\dfrac{32x^4y^6}{6x^{12}y^2} =$

3. $\dfrac{20x^{10}y^6}{5x^2y^6} =$

4. $\dfrac{10x^4y^6}{x^5y^4} =$

5. $\dfrac{14x^2y^3}{21x^6y^3} =$

6. $\dfrac{xy^6}{12xy^2} =$

7. $\dfrac{21x^4y^6}{7x^{12}y^2} =$

8. $\dfrac{3y^6}{9x^{10}y^4} =$

9. $\dfrac{16x^4}{6y^2} =$

10. $\dfrac{25x^4}{15x^3y} =$

11. $\dfrac{x^6y^6}{6x^2y^2} =$

12. $\dfrac{2x^2y^9}{y^{14}} =$

13. $\dfrac{100x^4}{5x^{10}y^5} =$

14. $\dfrac{150x^{50}y^6}{10x^{100}y^{60}} =$

Multiplying Binomials

For multiplying binomials, follow steps below.

- ❖ Multiply the first term of each binomial together.
- ❖ Multiply the outer terms together.
- ❖ Multiply the inner terms together.
- ❖ Multiply the last term of each expression together.
- ❖ Write the result in standard form.
- ❖ Combine like terms.

$(x+1)(3x-2) = 3x^2 - 2x + 3x - 2 = 3x^2 - x - 2$

10. Multiply the following.

1. $(x-1)(5-3x)$

17. $(x-1)(x-5)$

2. $21x(2y-8)$

3. $(x^2-1)(63-60)$

4. $(6x-4)(\frac{x}{2}+1)$

5. $(x+2)^2$

6. $(x-7)(x+1)$

7. $(x-3)(x-2)$

8. $(-4x-1)(x-7)$

9. $(3x-5)(x-1)$

10. $(x-5)(x-8)$

11. $(9-x)(2x-1)$

12. $(x-6)(3x-1)$

13. $(x-2)(6x-4)$

14. $(x+\frac{1}{2})(x-1)$

18. $(-3x+5)(-x+4)$

19. $(-x+6)(4x-1)$

20. $(x+6)^2$

21. $(2x+3)(x-9)$

22. $(x-4)(x-7)$

23. $(x-3)(x-1)$

24. $(x-7)(x-6)$

25. $(\frac{1}{3}+x)(x-\frac{1}{6})$

26. $(x-8)(x-12)$

27. $(6x-7)(9-x)$

28. $(x-5)(x+6)$

29. $(x+7)(x-1)$

30. $(x+7)(\frac{3}{4}+5x)$

15. $(x+11)(x-11)$

31. $(x+8)(x-3)$

Factoring Trinomials

Factoring is when you break a large number down into its simplest divisible parts. Each one of these parts is called a "factor."

$$y = ax^2 + bx + c$$

For factoring, find two numbers that if they multiply, equals to "c" and if they add or subtract equals to "b".

$m \times n = c$ $\qquad$ $m + n = b$ $\qquad$ $(x+m)(x+n) = 0$

11. Factor each Trinomial and write them in blocks.

1. $x^2 + 7x + 12 =$
2. $x^2 - 6x + 9 =$
3. $x^2 - 9 =$
4. $x^2 - 6x + 8 =$
5. $x^2 - 7x + 12 =$
6. $x^2 - 6x + 8 =$
7. $x^2 + 3x - 10 =$
8. $x^2 - 2x - 15 =$
9. $6x^2 + 13x + 6 =$
10. $x^2 - 169 =$
11. $x^2 - 5x + 6 =$
12. $x^2 - x - 6 =$
13. $10x^2 + 16x + 6 =$

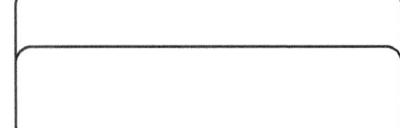

14. $6x^2 + 23x + 15 =$ ☐ ☐

15. $12x^2 + 17x - 7 =$ ☐ ☐

Operations with Polynomials

Adding Polynomials with More Than One Variable

- Identify like terms
- Combine them according to the correct integer operations

(2x + 3y) + (1 - 4x + 5y) = (2x - 4x) + (3y + 5y) + 1 = - 2x + 8y + 1

Subtracting polynomials is done like adding.

In order to remove the parentheses following a subtraction sign, you must multiply each term by −1.

(2x + 3y) - (1 - 4x + 5y) = 2x + 3y - 1 + 4x - 5y = 6x - 2y - 1

Multiplying Polynomials
- Multiply factors.
- If you have same variables, write one of them and add their powers.
- If you do not have same variables, multiply them and write.

$(2x + 3y)(1 - 4x + 5y) = 2x - 8x^2 + 10xy + 3y - 12xy + 15y^2 = 15y^2 - 8x^2 - 2xy + 2x + 3y$

Dividing Polynomials
- Divide factors.
- If you have same variables, write one of them and subtract their powers.
- If you do not have same variables, divide them and write.

$$\frac{14(x-1) + 20(x+2)}{2(x-1)(x+2)} = \frac{14(x-1)}{2(x-1)(x+2)} + \frac{20(x+2)}{2(x-1)(x+2)} = \frac{7}{(x+2)} + \frac{10}{(x-1)}$$

12. Perform all the defined steps on the following polynomial expressions.

Step 1: Find the **opposite** of Polynomials

Step 2: **Add** the answer of step 1 to $6x^2 + 2x + 12$

Step 3: **Subtract** the answer of step 2 from $-12x^2 + 12x + 1$

Step 4: **Multiply** the answer of step 3 by $2x$

Step 5: **divide** the answer of step 4 by x

Step 6: Find the **opposite** of answer of step 5

1. $x^2 - 2x - 15$

   Step 1:   Step 2:   Step 3:
   Step 4:   Step 5:   Step 6:

2. $11x^2 + 17x - 4 =$

   Step 1:   Step 2:   Step 3:
   Step 4:   Step 5:   Step 6:

Answers of Worksheets – Chapter 9

Simplify Polynomials

1.
   1. *Trinomial*
   2. *Bionomial*
   3. *Plynomial*
   4. *Polynomial*
   5. *Monomial*
   6. *Polynomial of 4 term*

2.
   1. *Degree* → 2
      Quadratic
   2. *Degree* → 0
      Constant
   3. *Degree* → 1
      Linear
   4. *Degree* → 4
      Quartic
   5. *Degree* → 1
      Linear
   6. *Degree* → 5
      Quintic

3.
   1. Degree → 3
      Name → Cubic
      Term → Trinomial
   2. Degree → 5
      Name → Quintic
      Term → Trinomial
   3. Degree → 2
      Name → Quadratic
      Term → Polynomial
   4. Degree → 1
      Name → Linear
      Term → Binomial
   5. Degree → 0
      Name → Constant
      Term → Monomial
   7. Degree → 2
      Name → Quadratic
      Term → Binomial
   8. Degree → 1
      Name → Liner
      Term → Polynomial
   9. Degree → 4
      Name → Quartic
      Term → Monomial
   10. Degree → 2
       Name → Quadratic
       Term → Trinomial
   11. Degree → 1
       Name → Linear
       Term → Polynomial

6. Degree → 2
    Name → Quadratic
    Term → Polynomials

12. Degree → 5
    Name → Quintic
    Term → Trinomial

Writing Polynomials in Standard Form

4.

1. $4x^5 + 5x^2$

2. $3x^3 + 3x^2 + 8x + 1$

3. $x^3 - 7x^2 + x + 80$

4. $x^4 + x^2 - 40$

5. $x^3 + 2x^2 + 2x$

6. $-7x^5 + 4x^2 + 6x$

7. $3x^6 + 4x^5 - 2x^3 + 2x - 10$

8. $5x^3 + 4x^2 - 3x + 60$

Simplify Polynomials

5.

1. $-6x - 4$

2. $-\dfrac{25x}{2} + 6$

3. $\dfrac{x^2}{2} + 9x + 8$

4. $5x^2 + 4x - 4$

5. $-4x^3 + 4x^2 + 60$

8. $-11x^3 - \dfrac{x^2}{5} - 16x + 40$

9. $3x^2 + 2x - 14$

10. No Change

11. $-10x - 28$

12. $2x^4 - 12x^2 - 4x - 12$

143

6. $4x^4 + 2x^3 - 4x - 3$

13. $-9x^2 + 10x$

7. $-8x^2 + 8x - 12$

14. $-5x^2 + 2x - 12$

Adding and Subtracting Polynomials

6.

1.

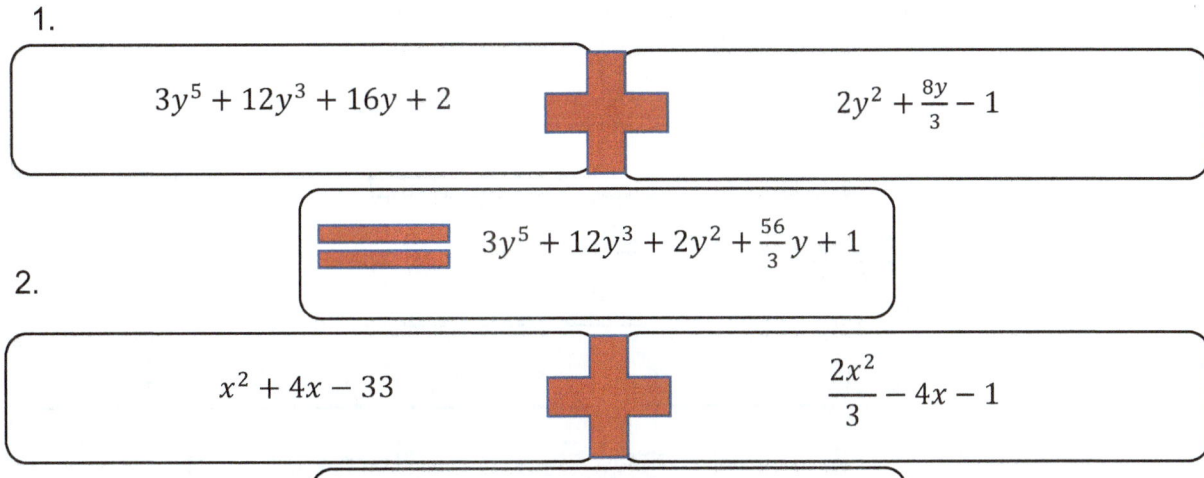

$3y^5 + 12y^3 + 16y + 2$ $+$ $2y^2 + \frac{8y}{3} - 1$

$=$ $3y^5 + 12y^3 + 2y^2 + \frac{56}{3}y + 1$

2.

$x^2 + 4x - 33$ $+$ $\frac{2x^2}{3} - 4x - 1$

$=$ $\frac{5x^2}{2} - 34$

3.

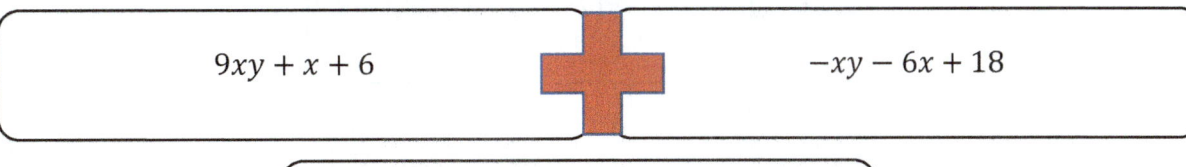

$9xy + x + 6$ $+$ $-xy - 6x + 18$

$=$ $8xy - 5x + 24$

4.

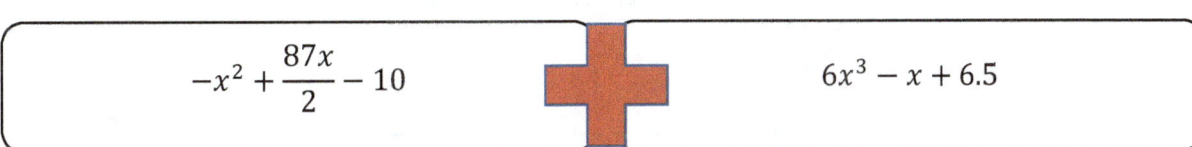

$-x^2 + \frac{87x}{2} - 10$ $+$ $6x^3 - x + 6.5$

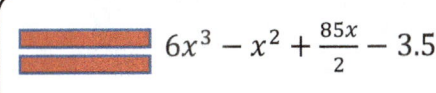

$= 6x^3 - x^2 + \frac{85x}{2} - 3.5$

7.

1.
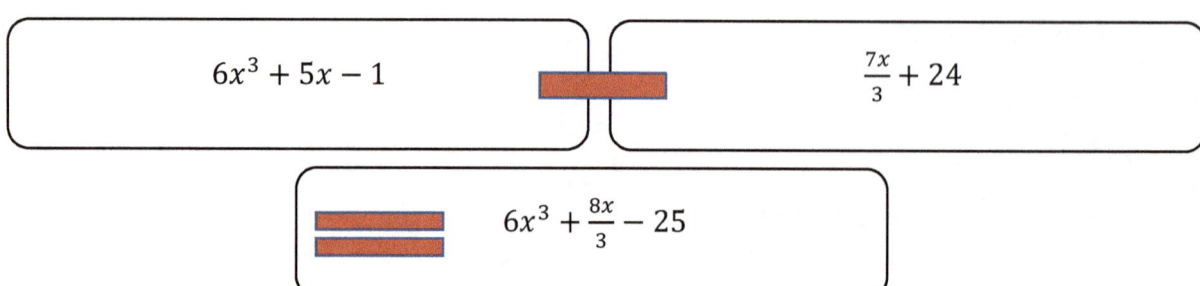

2.
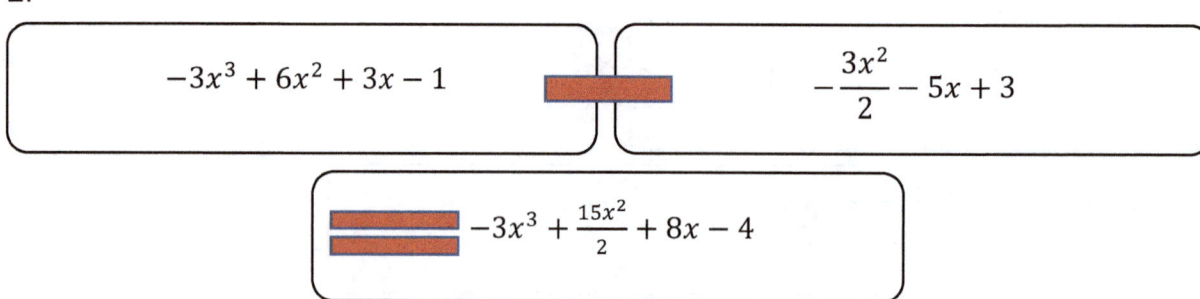

3.
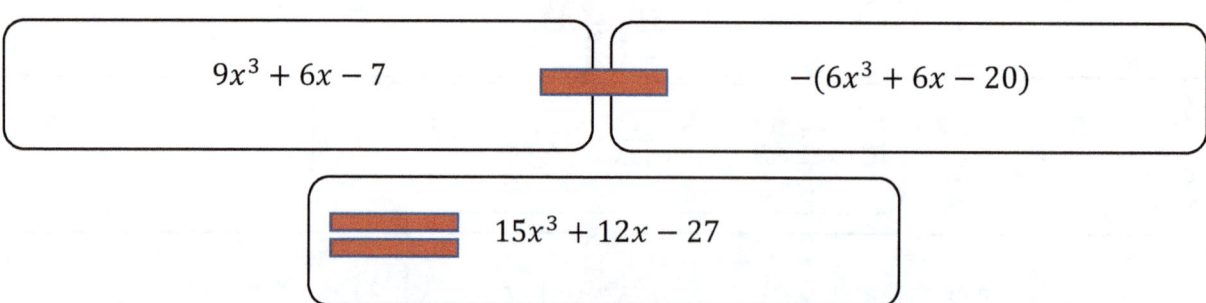

4.
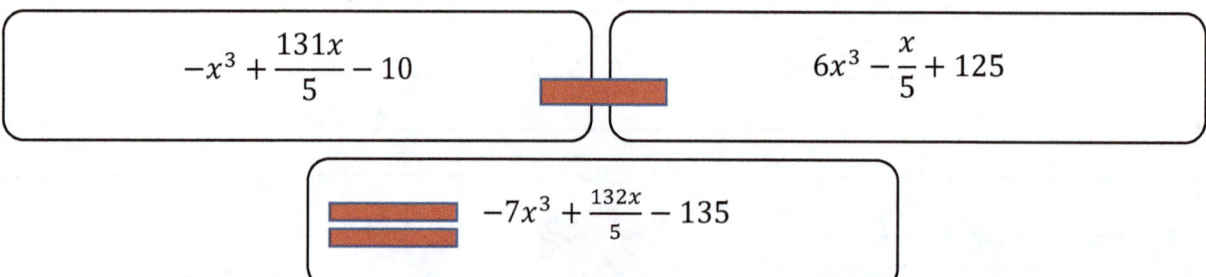

MathePathics

Multiplying Monomials

8.

1. $x^5 + 2x^4$
2. $5x^3 - 5x - 30$
3. $-2xy(xy - 3)$
4. $2x^2 + 2x - 12$
5. $18x^2y^3 + 12xy + 9x^2y^3$
6. $3x^2y + 6xy^2 - 7y^2$
7. $-6y^2 - 6xy + 6x - 36$
8. $-18x^2 - 21xy + 12x^3 - 15x$
9. $-4x^2 - x$
10. $-15x^2 + 66x - 24$
11. $15(xy)^2$
12. $-3x^2 - \dfrac{9x}{2} + \dfrac{8}{3}$
13. $3x^2 - 2x - 18$
14. $6x^4 + 90yx^3$
15. $4y^4 - 8y^2 + 20y)$
16. $30x^2 + 60x + 360$
17. $3x^4y + 2x^2y$
18. $88x^2 - 41x - 60$
19. $20x^3 - 4x^2$
20. $4xy - 4x^2y^2$

Multiply and Dividing Monomials

9.

1. $\dfrac{3}{x^2y^{11}}$
2. $\dfrac{16y^4}{3x^8}$
6. $\dfrac{y^4}{12}$
7. $\dfrac{3y^4}{x^8}$
11. $\dfrac{(xy)^4}{6}$
12. $\dfrac{2x^2}{y^5}$

3. $4x^8$

4. $\dfrac{10y^2}{x}$

5. $\dfrac{2}{3x^4}$

8. $\dfrac{y^2}{3x^{10}}$

9. $\dfrac{8x^4}{3y^2}$

10. $\dfrac{5x}{3y}$

13. $\dfrac{20}{x^6 y^5}$

14. $\dfrac{15}{x^{50} y^{54}}$

Multiplying Binomials

10.

1. $-3x^2 + 8x - 5$
2. $4xy - 168x$
3. $3x^2 - 3$
4. $(3x^2 + 4x - 4)$
5. $x^2 + 4x + 4$
6. $x^2 - 6x - 7$
7. $x^2 - 5x + 6$
8. $-4x^2 + 27x + 7$
9. $3x^2 - 8x + 5$
10. $x^2 - 13x + 40$
11. $-2x^2 + 19x - 9$
12. $3x^2 - 19x + 6$
13. $6x^2 - 16x + 8$
14. $x^2 - \dfrac{x}{2} - \dfrac{1}{2}$
15. $x^2 - 121$
16. $x^2 - 6x + 5$
17. $3x^2 - 17x + 20$
18. $-4x^2 + 25x - 6$
19. $x^2 + 12x + 36$
20. $2x^2 - 15x - 27$
21. $x^2 - 11x + 28$
22. $x^2 - 4x + 3$
23. $x^2 - 13x + 42$
24. $x^2 + \dfrac{x}{6} - \dfrac{1}{16}$
25. $x^2 - 20x + 96$
26. $-6x^2 + 61x - 63$
27. $x^2 + x - 30$
28. $x^2 + 6x - 7$
29. $5x^2 + \dfrac{143x}{4} + \dfrac{21}{4}$
30. $x^2 + 5x - 24$

Factoring Trinomials

11.

1. $(x + 3)(x + 4)$
2. $(x - 3)(x - 3) = (x - 3)^2$
3. $(x - 3)(x + 3)$
9. $(2x + 3)(3x + 2)$
10. $(x - 13)(x + 13)$
11. $(x - 3)(x - 2)$

4. $(x-4)(x-2)$
5. $(x-4)(x-3)$
6. $(x-4)(x-2)$
7. $(x-2)(x+5)$
8. $(x-5)(x+3)$

12. $(x-3)(x+2)$
13. $(2)(x+1)(5x+3)$
14. $(x+3)(6x+5)$
15. $(4x+7)(3x-1)$

Operations with Polynomials

12.

1. Step 1:   Step 2:   Step 3:
   $-x^2 + 2x + 15$ $5x^2 + 4x + 27$ $-22x^2 + 9x - 26$

   Step 4:   Step 5:   Step 6:
   $44x^3 + 18x^2 - 52x$ $44x^2 + 18x - 52$ $-44x^2 - 18x + 52$

2. Step 1:   Step 2:   Step 3:
   $-11x^2 - 17x + 4$ $-5x^2 - 15x + 16$ $-7x^2 + 27x - 15$

   Step 4:   Step 5:   Step 6:
   $-14x^3 + 4x^2 - 30x$ $-14x^2 + 4x - 30$ $+14x^2 - 4x + 30$

Extra Note for Chapter 9:

Chapter 10:
Quadratic and System of Equations

Solve a Quadratic Equation

Solving Systems of equations by Elimination

Systems of Equations Word Problems

Answers of Worksheets – Chapter 10

Solving Quadratic Equation

Look at following example:

$x^2 + 7x + 6 = 0$

First, we find factors. $a = 1$ $b = 7$ $c = 6$

Now we should find Δ. $\Delta = b^2 - 4ac = (7)^2 - 4(1)(6) = 49 - 24 = 25$

After finding Δ, we should find roots.

$x_1 = \dfrac{-b + \sqrt{\Delta}}{2a} = \dfrac{-7 + \sqrt{25}}{2(1)} = \dfrac{-7 + 5}{2} = -1$

$x_2 = \dfrac{-b - \sqrt{\Delta}}{2a} = \dfrac{-7 - \sqrt{25}}{2(1)} = \dfrac{-7 - 5}{2} = -6$

1. Solve each quadratic for "x".

   1. $x^2 + 11x + 30 = 0$

   2. $x^2 - 8x + 4 = 0$

   3. $x^2 - 9x + 7 = 0$

   4. $x^2 + 18x - 9 = 0$

   5. $x^2 + 6x - 7 = 0$

   7. $x^2 + 61x - 3 = 0$

   8. $x^2 + x - 4 = 0$

   9. $x^2 - 2x + 1 = 0$

   10. $x^2 + 2x - 11 = 0$

   11. $x^2 + 65x + 90 = 0$

6. $x^2 - 4x - 5 = 0$

12. $x^2 + 6x - 16 = 0$

2. Factor the following Quadratic then solve them for every possible "x".

1. $x^2 - 6x + 8$

7. $x^2 - 5x - 36$

2. $x^2 + 16x + 64$

8. $x^2 + 2x + 1$

3. $x^2 + 6x - 27$

9. $x^2 + 2x - 8$

4. $x^2 - 11x + 24$

10. $x^2 - 25$

5. $x^2 - 36$

11. $x^2 + 6x - 36$

6. $x^2 - 7x + 6$

12. $x^2 - 81$

MathePathics

Solving Systems of equations by Elimination

The Elimination Method is based on the Addition Property of Equality.

The Addition Property of Equality is:

Add the same quantity to both sides of an equation.

When you add equal quantities to both sides of an equation, the results are equal.

For any expressions a, b, c, and, d,

If a=b and c=d,

Then $a+c=b+d$

3. Solve the systems using elimination.

1. $5X - 3Y = 6$
   $6X + 2Y = 0$

2. $11X - 9Y = 0$
   $X + 6Y = 12$

3. $-X + Y = 6$
   $3X + 3Y = 1$

4. $10X + 11Y = 0$
   $3X - 7Y = 11$

6. $-X + 3Y = 5$
   $2X + 6Y = 2$

7. $12X - 6Y = \dfrac{1}{2}$
   $12X + 8Y = 18$

8. $-3X + Y = 10$
   $-X - 5Y = 0$

9. $-\dfrac{1}{6}X + 3Y = 3$
   $-4X - Y = 9$

5. $6X - 8Y = -6$
    $4X - 10Y = 10$

10. $10X + 3Y = 22$
    $6X + 5Y = -22$

Systems of Equations Word Problems

There are some steps for solving real word problems.

- Define your variables.
- Write two equations by using important information.
- Use one of the methods for solving systems of equations to solve.

Write your answer in complete sentences

4. Jose and Rose each bought from the same store. Jose spent $100 on 3 shoes and a bag. Rose spent $75 on a shoe and 2 bags. Find the cost of one shoe and the cost of one bag.

5. At an American restaurant, the cost of 2 plates of spaghetti and 4 salads is $50. The cost for 4 plates of spaghetti and 3 salads is $70 find the cost of a plate of spaghetti and a salad.

6. A hotel in British Colombia of Canada is offering 2 weekends special. One includes a 4-night stay with 3 meals which costs $200. The other includes 2-night with 4 meals which costs $120. How much does a single meal cost?

7. Mary ordered 6 pizzas and 2 salads for a total of $60. John ordered 3 pizzas and 4 salads for a total of $55. How much does a pizza cost?

MathePathics

Answers of Worksheets – Chapter 10

Solving Quadratic Equation

1.

1. $x = -6, x = -5$
2. $x = 7.46, x = 0.53$
3. $x = 8.14, x = 0.86$
4. $x = 0.84, x = -18.48$
5. $x = -7, x = 1$
6. $x = -1, x = 5$
7. $x = 0.049, x = -61.049$
8. $x = 1.56, x = -2.56$
9. $x = 1$
10. $x = 2.46, x = -4.46$
11. $x = -1.41, x = -63.58$
12. $x = -8, x = 2$

2.

1. $x = 4$
   $x = 2$
2. $x = -8$
3. $x = -9$
   $x = 3$
4. $x = 3$
   $x = 8$
5. $x = 6$
   $x = -6$
6. $x = 1$
   $x = 6$
7. $x = -4$
   $x = 9$
8. $x = -1$
9. $x = -4$
   $x = 2$
10. $x = 5$
    $x = -5$
11. $x = 3.70$
    $x = -9.70$
12. $x = 9$
    $x = -9$

Solving Systems of equations by Elimination

3.

1. $X = \dfrac{3}{7}$
5. $X = -5$
   $Y = -3$
9. $X = -\dfrac{180}{73}$

156

$$Y = -\frac{9}{7}$$

$$Y = \frac{63}{73}$$

2. $X = \frac{36}{13}$

   $Y = \frac{32}{13}$

6. $X = -2$

   $Y = 1$

10. $X = \frac{11}{2}$

    $Y = -11$

3. $X = -\frac{17}{6}$

   $Y = \frac{19}{6}$

7. $X = \frac{2}{3}$

   $Y = \frac{5}{4}$

4. $X = \frac{121}{103}$

   $Y = -\frac{110}{103}$

8. $X = \frac{28}{5}$

   $Y = \frac{5}{8}$

Systems of Equations Word Problems

4. B → Bag → B = 25

   S → Shoe → S = 25

5. P → Plate of spaghetti → P = 10

   S → Salad → S = 10

6. N → Night → N → 44

   M → Meal → M → 8

7. P → Pizza → P → $\frac{65}{9}$

   S → Salad → S → $\frac{25}{3}$

157

Extra Note for Chapter 10:

Chapter 11:
Quadratic Functions

Graphing Quadratic Functions

Solving Quadratic Equations

Use the Quadratic Formula and the Discriminate

Solve quadratic Inequalities

Answers of Worksheets – Chapter 11

MathePathics

Graphing Quadratic functions

A **quadratic function** is a polynomial function of degree 2 and it can be written in the general form.

$$y = ax^2 + bx + c$$

Here *a*, *b* and *c* represent real numbers where $a \neq 0$.

The simplest Quadratic Equation is $y = x^2$.

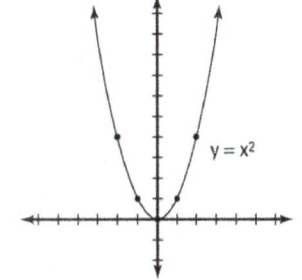

1. Sketch the graph of each function.

   1. $f(x) = 2x^2 - 12x + 22$

x	1	2	3	4	5
f(x)					

   2. $f(x) = 6x^2$

x	-2	-1	0	1	2
f(x)					

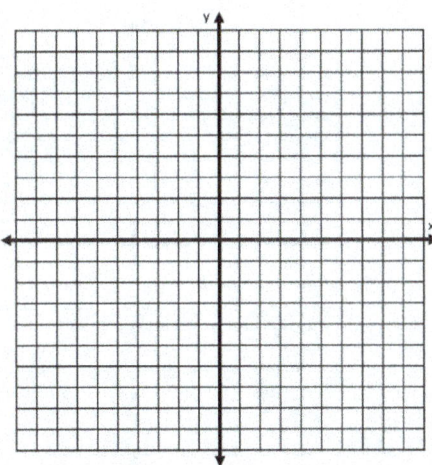

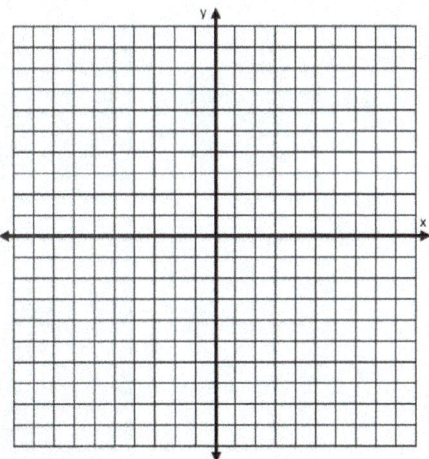

3. $f(x) = -x(x-9)$

x	0	1	2	3	4
f(x)					

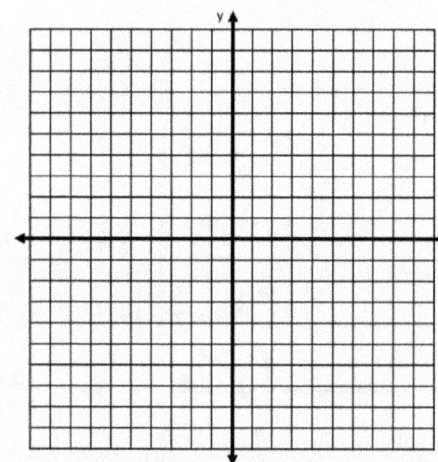

4. $f(x) = x^2 - 8x + 16$

x	2	3	4	5	6
f(x)					

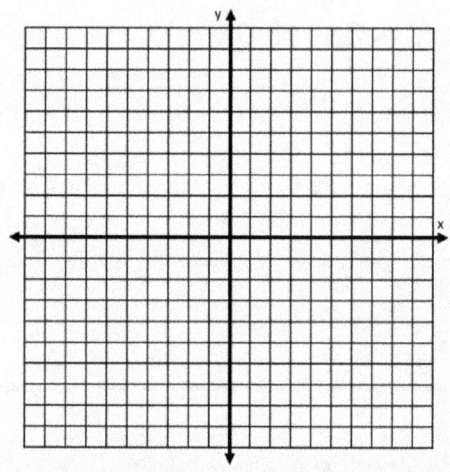

5. $f(x) = (x-2)^2 - 2$

x	-1	0	2	3	4
f(x)					

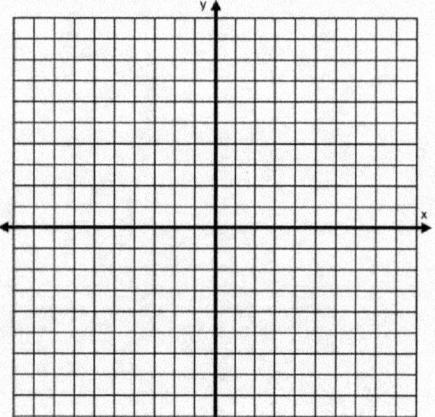

6. $f(x) = x^2 - 4$

x	-1	-1	0	1	2
f(x)					

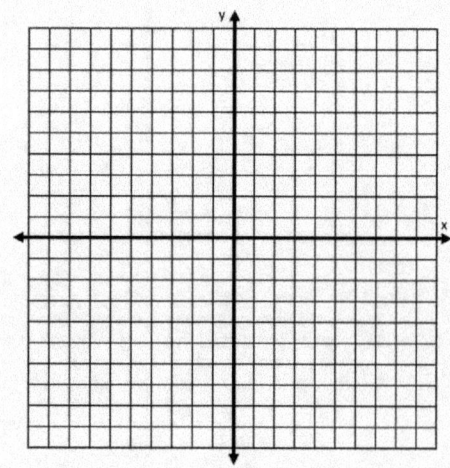

7. $f(x) = -3x^2 - 12x - 6$

x	-3	-2	-1	0	1
f(x)					

8. $f(x) = -x^2$

x	-3	-1	0	1	3
f(x)					

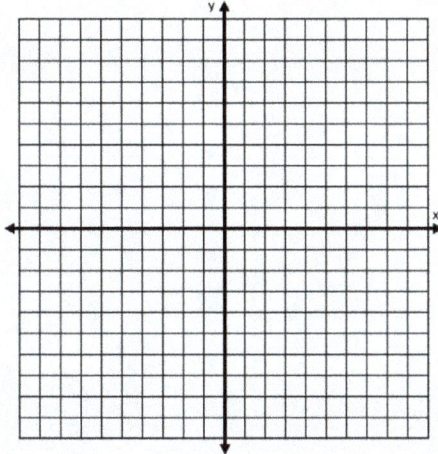
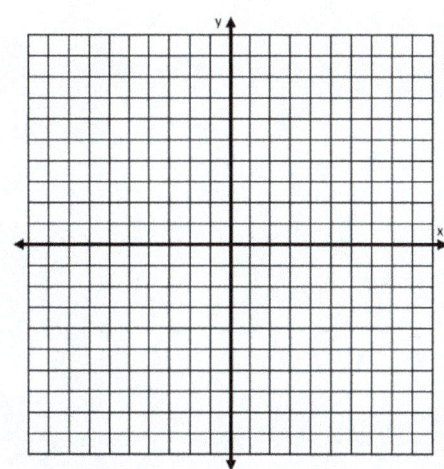

2. Write the quadratic function for each graph.

1.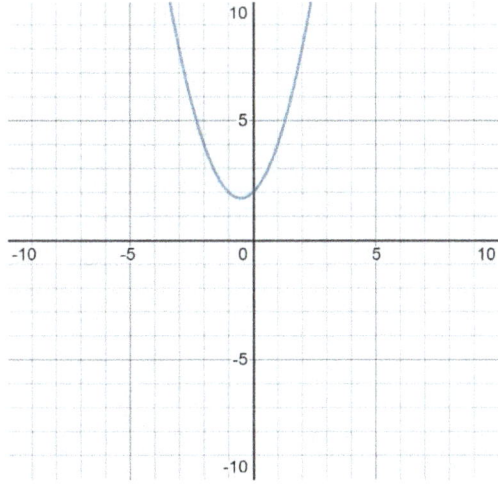

_____

2.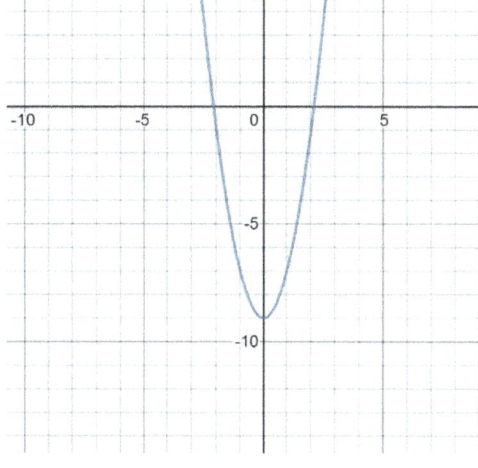

_____

3.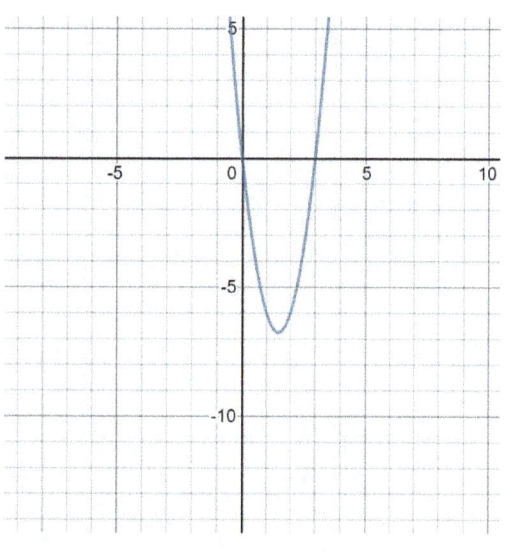

_____

4.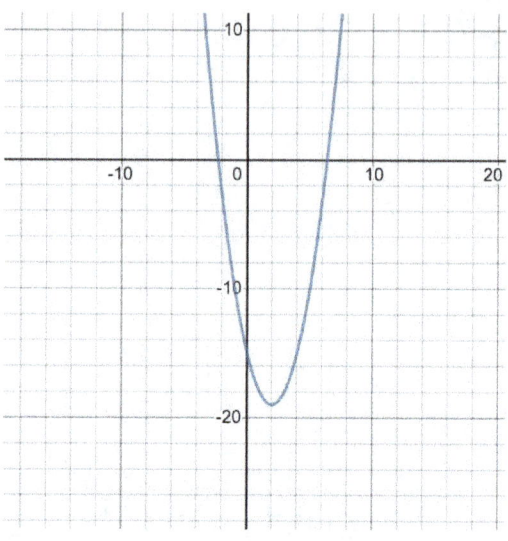

_____

5.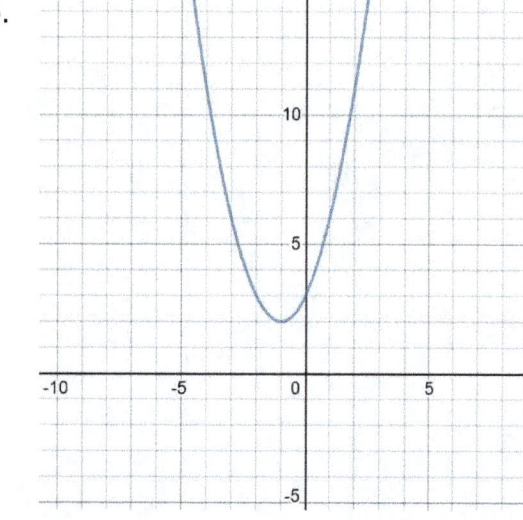

_____

6.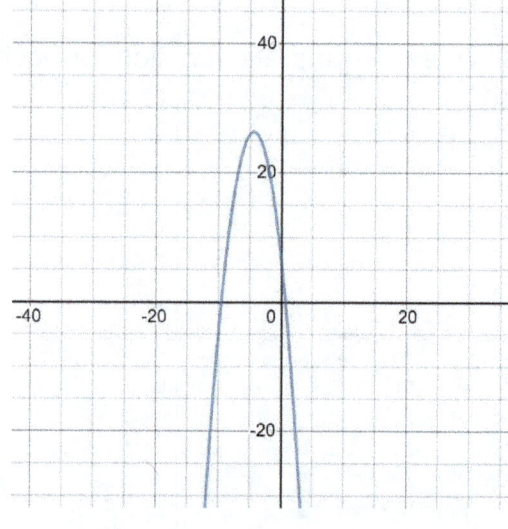

_____

7.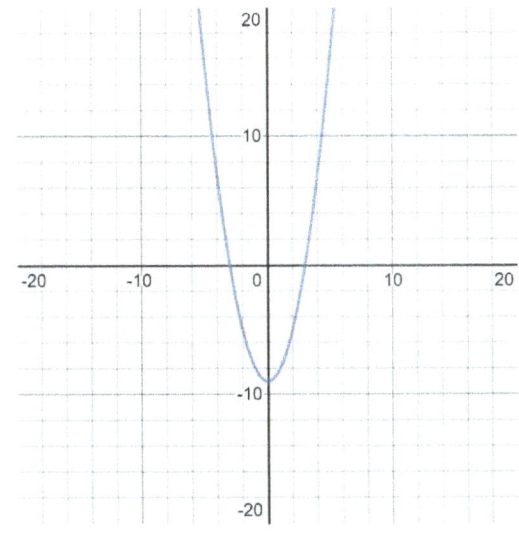

_____

8.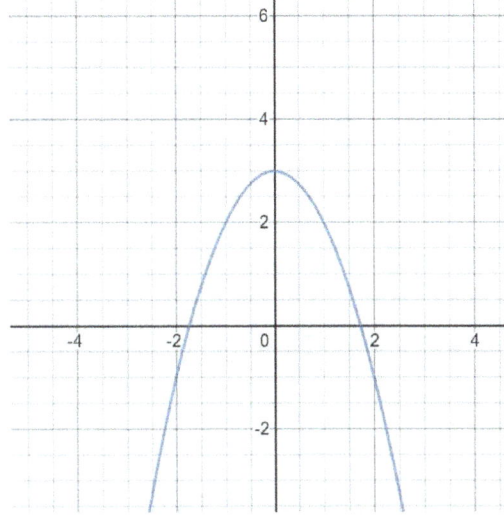

_____

Solving Quadratic Equations

Look at following example:

$x^2 + 7x + 6 = 0$

First, we find factors. $\quad a = 1 \quad b = 7 \quad c = 6$

Now we should find Δ. $\quad \Delta = b^2 - 4ac = (7)^2 - 4(1)(6) = 49 - 24 = 25$

After finding Δ, we should find roots.

$x_1 = \dfrac{-b + \sqrt{\Delta}}{2a} = \dfrac{-7 + \sqrt{25}}{2(1)} = \dfrac{-7 + 5}{2} = -1$

$x_2 = \dfrac{-b - \sqrt{\Delta}}{2a} = \dfrac{-7 - \sqrt{25}}{2(1)} = \dfrac{-7 - 5}{2} = -6$

3. Solve each equation for "x".

1. $x^2 + 2x - 8 = 0$

2. $x^2 - 5x - 14 = 0$

3. $x^2 + 7x + 12 = 0$

4. $x^2 - 6x - 16 = 0$

5. $x^2 - 10x + 25 = 0$

6. $x^2 - 49 = 0$

7. $x^2 - 16x = 15$

8. $3x^2 + 9x = 0$

9. $15x^2 - 3x = 0$

10. $2x^2 + 14x = 0$

13. $x^2 + 11x = -18$

14. $x^2 + 11x + 30 = 0$

15. $x^2 + 3x = 0$

16. $x^2 - 4x = 5$

17. $x^2 - 8x = -9$

18. $3x^2 - 2x - 5 = 0$

19. $x^2 - 196 = 0$

20. $2x^2 + 5x + 1 = 0$

21. $5x^2 - 40x = 0$

22. $x^2 - 9x - 8 = 0$

11. $x^2 + 12x = -36$

23. $x^2 - 75x - 4 = 0$

12. $x^2 + 6x = 0$

24. $x^2 + x - 2 = 0$

Use the Quadratic Formula and the Discriminate

The number $\Delta = b^2 - 4ac$ determined from the coefficients of the equations $y = ax^2 + bx + c$. The discriminant reveals what type of roots the equation has.

$$y = ax^2 + bx + c$$

$$\Delta = b^2 - 4ac \qquad x_1 = \frac{-b + \sqrt{\Delta}}{2a} \qquad x_2 = \frac{-b - \sqrt{\Delta}}{2a}$$

4. Find the value of the discrimination of each quadratic equation.

1. $x^2 - 10x + 24 = 0$

13. $9x^2 + 8x = -1$

2. $3x^2 - 4 = x$

14. $-5x^2 + 8x = 0$

3. $8x^2 + 14x = -3$

15. $3x^2 - 6x = 32$

4. $x^2 + 4 = 7x - 3$

16. $2x^2 - 21x = -49$

5. $2x^2 = 3x + 23$

17. $x^2 - 2x + 15 = 0$

6. $x^2 + 2x - 3 = 0$

18. $6x^2 - 17x - 7 = 0$

7. $(x+4)(x+7) = 0$

8. $x^2 - 1 = 0$

9. $(x-2)^2 = 0$

10. $(x+1)^2 + 2$

11. $(x-3)^2 - 3$

12. $5x^2 + 6x = -63$

19. $4x^2 + 11x = -6$

20. $21x^2 - 43x = -14$

21. $6x^2 + 5x - 21 = 0$

22. $x^2 + 2x - 1 = 0$

23. $x^2 - 6x = -13$

24. $(x+1)^2 - 2$

5. Solve quadratic equations by following defined steps.

A.

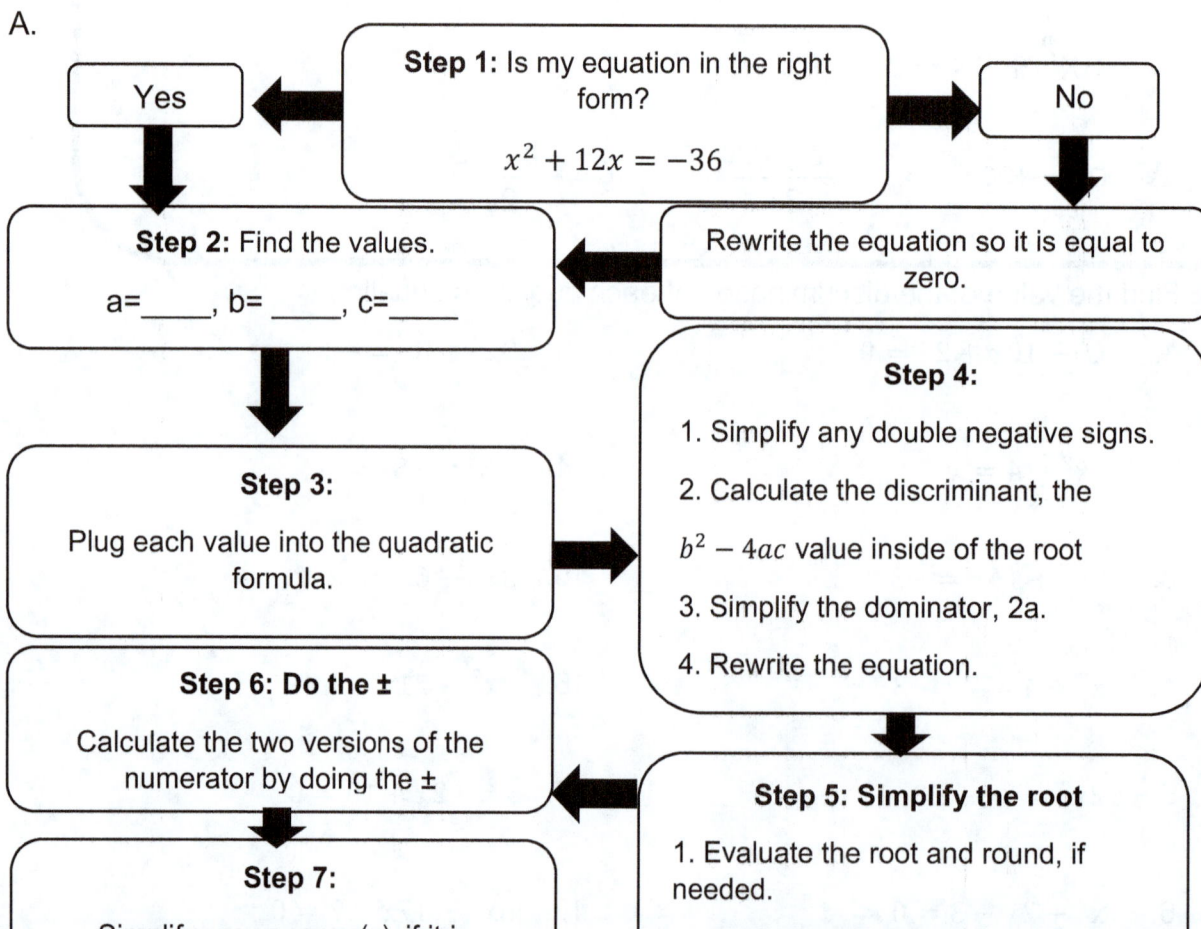

B.

Step 1:

Is my equation in the right form?

$x^2 - 1 = 0$

Yes →

No → Rewrite the equation so it is equal to zero.

Step 2:

Find the values.

a=____, b= ____, c=____

Step 3:

Plug each value into the quadratic formula.

Step 4:

1. Simplify any double negative signs.
2. Calculate the discriminant, the $b^2 - 4ac$ value inside of the root
3. Simplify the dominator, 2a.
4. Rewrite the equation.

Step 5: Simplify the root

1. Evaluate the root and round, if needed.
2. Rewrite the equation with the value of the root.

Step 6: Do the ±

Calculate the two versions of the numerator by doing the ±

Step 7:

Simplify your answer(s), if it is possible.

Solve quadratic Inequalities

A quadratic inequality may write like one of the below forms.

$ax^2 + bx + a > 0$ $\quad\quad$ $ax^2 + bx + c < 0$ $\quad\quad$ $ax^2 + bx + c \leq 0$ $\quad\quad$ $ax^2 + bx + c \geq 0$

To solve a quadratic inequality, follow these steps.

1. Change inequality to an equation.
2. Solve the equation.
3. After finding value of variable change equation to an inequality.
4. If a test point satisfies the original inequality, then the region that contains that test point is part of the solution.

6. Solve each quadratic inequality.

   1. $10 - 3x \leq x^2$

   2. $3x^2 + 7x \leq 2$

   3. $2k^2 + 3k - 2 > 0$

   4. $a^2 + 3a + 2 < -3(a - 3)$

   5. $x^2 + 3x \geq 14$

   12. $3x^2 < 6x$

   13. $2x^2 + 7x - 1 < 0$

   14. $4x^2 - 64 > 0$

   15. $2x^2 + 9x > 0$

   16. $y^2 \geq 81$

6. $-8 < -(1-x^2)$

7. $4x(x-1) > x(x+5)$

8. $b^2 + 3b \leq -2$

9. $t^2 + 18 \geq 11t$

10. $x^2 < 8$

11. $x^2 + 2x - 24 > 0$

17. $7 - 5x^2 > 2x$

18. $b^2 + 2b \geq 15$

19. $2x^2 + 6x \leq 8$

20. $r^2 - 18 < -3r$

21. $q^2 - 10q > -11$

22. $p(p-4) \geq -12$

MathePathics

Answers of worksheets – Chapter 11

Graphing Quadratic Functions

1.

1. $f(x) = 2x^2 - 12x + 22$

2. $f(x) = 6x^2$

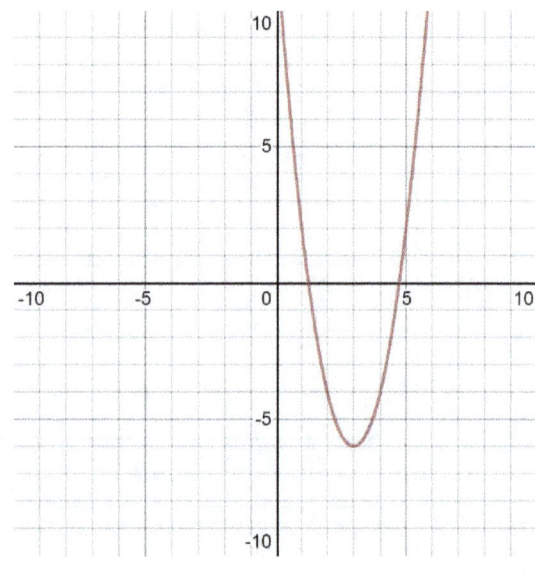
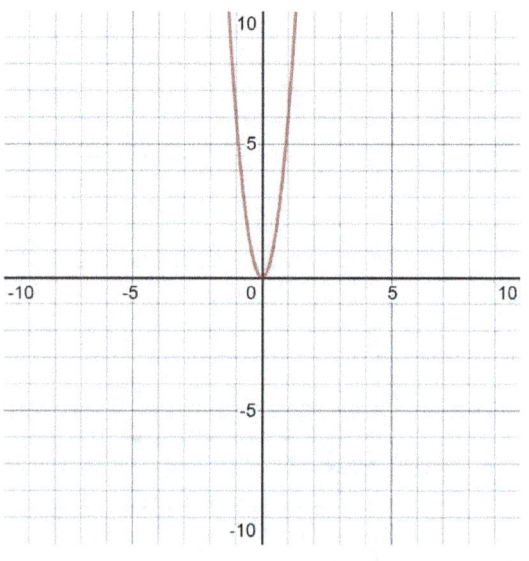

3. $f(x) = -x(x - 9)$

4. $f(x) = x^2 - 8x + 16$

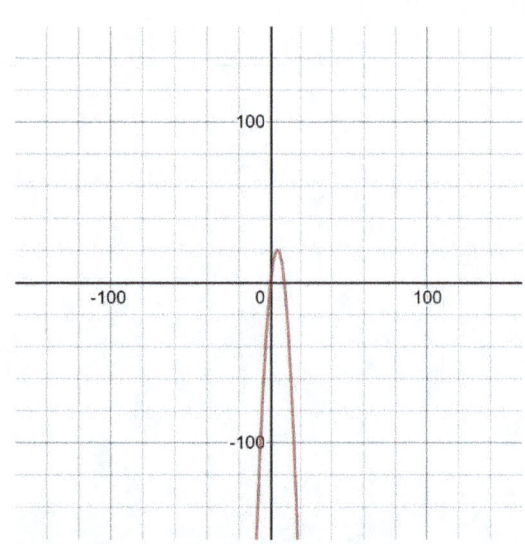
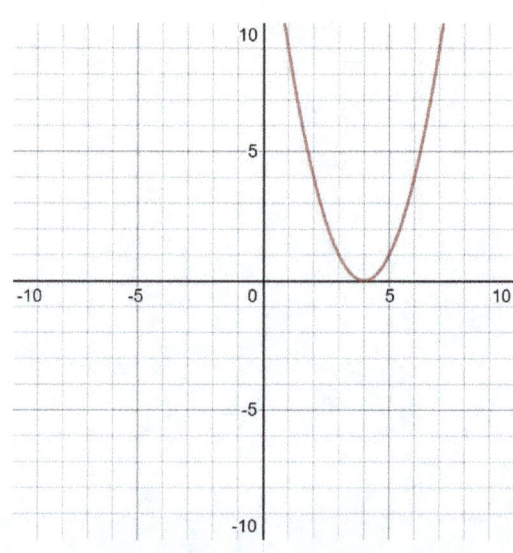

171

5. $f(x) = (x-2)^2 - 2$

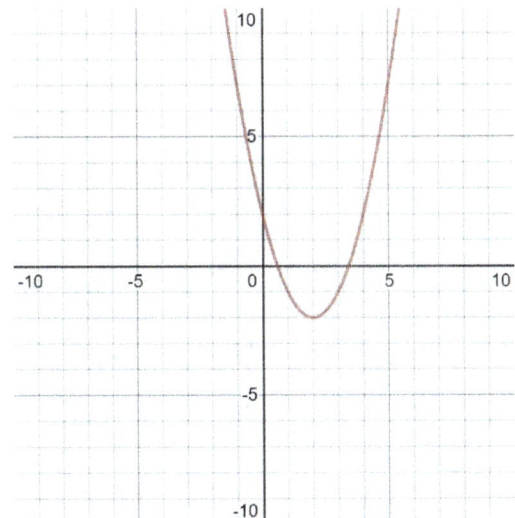

6. $f(x) = x^2 - 4$

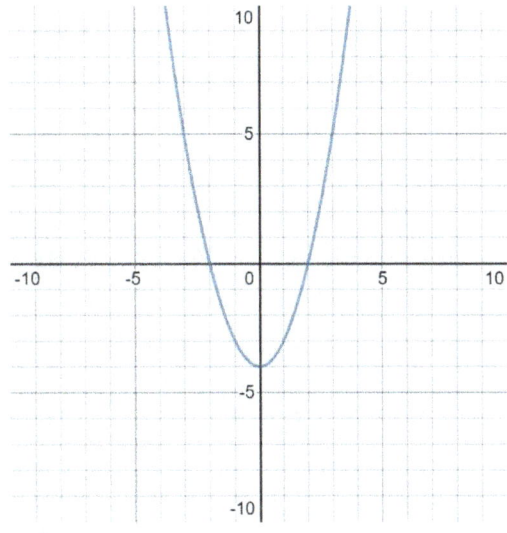

7. $f(x) = -3x^2 - 12x - 6$

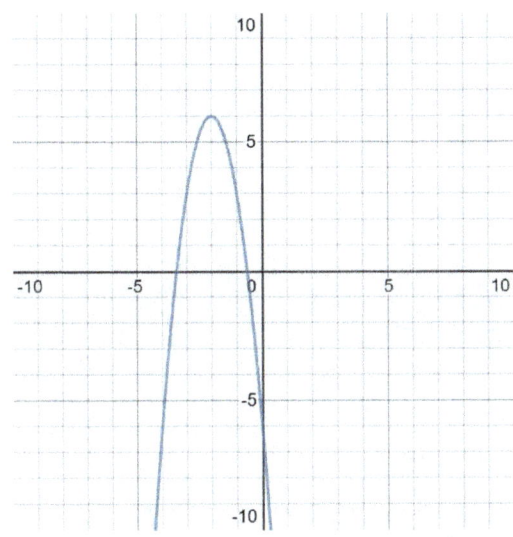

8. $f(x) = -x^2$

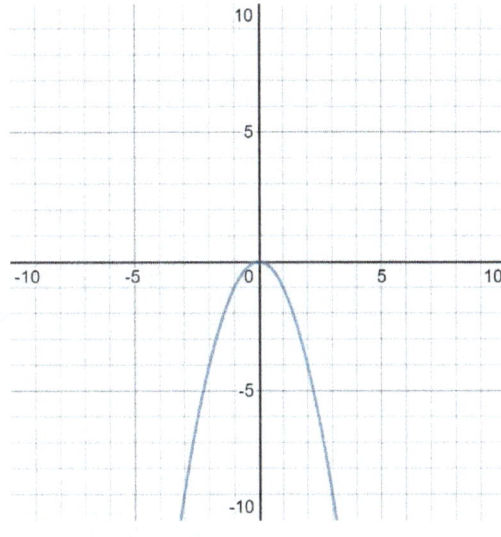

2.

1. $x^2 + x + 2$
2. $2x^2 - 9$
3. $3x^2 + 9x$
4. $x^2 - 6x - 16$
5. $(x+1)^2 + 2$
6. $-x^2 - 9x + 6$
7. $x^2 - 9$
8. $-7x^2$

Solving Quadratic Equations

3.

1. $x = -4, x = 2$
2. $x = -2, x = 7$
3. $x = -4, x = -3$
4. $x = -2, x = 8$
5. $x = 5$
6. $x = 7, x = -7$
7. $x = 16.8, x = -0.8$
8. $x = -3, x = 0$
9. $x = 0.5, x = 0$
10. $x = -7, x = 0$
11. $x = -6$
12. $x = -6, x = 0$
13. $x = -9, x = -2$
14. $x = -6, x = -5$
15. $x = -3, x = 0$
16. $x = -1, x = 5$
17. $x = 6.6, x = 1.3$
18. $x = -1, x = \dfrac{5}{3}$
19. $x = -14, x = 14$
20. $x = -0.2, x = -2.2$
21. $x = 8, x = 0$
22. $x = 9.8, x = -0.8$
23. $x = 75.05, x = -0.5$
24. $x = -2, x = 1$

Use the Quadratic Formula and the Discriminate

4.

1.

$(x-4)(x-6) = 0 \;\to\; x = 4, \; x = 6$

2.

$3x^2 - x - 4 = 0 \quad \Delta = b^2 - 4ac = (-1)^2 - 4(3)(-4) = 49$

$x_{1,2} = \dfrac{-b \pm \sqrt{\Delta}}{2a} \quad x_1 = \dfrac{1 + \sqrt{49}}{6} = \dfrac{4}{3} \quad x_2 = \dfrac{1 - \sqrt{49}}{6} = -1$

3.

$8x^2 + 14x + 3 = 0 \quad \Delta = b^2 - 4ac = (14)^2 - 4(3)(-4) = 100$

$x_{1,2} = \dfrac{-b \pm \sqrt{\Delta}}{2a} \quad x_1 = \dfrac{-14 + \sqrt{100}}{16} = -\dfrac{1}{4} \quad x_2 = \dfrac{-14 - \sqrt{100}}{16} = -\dfrac{2}{3}$

4.

$x^2 - 7x + 4 + 3 = 0 \;\to\; x^2 - 7x + 7 = 0 \quad \Delta = b^2 - 4ac = (-7)^2 - 4(1)(7) = 21$

$$x_{1,2} = \frac{-b \pm \sqrt{\Delta}}{2a} \quad x_1 = \frac{-7+\sqrt{21}}{2} = -1.25 \quad x_2 = \frac{-7-\sqrt{21}}{2} = -2.75$$

5.
$$2x^2 - 3x - 23 = 0 \quad \Delta = b^2 - 4ac = 193$$
$$x_{1,2} = \frac{-b \pm \sqrt{\Delta}}{2a} \quad x_1 = \frac{3+\sqrt{193}}{4} \quad x_2 = \frac{3-\sqrt{193}}{4}$$

6.
$$(x+3)(x-1) = 0 \rightarrow x = -3, \; x = 1$$

7.
$$x = -4, \; x = -7$$

8.
$$(x-1)(x+1) = 0 \rightarrow x = 1, \; x = -1$$

9.
$$x - 2 = 0 \rightarrow x = 2$$

10.
$$x^2 + 2x + 1 + 2 = x^2 + 2x + 3 \quad \Delta = b^2 - 4ac = (2)^2 - 4(1)(3) = -8 < 0 \; (\text{Doesn't have a real root})$$

11.
$$x^2 - 6x + 9 - 3 = x^2 - 6x + 6 = 0 \quad \Delta = b^2 - 4ac = 12$$
$$x_{1,2} = \frac{-b \pm \sqrt{\Delta}}{2a} \quad x_1 = \frac{6+\sqrt{12}}{2} \quad x_2 = \frac{6-\sqrt{12}}{2}$$

12.
$$5x^2 + 6x - 63 = 0 \quad \Delta = b^2 - 4ac = 1296$$
$$x_{1,2} = \frac{-b \pm \sqrt{\Delta}}{2a} \quad x_1 = \frac{-6+\sqrt{1296}}{10} = \frac{-6+36}{10} = 1 \quad x_2 = \frac{-6-\sqrt{1296}}{10} = \frac{-6-36}{10} = -\frac{42}{10}$$

13.
$$9x^2 + 8x + 1 = 0 \quad \Delta = b^2 - 4ac = 28$$
$$x_{1,2} = \frac{-b \pm \sqrt{\Delta}}{2a} \quad x_1 = \frac{-8+\sqrt{28}}{18} \quad x_2 = \frac{-8-\sqrt{28}}{18}$$

14.

$x(5x+8)=0 \quad x=0 \quad 5x+8=0 \to x=-\dfrac{8}{5}$

15.

$3x^2-6x-32=0 \quad \Delta=b^2-4ac=420$

$x_{1,2}=\dfrac{-b\pm\sqrt{\Delta}}{2a} \quad x_1=\dfrac{6+\sqrt{420}}{6} \quad x_2=\dfrac{6+\sqrt{420}}{6}$

16.

$2x^2-21x+49=0 \quad \Delta=b^2-4ac=49$

$x_{1,2}=\dfrac{-b\pm\sqrt{\Delta}}{2a} \quad x_1=\dfrac{21+\sqrt{49}}{4}=7 \quad x_2=\dfrac{21-\sqrt{49}}{4}=\dfrac{7}{2}$

17.

$\Delta=b^2-4ac=(-2)^2-4(1)(15)=-56<0 \quad \text{(Doesn't have a real root)}$

18.

$\Delta=b^2-4ac=457 \quad x_{1,2}=\dfrac{-b\pm\sqrt{\Delta}}{2a} \quad x_1=\dfrac{-17+\sqrt{457}}{12} \quad x_2=\dfrac{-17+\sqrt{457}}{12}$

19.

$4x^2+11x+6=0 \quad \Delta=b^2-4ac=25$

$x_{1,2}=\dfrac{-b\pm\sqrt{\Delta}}{2a} \quad x_1=\dfrac{-11+\sqrt{25}}{8}=-\dfrac{3}{4} \quad x_2=\dfrac{-11-\sqrt{25}}{8}=-2$

20.

$21x^2-43x+14=0 \quad \Delta=b^2-4ac=673$

$x_{1,2}=\dfrac{-b\pm\sqrt{\Delta}}{2a} \quad x_1=\dfrac{43+\sqrt{673}}{42} \quad x_2=\dfrac{43-\sqrt{673}}{42}$

21.

$(x+7)(x-3)=0 \quad x=-7 \;,\; x=3$

22.

$\Delta=b^2-4ac=4-4=0 \quad x_1=x_2=-\dfrac{b}{2a}=-\dfrac{2}{2}=-1$

23.

$x^2 - 6x + 13 = 0 \quad \Delta = b^2 - 4ac = -16 < 0$ (Doesn't have a real root)

24.

$x^2 + 2x + 1 - 2 = x^2 + 2x - 1 = 0$, $\Delta = (2)^2 - 4(1)(-1) = 4 + 4 = 8$

$x_1 = \dfrac{-2 + \sqrt{8}}{2(1)} = \dfrac{-2 + 2\sqrt{2}}{2} = \dfrac{2(-1 + \sqrt{2})}{2} = -1 + \sqrt{2}$

$x_2 = \dfrac{-2 - \sqrt{8}}{2(1)} = \dfrac{-2 - 2\sqrt{2}}{2} = \dfrac{2(-1 - \sqrt{2})}{2} = -1 - \sqrt{2}$

Quadratic Equation

5. A.

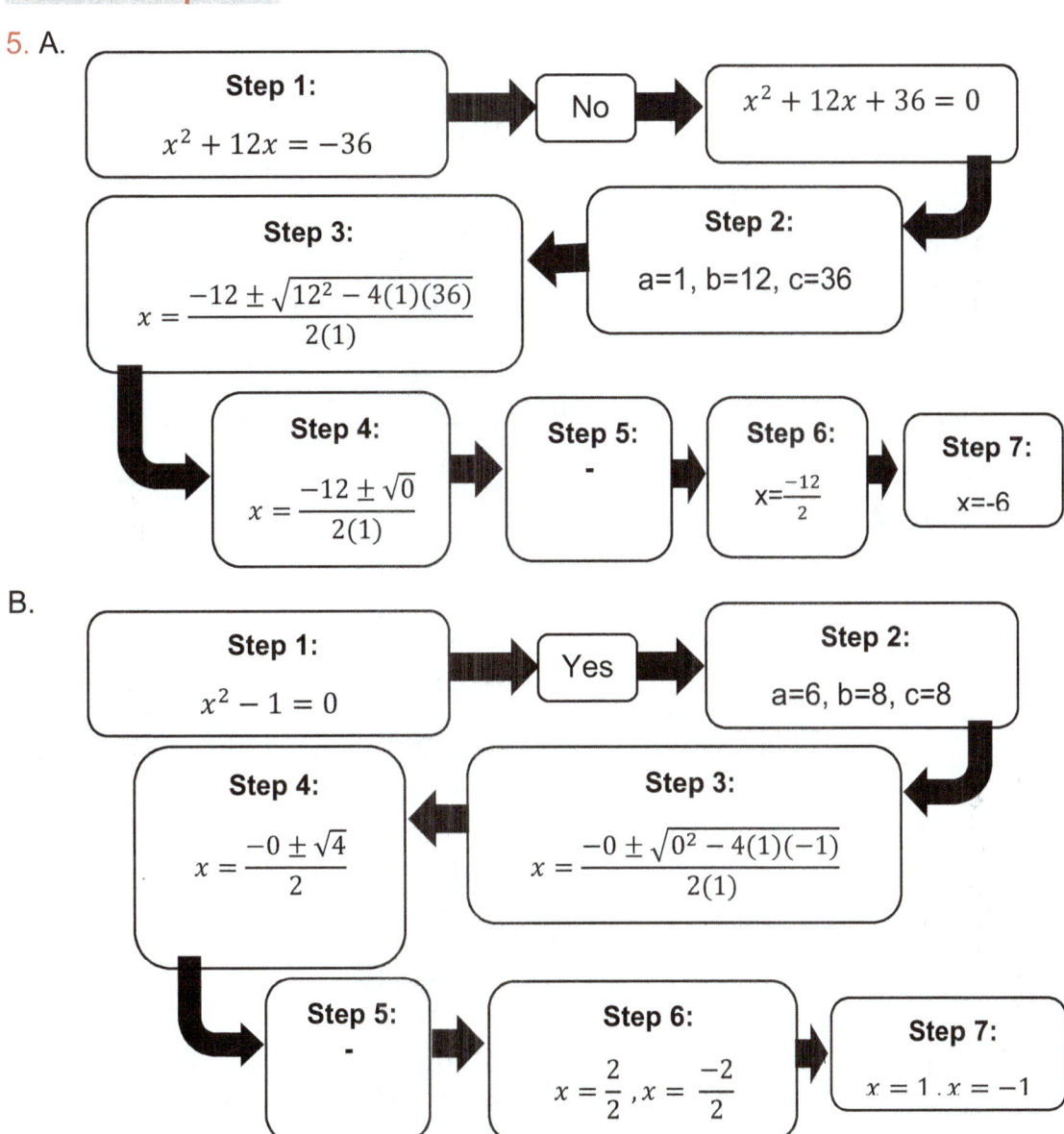

B.

176

Solve quadratic Inequalities

6.

1. $x \leq -5$
   $x \geq 2$

2. $x \in \left[\dfrac{-\sqrt{73}-7}{6}, \dfrac{+\sqrt{73}-7}{6}\right]$

3. $k < -2$
   $k > \dfrac{1}{2}$

4. $a \in (-7, 1)$

5. $x \leq \dfrac{-\sqrt{65}-3}{2}$
   $x \geq \dfrac{\sqrt{65}-3}{2}$

6. $x \in \mathbb{R}$

7. $x < 0$
   $x > 3$

8. $b \in [-2, -1]$

9. $t \leq 2$

12. $x \in (0, 2)$

13. $x \in \left(\dfrac{-\sqrt{57}-7}{4}, \dfrac{+\sqrt{57}-7}{4}\right)$

14. $x < -4$
    $x > 4$

15. $x < -\dfrac{9}{2}$
    $x > 0$

16. $y \geq 9$
    $y \leq -9$

17. $x \in \left(\dfrac{-7}{5}, 1\right)$

18. $b \leq -5$
    $b \geq 3$

19. $x \in [-4, 1]$

20. $r \in (-6, 3)$

$t \geq 9$

10. $x \in \left(-2\sqrt{2}, 2\sqrt{2}\right)$

11. $x < -6$
    $x > 4$

21. $q < 5 - \sqrt{14}$
    $q > \sqrt{14} + 5$

22. $p \in R$

Extra Note for Chapter 11:

Chapter 12: Complex Numbers

Adding and Subtracting Complex Numbers

Multiplying and Dividing Complex Numbers

Graphing Complex Numbers

Rationalizing Imaginary Denominators

Answers of Worksheets – Chapter 12

Adding and Subtracting Complex Numbers

A complex number is consisted of two parts, a real number, and an imaginary number.

$$\underset{\text{Imaginary}}{ai} + \underset{\text{Real}}{b} \qquad i = \sqrt{-1} \rightarrow i^2 = -1$$

To add and subtract complex numbers:
- Add or subtract real part together.
- Add or subtract imaginary number together.

Example:
$2i + 9 - 5i - 10 = 2i - 5i + 9 - 10 = -3i - 1$

1. Add or Subtract the following complex numbers.

1. $(3 + 4i) + (6 - i)$
2. $6 + (3 - 9i)$
3. $(9 + 3i) - (3 + 6i)$
4. $(8 - i) - (-7i)$
5. $(3 - 10i) + (18 + 3i)$
6. $(4 + 3i) + (6 + 2i)$
7. $4 - 3i + 7$
8. $(-3 + 8i) - (2 - 1i)$
9. $(3 + 13i) - (-3 + i)$
10. $(6 - 8i) + (5)$
11. $(3 - 2i) + (-9 - 8i)$
12. $(2 - i) - (3 + 11i)$
13. $(4) + (3 + 2i)$
14. $(18 - 6i) - (1 - 2i)$
15. $(13 + 13i) - (13i)$
16. $(8 - i) + (5 + 4i)$
17. $(3 + 3i) - (9 - i)$
18. $(13 - 5i) - (15 + 17i)$
19. $-(6 - 2i) + 4i$
20. $(-15) + (6 + 7i)$
21. $(9 - 2i) + (-4 + i)$
22. $(-10 + 12i) + (5 + i)$
23. $(12 + i) + (6 - 6i)$
24. $(-8 + 8i) - (-2 + i)$

2. Simplify.

1. $i + 10i$
2. $-4 - 8i + 54 - 2i$
3. $+3 + 9i + 2 - i$
4. $-3 + 5i - (-6 - 6i) + 10i$
5. $3 + 5i - 4 + 7i$
6. $6 + 41 - 3i$
7. $9 + 18i - 6 + 2$
8. $+9 - 5i + 6 - 7i + 31$
9. $-7i - 9i + 3 - 12i$
10. $-4i - (-5 + 3i) - 12$

3. How are the following problems different?

Simplify: $2 + x - (3 - 2x)$

Simplify: $2 + i - (3 - 2i)$

Answer:

Multiplying and Dividing Complex Numbers

For **multiplying** (a + bi) and (c + di), each term of first parenthesis gets multiplied by each term of second parenthesis.

$$(a + bi)(c + di) = ac + adi + bci + bdi^2 = (ac - bd) + (ad + bc)i$$

Example: $(2 + 4i)(6 + 3i) = ((12 - 12) + (6 + 24)i) = 0 + 30i = 30i$

For **dividing**, you must multiply numerator and denominator by conjugate of the denominator.

$$\frac{a+bi}{c+di} \times \frac{c-di}{c-di}$$

$$a+bi \xrightleftharpoons[\text{conjugate}]{\text{conjugate}} a-bi$$

4. Find the answer of each expression.

1. $(2 + 4i)(6 + 4i)$

9. $-\frac{1}{2} + \frac{5}{2}i$

2. $(6+3i)(7-i)$

3. $(\dfrac{3+i}{3-i})(\dfrac{1-2i}{5i})$

4. $\dfrac{(4+2i)}{(9-i)}$

5. $(-10-8i)(2-6i)$

6. $\dfrac{(-9-3i)}{(5+3i)}$

7. $(8+2i)^2$

8. $\dfrac{(-1+3i)}{-(3+4i)}$

10. $\dfrac{1}{10} - \dfrac{3}{10}i$

11. $\dfrac{2-6i}{3+i}$

12. $(6+2i)-(3-7i)$

13. $\left(\dfrac{1}{5}+i\dfrac{2}{5}\right)-(4+i\dfrac{5}{2})$

14. $(9+3i)(8-2i)$

15. $\dfrac{2i}{-(1+i)}$

16. $(2+3i)(2-6i)$

5. Write the expression as a complex number in standard form.

1. $\dfrac{|2-3i|-|-3-4i|}{|2+3i|}$

2. $(2i)(1-4i)(1+i)$

3. $(5-2i)^2$

4. $3i(1-7i)$

5. $\dfrac{2(5-6i)}{4i}$

6. $(2i)(8-5i)(3+2i)$

7. $\dfrac{i(1-i)}{-i}$

8. $\dfrac{(-10+4i)(4i)}{(1+9i)}$

9. $\dfrac{i^6}{i^{11}}$

10. $\dfrac{(2i)(4+3i)}{-i}$

11. $(3+9i)(3i)(9-i)$

12. $(3-i)\dfrac{4i}{2}$

13. $\dfrac{(2-2i)(14+i)}{(2i)}$

14. $(1+i)^2$

15. $(9-11i)(12+2i)(4)$

16. $\dfrac{-2(9-4i)}{-i}$

MathePathics

Graphing Complex Numbers

Y – axis is used for imaginary numbers..

X – axis is used for real numbers.

Example: 1 – 4i

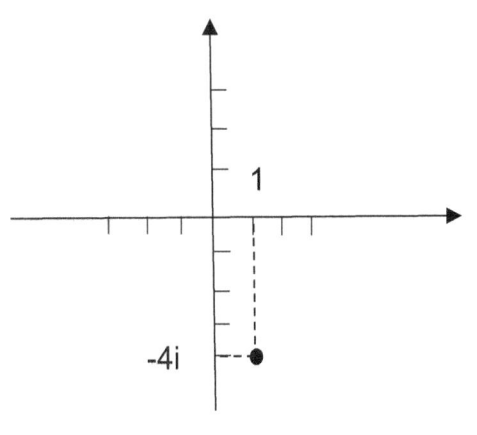

6. Show each complex number in a complex plane.

$-4 + i$

1.

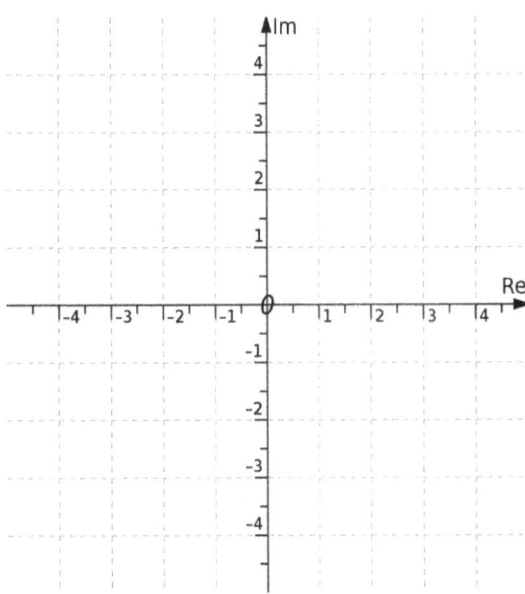

$2 - 4i$

5.

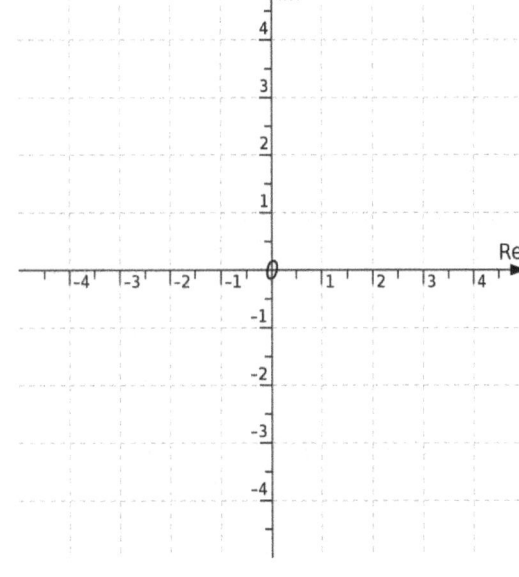

184

2. $-(3-i)$

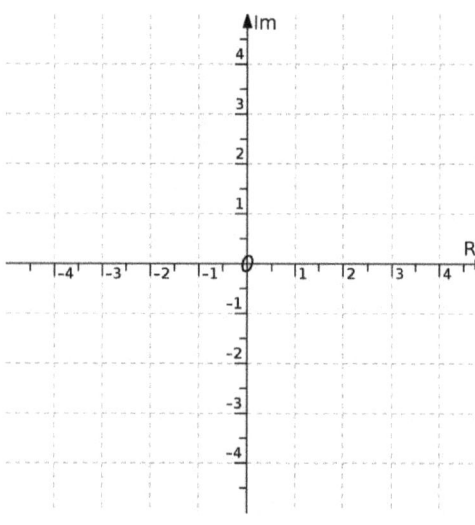

6. $3-2i$

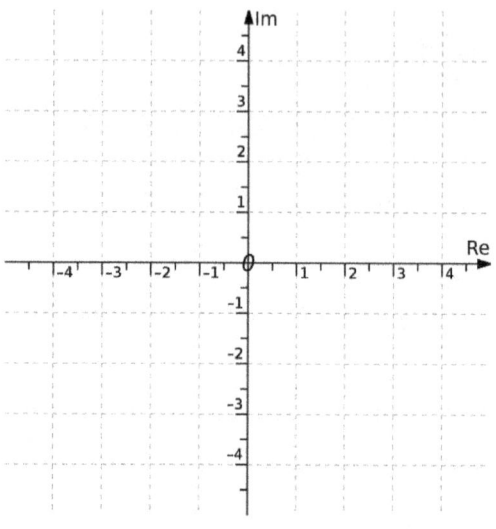

7. Two complex numbers are graphed below.

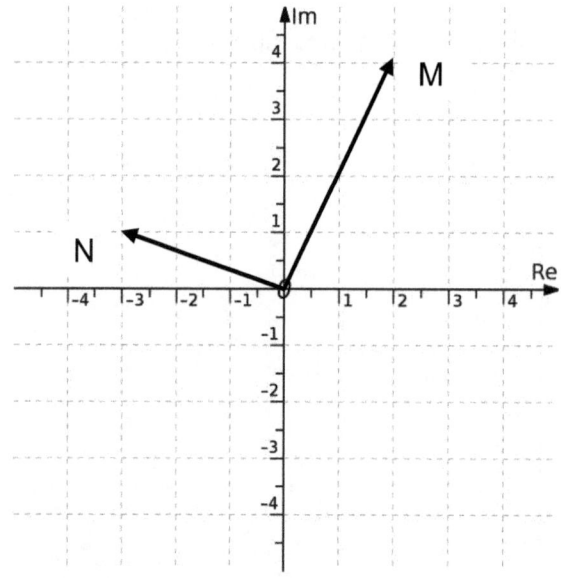

Write the sum of M and N, expressed in standard complex number form.

Standard form →

8. On a graph show, if point D represents $8-i$ and point E represents $(2+2i)$ which quadrant contains $D-2E$?

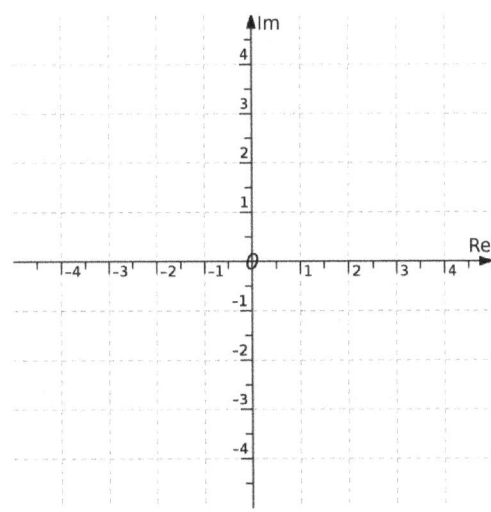

9. The graph of the product of $(4 + 3i)$ and $6i$ lies in which quadrant?

10. When the sum of $-8 + i$ and $-1 - 2i$ graphed, in which quadrant dose does it lay?

11. Find the sum of $-i$ and $4 + 4i$, graph the resultant on the accompanying set of axes.

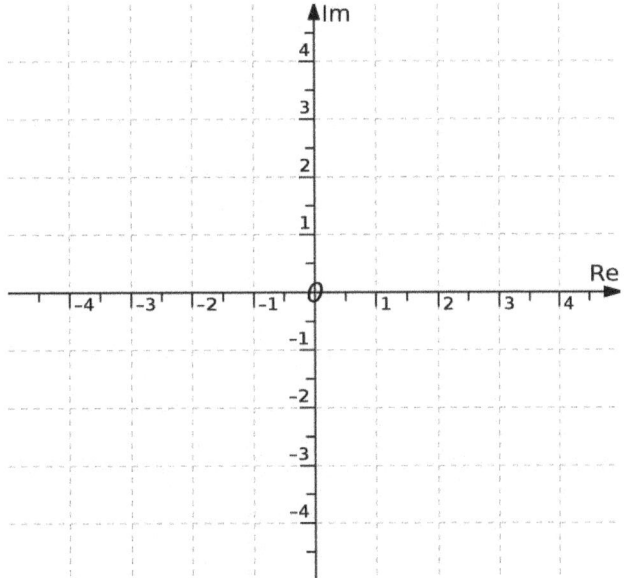

Rationalizing Imaginary Denominators

 You must delete imaginary part from denominator.

There are two states.

- If denominator is combination of real and imaginary numbers, multiply both numerator and denominator by conjugate of the denominator.
- If denominator includes just imaginary part, multiply both numerator and denominator by absolute value of denominator.

Example: $i = \sqrt{-1} \to i^2 = -1$

$$\frac{5}{-i} \xrightarrow{|-i|=i} \frac{5}{-i} \times \frac{i}{i} = \frac{5i}{-i^2} = 5i$$

$$\frac{2+3i}{5+2i} \times \frac{5-2i}{5-2i} = \frac{10-4i+15i-6i^2}{(5)^2-(2i)^2} = \frac{(10+6)+(-4+15)i}{25+4} = \frac{16+11i}{29}$$

12. Simplify.

1. $\dfrac{-4+10i}{-5i}$

2. $\dfrac{3}{-5i}$

3. $\dfrac{-6+3i}{9+8i}$

4. $\dfrac{a}{-bi}$

5. $\dfrac{-8+6i}{4i}$

6. $\dfrac{2+i}{5-5i}$

7. $\dfrac{15+i}{9-7i}$

8. $\dfrac{5}{5-10i}$

9. $\dfrac{-9}{-9i}$

10. $\dfrac{5-5i}{-10i}$

11. $\dfrac{6+12i}{6i}$

12. $\dfrac{-4i}{-1+2i}$

13. $\dfrac{-i}{-4-5i}$

14. $\dfrac{-1-i}{5i}$

15. $\dfrac{3i}{1-i}$

16. $\dfrac{6-6i}{2-i}$

MathePathics

Answers of Worksheets – Chapter 12

Adding and Subtracting Complex Numbers

1.

1.	$9 + 3i$	9.	$6 + 12i$	17.	$-6 + 4i$
2.	$9 - 9i$	10.	$11 - 8i$	18.	$-2 - 22i$
3.	$6 - 3i$	11.	$-6 - 10i$	19.	$-6 + 6i$
4.	$8 + 6i$	12.	$-1 - 12i$	20.	$-9 + 7i$
5.	$21 - 7is$	13.	$7 + 2i$	21.	$5 - i$
6.	$10 + 5i$	14.	$17 - 4i$	22.	$-5 + 13i$
7.	$11 - 3i$	15.	13	23.	$18 - 5i$
8.	$-5 + 9i$	16.	$13 + 3i$	24.	$-6 + 7i$

2.

1.	$11i$	5.	$-1 + 12i$	9.	$3 - 28i$
2.	$20 - 10i$	6.	$47 - 3i$	10.	$-7 - 7i$
3.	$5 + 8i$	7.	$5 + 18i$		
4.	$3 + 21i$	8.	$46 - 12i$		

3. There is no difference.

Multiplying and Dividing Complex Numbers

4.

1.	$-4 + 32i$	7.	$60 + 32i$	13.	$\left(\dfrac{19}{5} - \dfrac{21}{10}i\right)$
2.	$45 + 15i$	8.	$-\dfrac{9}{25} - \dfrac{13}{25}i$	14.	$78 + 6i$
3.	$-\dfrac{1}{5} - \dfrac{2}{5}i$	9.	$-\dfrac{1}{2} + \dfrac{5}{2}i$	15.	$-1 - i$
4.	$\dfrac{17}{41} + \dfrac{11}{41}i$	10.	$\dfrac{1}{10} - \dfrac{3}{10}i$	16.	$22 - 6i$

5. $-68 + 44i$
6. $-\dfrac{27}{17} + \dfrac{6}{17}i$
11. $-2i$
12. $3 + 9i$

5.

1. $\dfrac{13 - 5\sqrt{13}}{13}$
2. $6 + 10i$
3. $21 - 20i$
4. $21 + 3i$
5. $-3 - \dfrac{5}{2}i$
6. $-2 + 68i$
7. $-1 + i$
8. $-\dfrac{188}{41} + \dfrac{52}{41}i$
9. $-i$
10. $-8 - 6i$
11. $-234 + 108i$
12. $2 + 6i$
13. $-13 - 15i$
14. $2i$
15. $520 - 456i$
16. $-8 - 18i$

Graphing Complex Numbers

6.

1.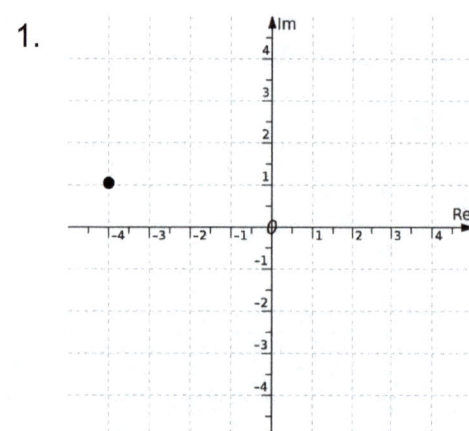

5.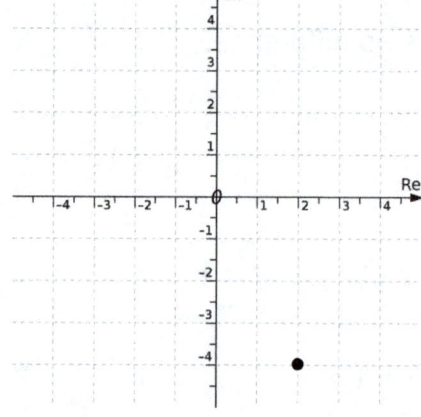

2.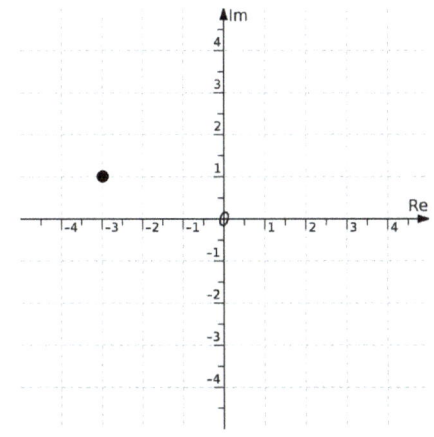

6.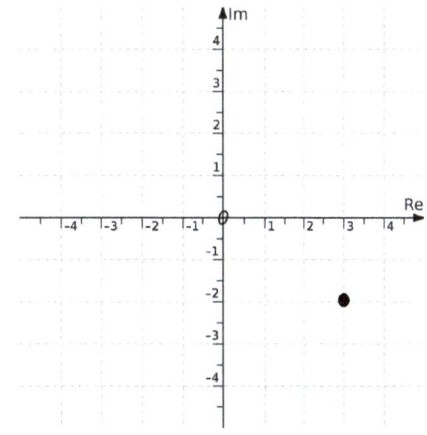

7. $(-1 + 5i)$

8. $(8 - i) - 2(2 + 2i) = 4 - 5i$ - IV

9. $(4 + 3i)(6i) = -18 + 24i$ - II

10. $-9 - i$ - III

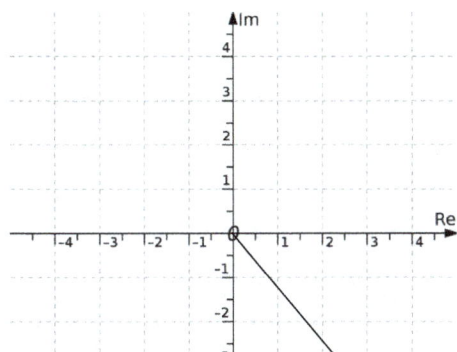

11. $-i + 4 + 4i = 4 + 5i$

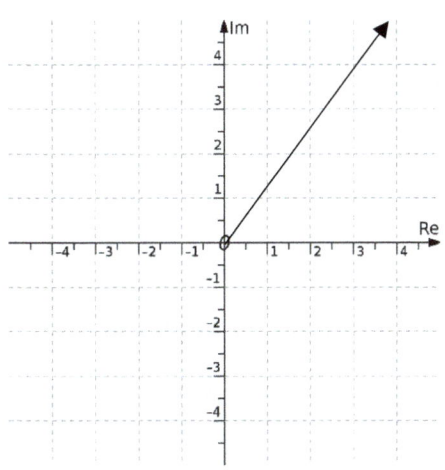

Rationalizing Imaginary Denominators

12.

1.

$$\frac{-4+10i}{-5i} \times \frac{i}{i} = \frac{-4i+10i^2}{-5i^2} = \frac{-4i+10(-1)}{-5(-1)} = \frac{-4i-10}{5}$$

2.

$$\frac{3}{5i} \times \frac{i}{i} = \frac{3i}{5i^2} = \frac{3i}{-5}$$

3.

$$\frac{-6+3i}{9+8i} \times \frac{9-8i}{9-8i} = \frac{-54+48i+27i-24i^2}{9^2-(8i)^2} = \frac{-54+75i-24(-1)}{81-64(-1)} = \frac{75i-30}{145}$$

4.

$$\frac{a}{-bi} \times \frac{i}{i} = \frac{ai}{-bi^2} = \frac{ai}{b}$$

5.

$$\frac{-8+6i}{4i} \times \frac{i}{i} = \frac{-8i+6i^2}{4i^2} = \frac{-8i-6}{-4} = 2i + \frac{3}{2}$$

6.

$$\frac{2+i}{5-5i} \times \frac{5+5i}{5+5i} = \frac{10+10i+5i+5i^2}{5^2-(5i)^2} = \frac{15i+5}{50} = \frac{i}{4} + \frac{1}{10}$$

7.

$$\frac{15+i}{9-7i} \times \frac{9+7i}{9+7i} = \frac{135+105i+9i-7}{9^2-(7i)^2} = \frac{114i+128}{130}$$

8.

$$\frac{5}{5-10i} \times \frac{5+10i}{5+10i} = \frac{25+15i}{5^2-(10i)^2} = \frac{25+15i}{25+100} = \frac{15i+25}{125} = \frac{3}{5}i + \frac{1}{5}$$

9.

$$\frac{-9}{-9i} \times \frac{i}{i} = \frac{-9i}{-9i^2} = \frac{-9i}{9} = -i$$

10.

$$\frac{5-5i}{-10i} \times \frac{i}{i} = \frac{5i-5i^2}{-10i^2} = \frac{5i+5}{10} = \frac{1}{2}i + \frac{1}{2}$$

11.

$$\frac{6+12i}{6i} \times \frac{i}{i} = \frac{6i+12i^2}{6i^2} = \frac{6i-12}{-6} = -i+2$$

12.

$$\frac{-4i}{-1+2i} \times \frac{-1-2i}{-1-2i} = \frac{4i+8i^2}{(-1)^2-(2i)^2} = \frac{4i-8}{1+4} = \frac{4i-8}{5}$$

13.

$$\frac{-i}{-4-5i} \times \frac{-4+5i}{-4+5i} = \frac{4i-5i^2}{(-4)^2-(5i)^2} = \frac{4i+5}{16+25} = \frac{4i+5}{41}$$

14.

$$\frac{-1-i}{5i} \times \frac{i}{i} = \frac{-i-i^2}{5i^2} = \frac{i+1}{-5}$$

15.

$$\frac{3i}{1-i} \times \frac{1+i}{1+i} = \frac{3i+3i^2}{1^2-i^2} = \frac{3i-3}{1+1} = \frac{3i-3}{2}$$

16.

$$\frac{6-6i}{2-i} \times \frac{2+i}{2+i} = \frac{12+6i-12i-6i^2}{2^2-i^2} = \frac{-6i+18}{4+1} = \frac{-6i+18}{5}$$

Extra Note for Chapter 12:

MathePathics

Chapter 13: Exponents and Radicals

- Multiplications Property of Exponents
- Division Property of Exponents
- Power of Products and Quotients
- Zero and Negative Exponents
- Negative Exponents and Negative Bases
- Writing Scientific Notation
- Square Roots

Answers of Worksheets – Chapter 13

MathePathics

Multiplication Property of Exponents

For multiplication of exponents which have same base:

> Write one of the bases
> Add exponents

$$x^a \cdot x^b = x^{a+b}$$

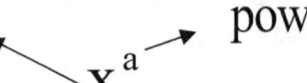

$x^a \longrightarrow$ Means multiply **a** factor of **x**

$$x^a = \underbrace{x \cdot x \cdot x \cdots x}_{a \text{ factors}}$$

1- Simplify.

a. $5^3 =$ b. $(\frac{1}{2})^2 =$ c. $(0.3)^4 =$

d. $(-7)^3 =$ e. $(\sqrt{3})^5 =$ f. $(\frac{5}{6})^2 =$

g. $(8)^3 =$ h. $(-10)^2 =$ i. $(0.2)^4 =$

2- What does $(8)^5$ mean?

3- Simplify.

a) $a^5 \cdot a^3 =$

b) $x^9 \cdot x^6 \cdot x =$

c) $y^2 \cdot y^4 =$

d) $b^{11} \cdot b^{12} =$

e) $4x^2 y x^3 =$

f) $(8a^2 b) \cdot (3b a^4) =$

g) $(10a^9 bc)(2ab^5)(5ac^3) =$

h) $(x^5 y^6 z^2)(3xy) =$

4- Jack wants to solve $(5x y^5 z^4)(6x^6 y^8)(11x^9 z^{12})$.

But he does not know how to solve. Can you help him?

5- How can you write 4^3?

6- Rosy wants to multiply 0.3 one-hundred times by itself. But it takes a long time and she does not have enough time to do it. How can she write it simpler?

Division Property of Exponents

To divide exponents with the same base:

- Write one of the bases.
- Subtract powers.

$$\frac{x^a}{x^b} = x^{(a-b)}$$

1- Simplify.

a) $\dfrac{x^8}{x^5} =$

b) $\dfrac{y^2}{y^3} =$

c) $\dfrac{a^{10}}{a^{12}} =$

d) $\dfrac{x^5 y}{x} =$

e) $\dfrac{4a^5 b}{ab^6} =$

f) $\dfrac{10 m^{11} n^4}{5 m^5 n^6} =$

g) $\dfrac{18 x^5 y z^3}{4 x y^{10} z} =$

h) $\dfrac{35 a^5 b c}{7 a^3 b} =$

i) $\dfrac{14 x y^4}{3 x y z^5} =$

2- Tim and Max simplified $\dfrac{(5a^5 b^4 c)(2x^3 y^8 z)(4a^5 b)(8x^9 y^2 z)}{(a^6 bc)(4x^7 yz^8)}$.

Which of them wrote correct answer?

Tim's solution

$$\dfrac{(5a^5 b^4 c)(2x^3 y^8 z)(4a^5 b)(8x^9 y^2 z)}{(a^6 bc)(4x^7 yz^8)} = \dfrac{320(a^{10} b^3 c)(x^{12} y^{10} z^2)}{20(a^6 bc)(x^7 yz^8)} = 16a^4 b^2 x^4 y^9 z^{-6}$$

Max's solution

$$\dfrac{(5a^5 b^4 c)(2x^3 y^8 z)(4a^5 b)(8x^9 y^2 z)}{(a^6 bc)(4x^7 yz^8)} = \dfrac{320(a^{10} b^3 c)(x^{12} y^{10} z^2)}{20(a^6 bc)(x^7 yz^8)} = 15a^5 b^7 x^3 y^9 z^{-6}$$

3- Simplify.

a) $\dfrac{(6a^{10} b)(2x^8 y^4)}{(3a^7 b)(5x^6 y)} =$

b) $\dfrac{(x^{10} y)(a^5 b)(m^6 n)}{(x^3 y^4)(m^8 n^2)} =$

c) $\dfrac{(5x^4 y^3 z^2)(2xyz)(3x y^2 z^7)}{(3x^5 yz)(2xyz)} =$

d) $\dfrac{(4a^5 b)(6ab^6)}{8a^2 b} =$

Power of Products and Quotients

Multiplication

Write each base by the power one by one and fine their answer. Then multiply them and write answer.

$(a.b)^m = a^m.b^m$

Division

Write numerator and denominator by the power separately and find the answer. Then divide numerator by denominator and write answer.

$(\frac{a}{b})^m = \frac{a^m}{b^m}$

1- Simplify expression.

a) $(2a)^3 =$

b) $(5x)^4 =$

c) $(7y)^2 =$

d) $(13ab)^2 =$

e) $(0.1bc)^3 =$

f) $(\frac{1}{2}x^2)^2 =$

g) $(4x^2y)^3 =$

h) $(6mn)^3 =$

i) $(9x^2y)^3 =$

2- Ted simplified below expression, but he isn't sure whether it's correct. Check his answer.

$$\left(\frac{(5a^5b^4c)(2x^3y^8z)(4a^5b)(8x^9y^2z)}{(5a^6bc)(4x^7yz^8)}\right)^2 = \left(\frac{(20a^{5+5}b^{4+1}c)(16x^{3+9}y^{8+2}z^{1+1})}{(5a^6bc)(4x^7yz^8)}\right)^2$$

$$\left(\frac{320(a^{10}b^5c)(x^{12}y^{10}z^2)}{20(a^6bc)(x^7yz^8)}\right)^2 = \left(16\, a^{10-6}\, b^{5-1}\, x^{12-7}\, y^{10-1}\, z^{2-8}\right)^2$$

$$= 256\, a^8\, b^8\, x^{10}\, y^{18}\, z^{-12}$$

3- Simplify below expression.

a) $(\dfrac{5x^2}{2xy})^2 =$

b) $(\dfrac{3a}{5})^3 =$

c) $(\dfrac{6}{2x^2})^4 =$

d) $(\dfrac{2x}{y})^2 =$

e) $(\dfrac{ab}{2a})^3 =$

f) $(\dfrac{3b^5c}{b})^2 =$

g) $(\dfrac{4x^2yz}{2xy})^3 =$

h) $(\dfrac{5ab^2c^3}{abc})^3 =$

i) $(\dfrac{36m^4n^2}{6mn})^2 =$

Zero and Negative Exponents

The Rule for Negative Exponents

The expression a^{-n} is the reciprocal of a^n. A **reciprocal** is when you "flip a fraction".

$$x^{-m} = \frac{1}{x^m} \quad (x \neq 0)$$

Example: $2^{-5} = \dfrac{1}{2^5} = \dfrac{1}{32}$

The Rule for Zero Exponents

Any number (except 0) to the zero power is equal to 1. $x^0 = 1 \, (x \neq 0)$

Example: $8^0 = 1$

1- Simplify.

a) $(5x)^0 =$

b) $(2ab)^{-1} =$

c) $(3x)^0 =$

d) $(\frac{1}{2}x)^{-1} =$

e) $(5)^{-1} =$

f) $(5z)^{-1} =$

2- Billy simplified below expression. Is his solution correct? Check it.

$$\left(\frac{(2ab)^3 (2a^2b)^2 (5ab)}{(2a^5b)^3} \right)^{-1}$$

$$\left(\frac{(2ab)^3 (2a^2b)^2 (5ab)}{(2a^5b)^3} \right)^{-1} = \left(\frac{(8a^3b^3)(16a^8b^4)(5ab)}{(8a^{15}b^3)} \right)^{-1} = (80a^{-3}b^5)^{-1} = \frac{a^3}{80b^5}$$

Negative Exponents and Negative Bases

The minus sign on the base does not belong to power. When a power has a minus sign, you should write the base with a positive power in the denominator

$$-X^{-a} = -\frac{1}{X^a}$$

Example: $-2^{-5} = \frac{1}{(-2^5)} = -\frac{1}{32}$

1- Rewrite following expressions without an exponent.

a) $(-5)^{(-3)} =$

b) $(-\frac{1}{2})^{(-2)} =$

c) $(-ab)^{(-3)} =$

d) $(-7x)^{(-2)} =$

e) $(-10)^{(-4)} =$

f) $(-\frac{x}{5})^{(-3)}$

2- Following expressions are Adam's math homework. Can you help him to solve them?

a) $(-2)^{(-3)} + (-5)^{(-2)} =$

b) $(-a)^{(-4)} + (-\frac{1}{a})^{(-2)}$

Writing Scientific Notation

Scientific notation is a standard way of writing very large and very small numbers so that they are easier to both compare and use in computations.

How can you do it?

- When the number is 10 or greater, the decimal point must move to the left, and the power of 10 is positive.
  Example: $257000 = 2.57 \times 10^5$

- When the number is smaller than 1, the decimal point must move to the right, so the power of 10 is negative.
  Example: $0.0000257 = 2.57 \times 10^{-5}$

1- Write following numbers in scientific notation.

a) 127000 =

b) 0.00037 =

c) 5460000 =

d) 0.009 =

e) 1500 =

f) 0.000789 =

2- A tiny box that is magnified by a microscope has 0.0002 length, 0.0003 height and 0.0004 width.

What is its volume?

Square Roots

A square root of a number is a value that can be multiplied by itself to give the original number.

$$a \xrightleftharpoons[\text{Square Root}]{\text{Square}} a^2 \qquad 5 \xrightleftharpoons[\text{Square Root}]{\text{Square}} 25$$

Radical is a special symbol that means "square root".

$\sqrt{25} = 5$ Square root of 25 equals to 5.

$\sqrt{25} = 5$ means $5^2 = 25$

1- Write the square roots of below numbers.

a) 9

b) 16

c) 4

d) 49

e) 100

f) 81

g) 10000

h) 121

i) 225

2- Write square of below numbers.

a) 14

b) 0.2

c) $\dfrac{1}{2}$

d) 5

e) 12

f) (−3)

MathePathics

Answers of Worksheets – Chapter 13

Multiplication Property of Exponents

1.

a. $5^3 = 5.5.5 = 125$

b. $(\frac{1}{2})^2 = \frac{1}{2} \cdot \frac{1}{2} = \frac{1}{4}$

c. $(0.3)^4 = (0.3).(0.3).(0.3).(0.3) = 0.0081$

d. $(-7)^3 = (-7).(-7).(-7) = -343$

e. $(\sqrt{3})^5 = (\sqrt{3}).(\sqrt{3}).(\sqrt{3}).(\sqrt{3}).(\sqrt{3}) = 9\sqrt{3}$

f. $(\frac{5}{6})^2 = (\frac{5}{6}).(\frac{5}{6}) = \frac{25}{36}$

g. $(8)^3 = 8.8.8 = 512$

h. $(-10)^2 = (-10).(-10) = +100$

i. $(0.2)^4 = (0.2).(0.2).(0.2).(0.2) = 0.0016$

2.

$(8)^5 = 8.8.8.8.8 = 32768$

3.

a) $a^5.a^3 = a^{5+3} = a^8$

b) $x^9.x^6.x = x^{9+6+1} = x^{16}$

c) $y^2.y^4 = y^{2+4} = y^6$

d) $b^{11}.b^{12} = b^{11+12} = b^{23}$

e) $4x^2yx^3 = 4x^{2+3}y$

f) $(8a^2b).(3ba^4) = 24a^{2+4}b^{1+1} = 24a^6b^2$

205

g) $(10a^9bc)(2ab^5)(5ac^3) = 100a^{9+1+1} \cdot b^{1+5} \cdot c^{1+3} = 100a^{11}b^6c^4$

h) $(x^5y^6z^2)(3xy) = 3x^{5+1}y^{6+1}z^2 = 3x^6y^7z^2$

4.

$(5xy^5z^4)(6x^6y^8)(11x^9z^{12}) = 330x^{1+6+9}y^{5+8}z^{4+12} = 330x^{16}y^{13}z^{16}$

5.

$4^3 = 4 \cdot 4 \cdot 4 = 64$

6.

$(0.3)^{100}$

Division Property of Exponents

1.

a) $\dfrac{x^8}{x^5} = x^{8-5} = x^3$

b) $\dfrac{y^2}{y^3} = y^{2-3} = y^{-1}$

c) $\dfrac{a^{10}}{a^{12}} = a^{10-12} = a^{-2}$

d) $\dfrac{x^5y}{x} = x^{5-1} \cdot y = x^4y$

e) $\dfrac{4a^5b}{ab^6} = 4a^{5-1}b^{1-6} = 4a^4b^{-5}$

f) $\dfrac{10m^{11}n^4}{5m^5n^6} = 2m^{11-5}n^{4-6} = 2m^6n^{-2}$

g) $\dfrac{18x^5yz^3}{4xy^{10}z} = \dfrac{9}{2}x^{5-1}y^{1-10}z^{3-1} = \dfrac{9}{2}x^4y^{-9}z^2$

h) $\dfrac{35a^5bc}{7a^3b} = 5a^{5-3}c = 5a^2c$

i) $\dfrac{14xy^4}{3xyz^5} = \dfrac{14y^3}{3z^5}$

2.

Tim's solution

3.

a) $\dfrac{(6a^{10}b)(2x^8y^4)}{(3a^7b)(5x^6y)} = \dfrac{12}{15}a^3x^2y^3$

b) $\dfrac{(x^{10}y)(a^5b)(m^6n)}{(x^3y^4)(m^8n^2)} = x^7y^{-3}a^5b$

c) $\dfrac{(5x^4y^3z^2)(2xyz)(3xy^2z^7)}{(3x^5yz)(2xyz)} = \dfrac{15x^5y^5z^9}{3x^5yz} = 5y^4z^8$

d) $\dfrac{(4a^5b)(6ab^6)}{8a^2b} = \dfrac{24a^6b^7}{8a^2b} = 3a^4b^6$

Power of Products and Quotients

1.

a) $(2a)^3 = 8a^3$

b) $(5x)^4 = 625x^4$

c) $(7y)^2 = 49y^2$

d) $(13ab)^2 = 169a^2b^2$

e) $(0.1bc)^3 = 0.001b^3c^3$

f) $(\dfrac{1}{2}x^2)^2 = \dfrac{1}{4}x^4$

g) $(4x^2y)^3 = 64x^5y^3$

h) $(6mn)^3 = 216m^3n^3$

i) $(9x^2y)^3 = 729x^6y^3$

2.

It is correct.

3.

a) $(\dfrac{5x^2}{2xy})^2 = \dfrac{25x^4}{4x^2y^2} = \dfrac{25x^2}{4y^2}$

b) $(\dfrac{3a}{5})^3 = \dfrac{27a^3}{125}$

c) $(\dfrac{6}{2x^2})^4 = \dfrac{1298}{8x^8} = \dfrac{162}{x^8}$

d) $(\dfrac{2x}{y})^2 = \dfrac{4x^2}{y^2}$

e) $(\dfrac{ab}{2a})^3 = \dfrac{a^3b^3}{8a^3} = \dfrac{b^3}{8}$

f) $(\dfrac{3b^5c}{b})^2 = \dfrac{9b^{10}c^2}{b^2} = 9b^8c^2$

g) $(\dfrac{4x^2yz}{2xy})^3 = \dfrac{64x^6y^3z^3}{4x^3y^3} = 16x^3z^3$

h) $(\dfrac{5ab^2c^3}{abc})^3 = 125b^3c^6$

i) $(\dfrac{36m^4n^2}{6mn})^2 = \dfrac{1296m^8n^4}{36m^2n^2} = 36m^6n^2$

Zero and Negative Exponents

1.

a) $(5x)^0 = 1$

b) $(2ab)^{-1} = \dfrac{1}{2ab}$

c) $(3x)^0 = 1$

d) $(\dfrac{1}{2}x)^{-1} = \dfrac{2}{x}$

e) $(5)^{-1} = \dfrac{1}{5}$

f) $(5z)^{-1} = \dfrac{1}{5z}$

2.

It is correct.

Negative Exponents and Negative Bases

1.

a) $(-5)^{(-3)} = \dfrac{1}{(-5)^3} = -\dfrac{1}{125}$

b) $(-\dfrac{1}{2})^{(-2)} = \dfrac{1}{(-\dfrac{1}{2})^2} = \dfrac{1}{\dfrac{1}{4}} = 4$

c) $(-ab)^{(-3)} = \dfrac{1}{(-ab)^3} = -\dfrac{1}{a^3 b^3}$

d) $(-7x)^{(-2)} = \dfrac{1}{(-7x)^2} = \dfrac{1}{49x^2}$

e) $(-10)^{(-4)} = \dfrac{1}{(-10)^4} = \dfrac{1}{10000}$

f) $(-\dfrac{x}{5})^{(-3)} = \dfrac{1}{(-\dfrac{x}{5})^3} = -\dfrac{125}{x^3}$

2.

a) $(-2)^{(-3)} + (-5)^{(-2)} = \dfrac{1}{(-2)^3} + \dfrac{1}{(-5)^2} = -\dfrac{1}{8} + \dfrac{1}{10} = \dfrac{-5+4}{40} = -\dfrac{1}{40}$

b) $(-a)^{(-4)} + (-\dfrac{1}{a})^{(-2)} = \dfrac{1}{(-a)^4} + \dfrac{1}{(\dfrac{1}{a})^2} = \dfrac{1}{a^4} + a^2 = \dfrac{1+a^6}{a^4}$

Writing Scientific Notation

1.

a) $127000 = 1.2 \times 10^5$

b) $0.00037 = 3.7 \times 10^{-4}$

c) $5460000 = 5.46 \times 10^6$

d) $0.009 = 9 \times 10^{-3}$

e) $1500 = 1.5 \times 10^3$

f) $0.000789 = 7.89 \times 10^{-4}$

2.

The volume of box = height × length × width

The volume of box $= 0.0003 \times 0.0002 \times 0.0004 = (3 \times 10^{-4})(2 \times 10^{-4})(4 \times 10^{-4})$

$= 24 \times 10^{(-4-4-4)} = 24 \times 10^{-12}$

Square Roots

1.

a) $9 \rightarrow \sqrt{9} = 3$

b) $16 \rightarrow \sqrt{16} = 4$

c) $4 \rightarrow \sqrt{4} = 2$

d) $49 \to \sqrt{49} = 7$　　　e) $100 \to \sqrt{100} = 10$　　　f) $81 \to \sqrt{81} = 9$

g) $10000 \to \sqrt{10000} = 100$　　　h) $121 \to \sqrt{121} = 11$　　　i) $225 \to \sqrt{225} = 15$

2.

a) $14 \to 14 \times 14 = 14^2 = 196$　　　b) $0.2 \to 0.2 \times 0.2 = 0.2^2 = 0.04$

c) $\dfrac{1}{2} \to \dfrac{1}{2} \times \dfrac{1}{2} = \dfrac{1^2}{2} = \dfrac{1}{4}$　　　d) $5 \to 5 \times 5 = 5^2 = 25$

e) $12 \to 12 \times 12 = 12^2 = 144$　　　f) $(-3) \to (-3) \times (-3) = (-3)^2 = 9$

Extra Note for Chapter 13:

Chapter 14:

Statistics

Mean, Median, Mode, and Range of the Given Data

Box and whisker

Bar Graph

Stem – And – Leaf Plot

The Pie Graph or Circle Graph

Scatter Plots

Probability Problems

Answers of Worksheets – Chapter 14

Mode, Mean, Median, and range of the given data

Mean: Average value of a set of numbers.

Example: 2, 4, 5, 6

- Adding the numbers. 2+5+4+6=16
- So divided the total by 4. (There are 4 numbers.) $\frac{16}{4}=4$

Median: Middle value of a set of numbers.

Example: 1, 5, 6, 1, 3, 5, 1, 6, 7, 6, 7

- Organize the numbers in increasing order.   1, 1, 1, 3, 5, 5, 6, 6, 6, 7, 7
- The median is the middle number. 5
- If there are two middle numbers, add them and divide by 2 to get the median.

Mode: Most common or frequent value of the set.

Example: 4, 8, 9, 8, 9, 4, 1, 9, 5, 1, 9

- Count how many times a number appears in the list of data.
- The mode is the one that is appeared the most.   9

Range: Range is the difference between the maximum and minimum number of the set.

Example: 12, 15, 14, 10, 16, 13, 12

- Organize the numbers in increasing order.   10, 12, 12, 13, 14, 15, 16
- Highest value: 16
- Lowest value: 10
- Range: 16 – 10 = 6

1-The following set of numbers is a recent survey that was done on people's weight. Find the maximum and minimum weight.

- 85,64,78,52,46,72,59,67

2-Find the mean, median, mode and range for the following lists of numbers.

A: 3,9,10,3,4,4,10,9,3,5,6

B: 1,2,4,2,7,11,11,2,5,7,11,7

3-Complete the chart.

Set of number	Maximum	Minimum	Mean	Median
5,5,6,9,3,9,3,5				
71,89,25,25,34,11,25				
11,14,18,11,12,11.12				

4- The following set of numbers is students' grade in final exam.

What is the mean grade?

100,95,84,75,84,96,84

Box and Whisker Plots

A Box and Whisker Plot (or Box Plot) is a convenient way of visually displaying the data distribution through their quartiles.

Example: Draw a box-and-whisker plot for the following data set.

- 2.9, 3.5, 3.7, 3.1, 4.0, 3.9, 3.5, 3.8, 3.1, 3.7, 3.6, 3.6, 3.7, 3.5

1-Order the set.

- 2.9, 3.1, 3.1, 3.5, 3.5, 3.5, <u>3.6</u>, 3.6, 3.7, 3.7, 3.8, 3.9, 4.0

2-Find the median.

- Median is 3.6.(A)

3-Find the median of two halves.

- First half: 2.9, 3.1, 3.1, 3.5, 3.5, 3.5   Median is 3.3.(B)
  $$\frac{3.1+3.5}{2} = 3.3$$

- Second half: 3.6, 3.7, 3.7, 3.8, 3.9, 4.0   Median is 3.75.(C)
  $$\frac{3.7+3.8}{2} = 3.75$$

4-Draw a box and Whisker plot.

📎 Since the values in the list are written with one decimal place and range from 2.9 to 4.0. Do not use a scale of one to ten. Draw a number line from 2.9 to 4.0 and mark off by tenths.

2.9   4.0

Mark off the minimum, maximum, median, and median of two halves. The box part of plots goes from B to C, and then the "whiskers" are drawn to the endpoints.

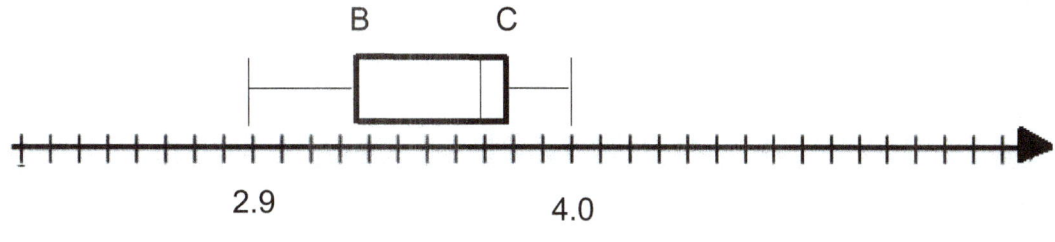

1. Construct a box plot for the following data.

A: 5.2, 5.6, 5.7, 4.9, 5.8, 6.1, 6.0, 5.3

B: 10.2, 10.4, 10.8, 9.8, 9.9, 11, 10.9, 10.5

C: 12.5, 12.7, 13.4, 13, 13.1, 13.5, 12.6, 13.3

2. According to information, construct a box-whisker plot.

A: Median = 6.5   Median of first half = 6.3   Median of second half = 6.9

Maximum = 7.3   Minimum = 5.9

B: Median = 11.2   Median of first half = 10.8   Median of second half = 11.5

Maximum = 11.9   Minimum = 10.4

Bar Graph

A Bar Graph (Bar Chart) is a graphical display of data using bars of different heights.

Bar graphs are commonly used in financial analysis for displaying data

Example

A survey of 125 people which asked them "How much is their monthly income?"

Income	100$	150$	200$	300$	400$
People	31	25	41	20	9

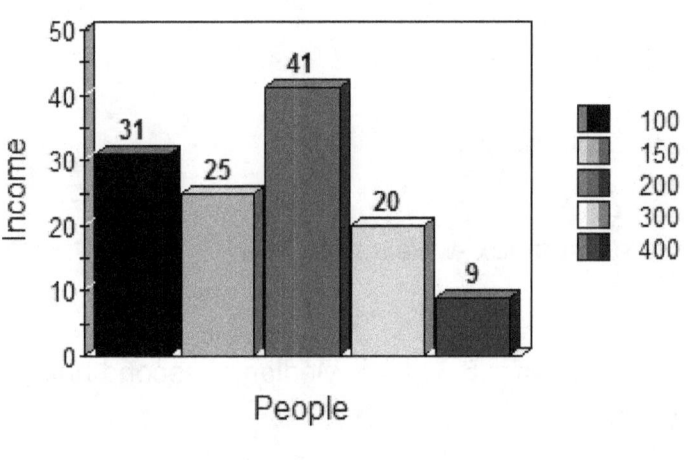

1- A survey has done on 50 students of a school and it is about their favorite sport. 18 students like football. 5 students like tennis. 12 students like basketball. 10 students like baseball and 5 students like chess. Draw a schematic bar graph.

2- The following set is students' grades. Draw a schematic bar graph for them.

Student's name	Sam	Tim	Joe	Adam	Mike
Student's grade	100	64	78	52	46

3- The following bar graph is about people's weight versus age. According to it, answer questions.

A: How old are the people who are 60 kg?

....

B: How old are the people who are 75 kg?

....

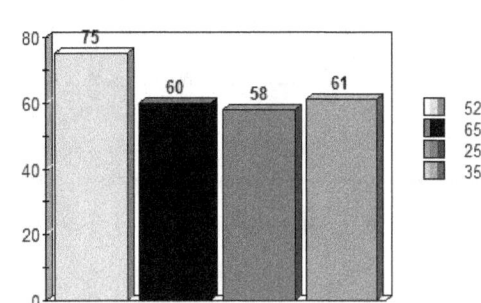

4- The following table shows result of a survey that is done on people's favorite movie. Draw a schematic bar graph for it.

Comedy	Romantic	Horror	Documentary	Action
15%	56%	23%	12%	42%

Stem and Leaf Plot

Stem-and-leaf plots are a method for showing the frequency which certain classes of values occur with. You could make a frequency distribution table or a histogram for the values, or you can use a stem-and-leaf plot and let the numbers themselves to show pretty much the same information.

Example: "21 is split into "2" (stem) and "1" (leaf).

13, 21, 34, 15, 26, 32, 18

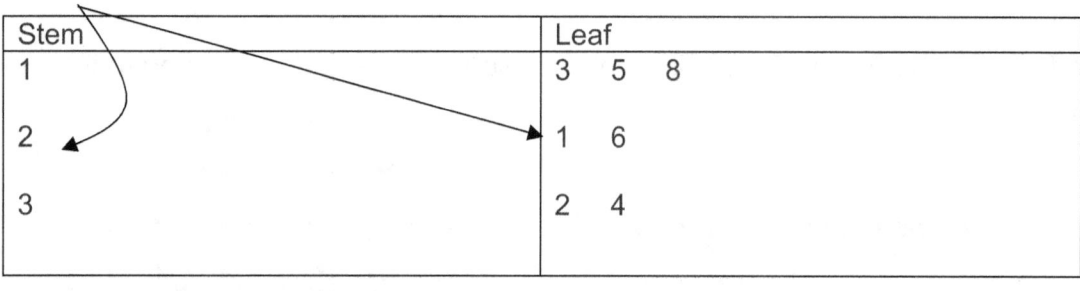

1-Draw a stem-and-leaf plot for the following list of people's weights.

85, 49, 60, 55, 72, 68, 62, 76

2-Calculate the mean and range of the following stem and leaf plot.

Stem	Leaf
1	2 6 8
2	1 4
3	2 3 7 8
4	5 9
5	0
6	3 6

3- Complete sentences.

A: "32" is split into ………………… and ………………………… .

B: What is the leaf of 57?   ……………………… .

C: "……" is split into 9 and 2.

D: "78" is split into 7 and………………………… .

E: Is 6 leaf of 32?   ………………………… .

4- Write T (True) and F (False).

A: "64" is split into 5 and 4.   ………………………

B: 2 is the stem of 29.   ………………………

C: "98" split into 9 and 8.   ………………………

D: 3 is the leaf of 53.   ………………………

The Pie Graph or Circle Graph

A Pie Chart is a type of graph that displays data in a circular graph.

Each slice of the pie is relative to the size of that category in the group.

The entire "pie" represents 100 percent of a whole, while the pie "slices" represent portions of the whole.

Example: You ask your friend which country they want to travel.

Spain	France	Brazil	Peru	India
12	5	8	4	10

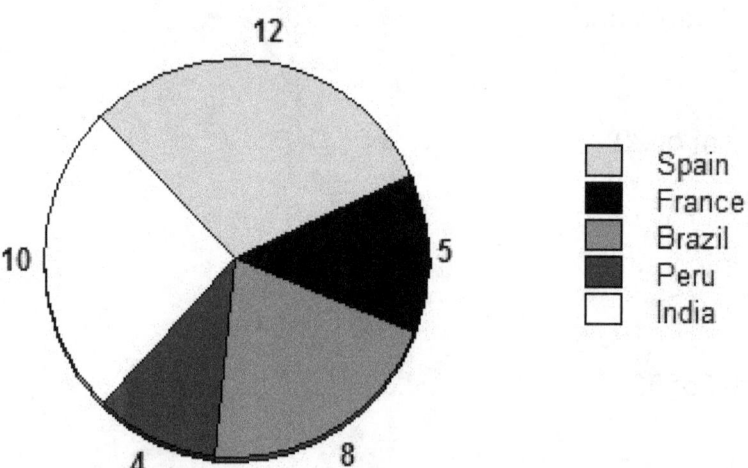

1- According to pie graph in 1963 what percent of death occurred?

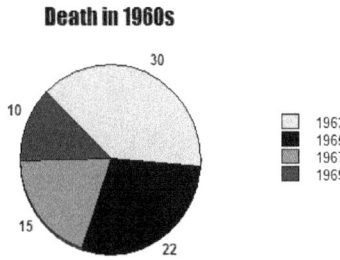

2- According to pie graph, answer questions.

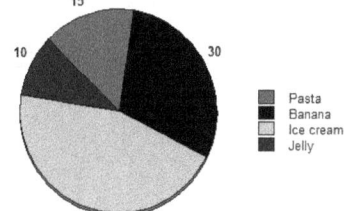

A: What percent of kids like pasta?   ....

B: What percent of kids do not like ice cream?
....

C: What percent of kids like jelly?   ....

D: What percent of kids do not like banana?   ....

3- The following table is the result of a survey that shows increasing of air pollution in recent years. Draw a pie graph schematically.

Years	1951	1954	1957	1959
Pollution	10%	20%	30%	40%

MathePathics

Scatter Plots

The scatter diagram graphs contain numerical data. If points are scattered in the diagram it shows the result is not closed to real one. But if most points lay on the right line it shows that the result is close to real answer.

Example: In the following diagram, each dot shows the price of Benz in 1990s.

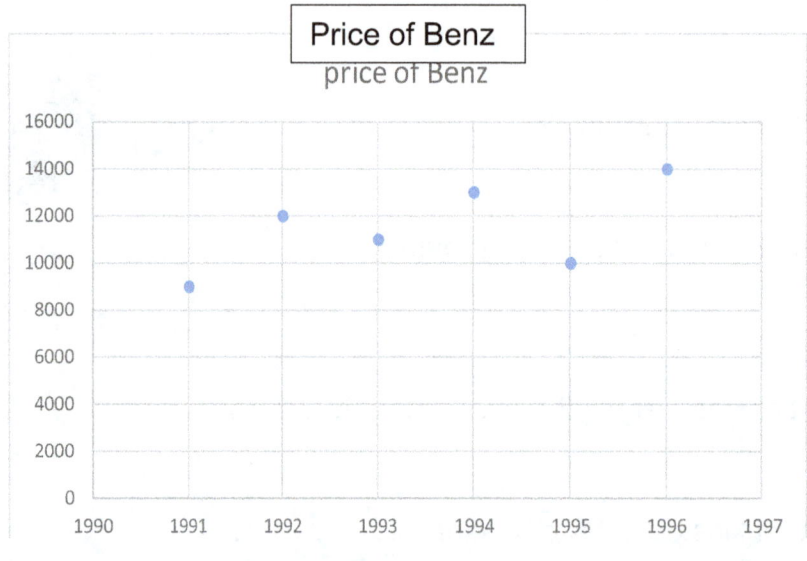

1- Draw a scatter plot for the following chart. It is person's weight versus height.

Weight(kg)	Height(cm)
55	163
68	168
72	160
65	158
52	169
75	157

2- The following scatter diagram shows two sets of data that show high positive correlation.

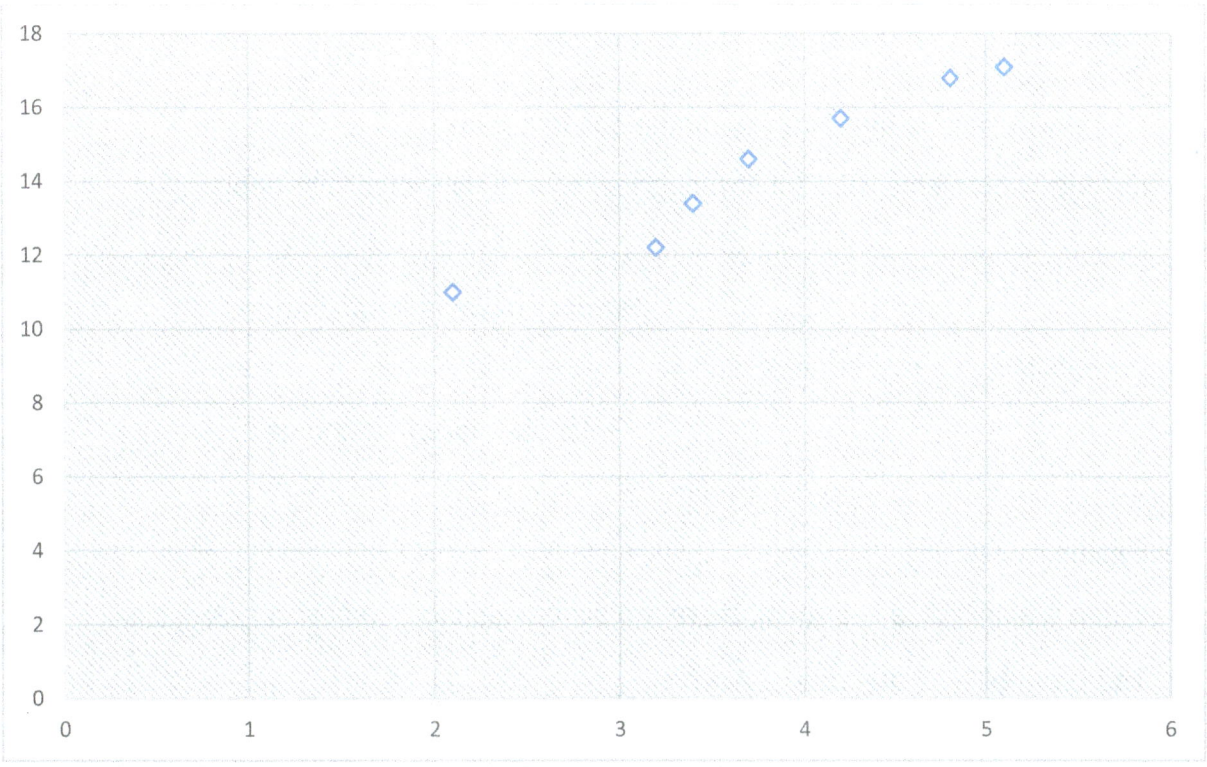

Draw a line of best fit, and then use interpolation to predict the value of y when x = 4

Probability Problems

Probability means how likely something is to happen.

For many problems we should recognize how likely they are to happen.

$$\text{Probability of an event happening} = \frac{\text{Number of ways it can happen}}{\text{Total number of outcomes}}$$

Example

When a single dice is thrown, there are six possible outcomes: 1, 2, 3, 4, 5, 6

The probability of any one of them is

1- Tim tosses a coin 50 times. How many Tails might come up?

2- Tim has 35 colorful balls in a box. 6 blue balls, 8 green balls, 11 red balls, 5 pink balls and 5 yellow balls. What is the probability that he picks green balls?

3- A dice is thrown twice. What is the probability that the number is a factor of 4?

4- There are 5 kinds of fruits in the basket. 2 bananas, 6 apples, 5 pineapples, 8 lemons and 3 cucumbers. What is the probability that Rosy picks pineapples?

5- Jack wrote 6 times SMART, 5 times SHY, 11times BRAVE on piece of papers and put them in a hat. What is the probability that he picks BRAVE?

6- A standard dice is rolled. What is the probability that 3, 5 or 6 rolls?

Answers of Worksheets – Chapter 14

Mode, Mean, Median, and range of the given data

1.

Max = 85   Min = 46

2.

Set of numbers	Mean	Median	Mode	Range
A	6	4.5	3	7
B	6	7	11	10

3.

Set of number	Maximum	Minimum	Mean	Median
5,5,6,9,3,9,3,5	9	3	5.6	5
71,89,25,25,34,11,25	11	89	40	25
11,14,18,11,12,11.12	11	18	12.7	11

4.

88.2

Box and Whisker Plot

1.

A

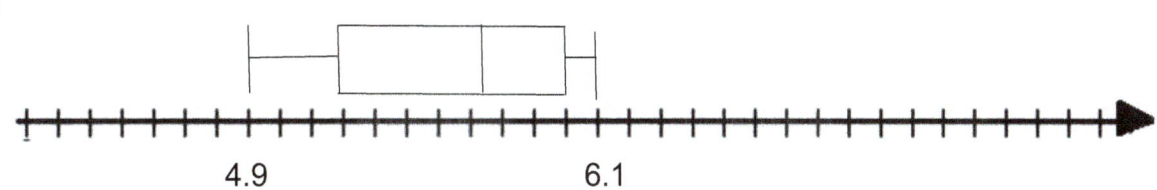

4.9   6.1

B

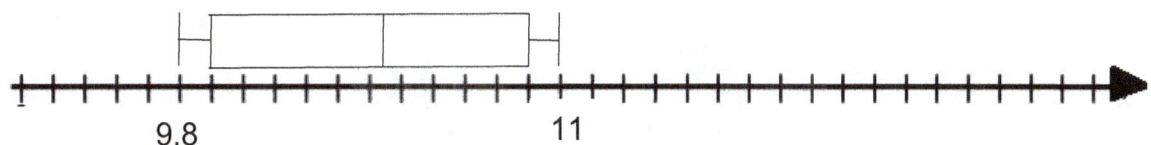

9.8   11

C

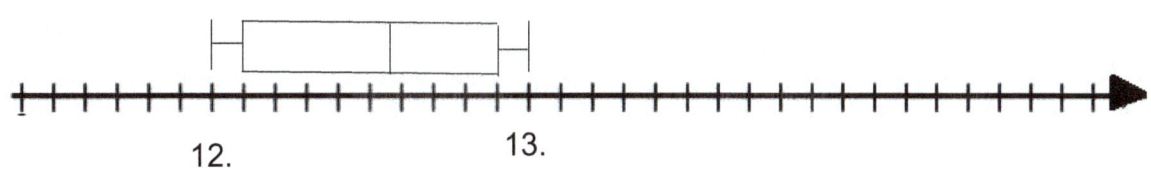

12.   13.

2.

A

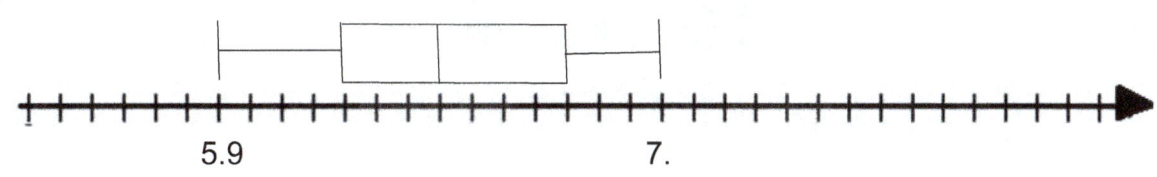

5.9   7.

B

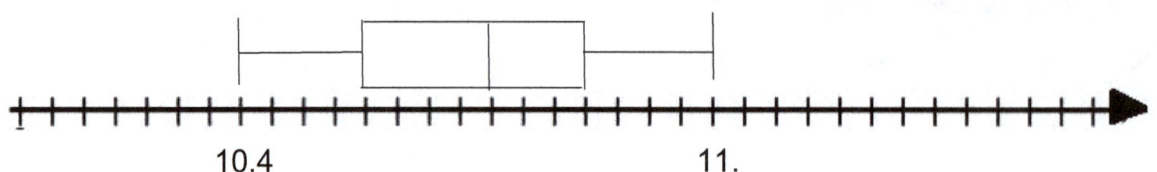

10.4   11.

Bar Graph

1.

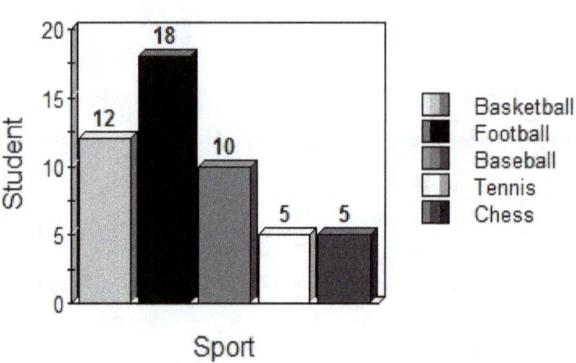

2.

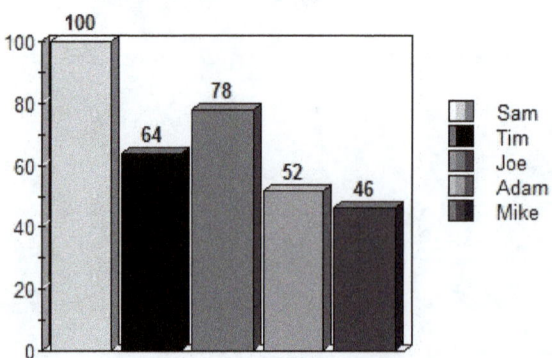

3.

A.65   B.35

4.

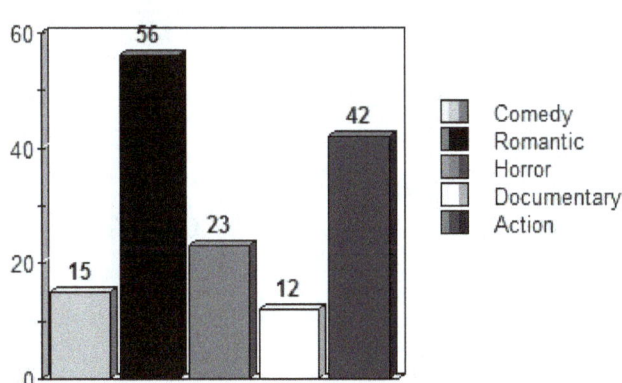

Stem and leaf plot

1.

Stem	Leaf
4	9
5	5
6	0 2 8
7	2 6
8	5

2.

Mean: 36

Range: 54

3.

A. 3 – 2   B. 7   C. 92   D. 8   E. NO

MathePathics

4.

A. F   B. F   C. T   D. T

The Pie Graph or Circle Graph

1.

30%

2.

A. 15%   B. 55%   C. 10%   D. 70%

3.

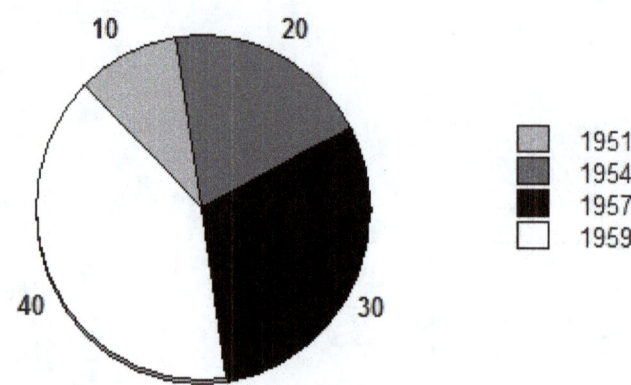

MathePathics

Scatter plots

1.

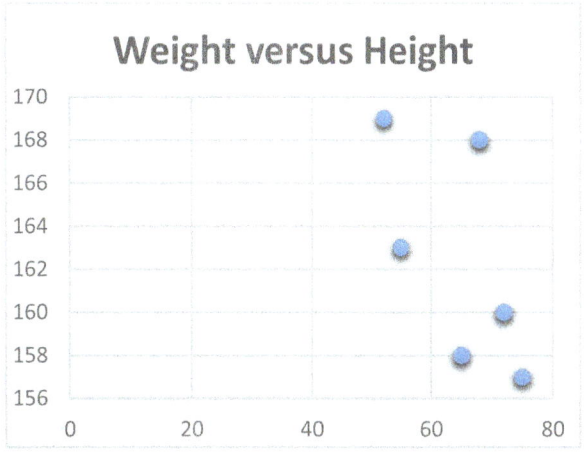

2. 14.9

Probability Problems

1.　$\dfrac{1}{100}$

2.　$\dfrac{8}{35}$

3.　$\dfrac{12}{3} = 4$

4.　$\dfrac{5}{24}$

5.　$\dfrac{11}{22} = \dfrac{1}{2}$

6.　$\dfrac{1}{2}$

232

Extra Note for Chapter 14:

Chapter 15:
Geometry

The Pythagorean Theorem

Area of Triangles

Perimeter of Polygons

Area and Circumferences of Circles

Area of Squares, Rectangles, and Parallelograms

Area of Trapezoids

Answers of Worksheets – Chapter 15

MathePathics

The Pythagorean Theorem

The Pythagorean Theorem is a statement about triangles which has a right angle. The Pythagorean Theorem states that:

"The area of the square built upon the hypotenuse of a right triangle is equal to the sum of the areas of the squares upon the remaining sides."

$$a^2 + b^2 = c^2$$

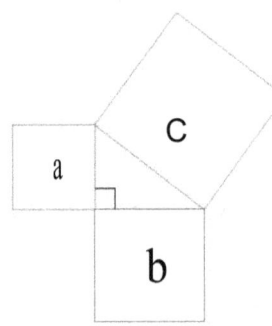

Example: Solve this triangle.

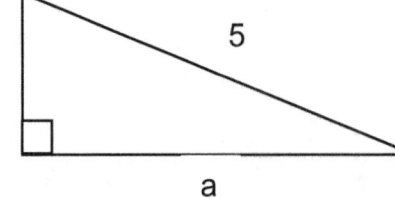

$$5^2 = a^2 + 3^2$$
$$25 = a^2 + 9$$
$$a^2 = 25 - 9$$
$$a^2 = 16$$
$$a = 4$$

1- Solve to find the missing value of the triangle.

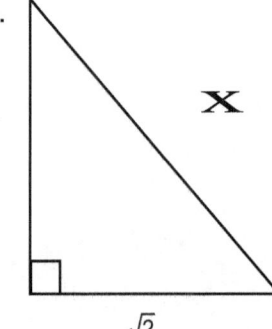

235

2. Billy wants to climb up the wall. He puts a 13 m ladder on the ground. The distance from the foot of the ladder to the bottom of the wall is 5 m.
Find height of the wall.

3- Mike rides his bicycle 1170 km south and then 18 km west. How far is he from his starting point?

4-Find the value of x.

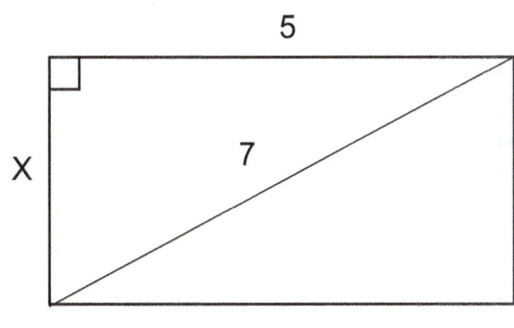

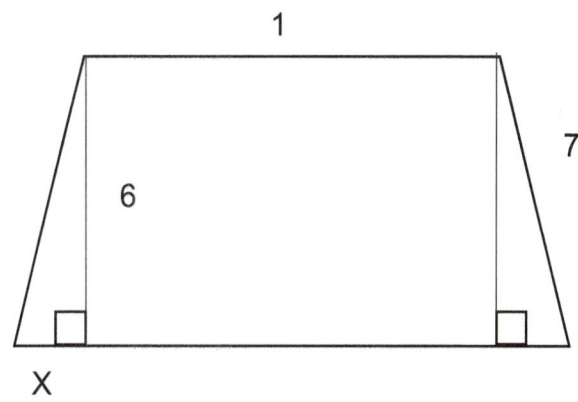

236

Area of Triangles

Area: $\frac{1}{2}bh$

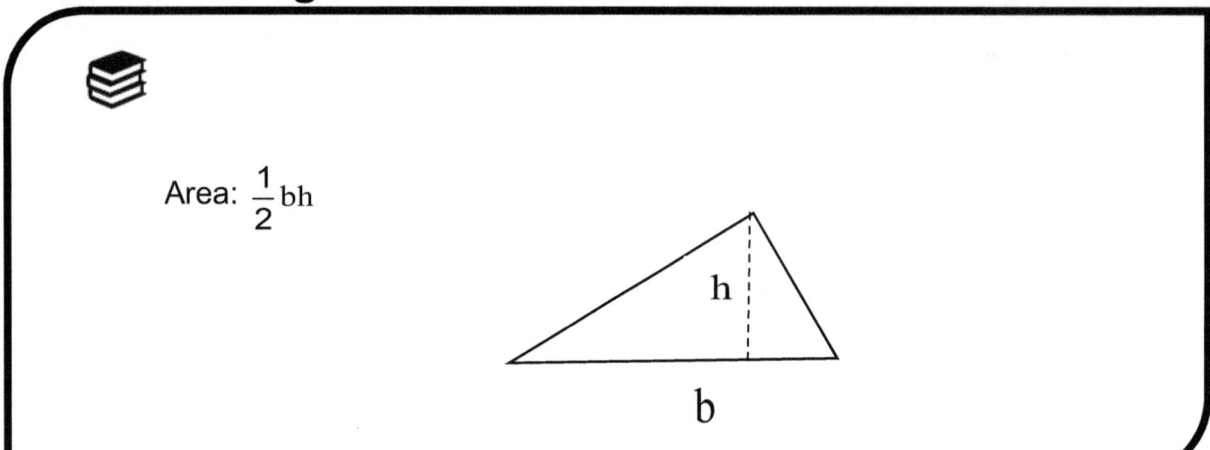

1- Find the area of below triangles.

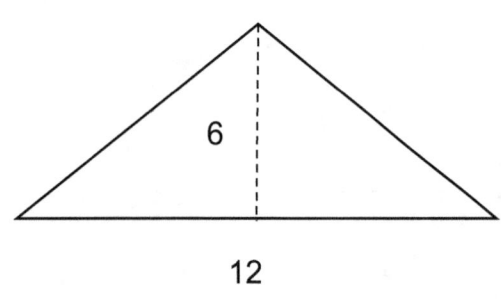

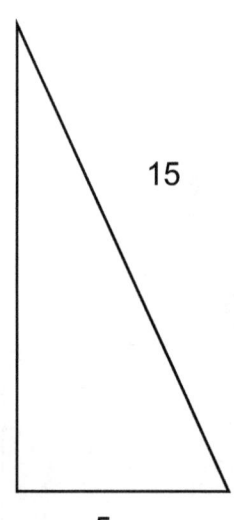

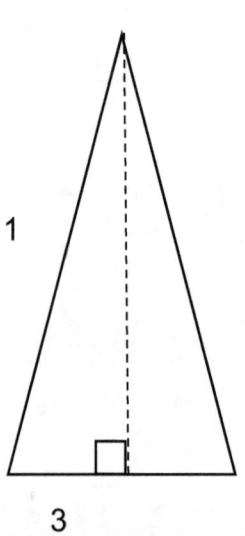

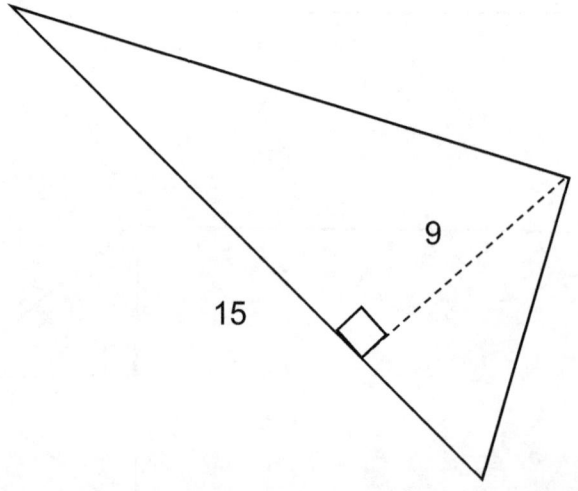

Perimeter of Polygon

Polygon: A polygon is defined as a plane figure that is enclosed by closed path or a closed circle.

Perimeter: Perimeter is surrounds of a shape. The perimeter of a polygon is the sum of the lengths.

1- Find the perimeter of the following figure.

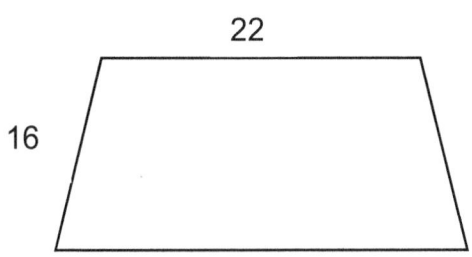

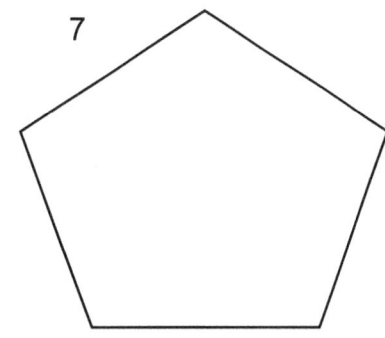

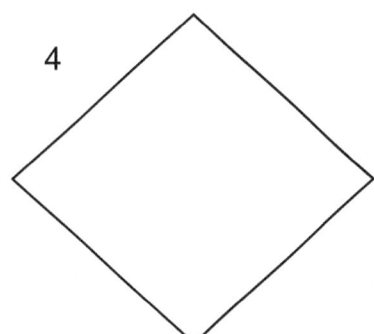

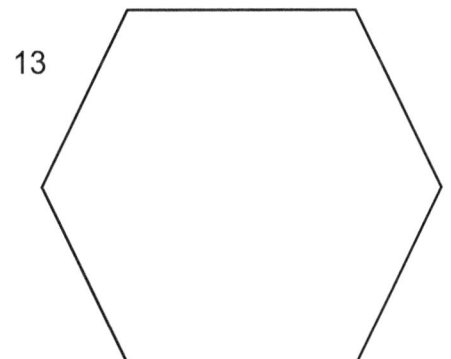

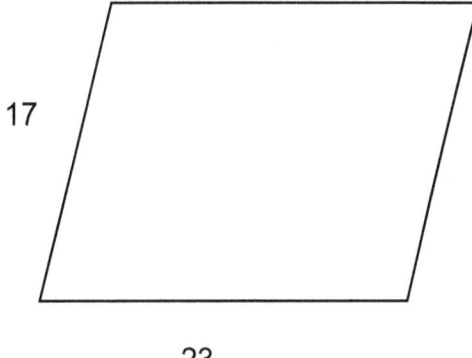

Area and Circumference of Circles

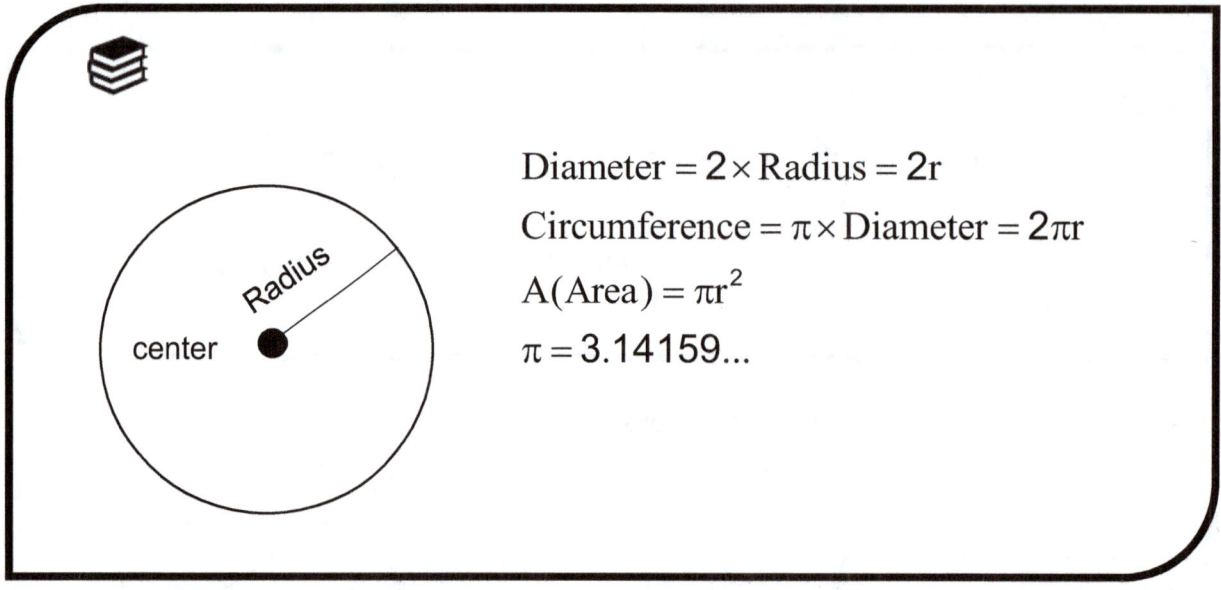

1- Tina makes a burger. The diameter of burger is 6 cm. What is the area of burger?

2- The circumference of a circle is 33 cm. What is its radius?

3- Alison wants to draw a round table which has a radius of 11 cm. What is its area?

4- Calculate the area and circumference of the circle.

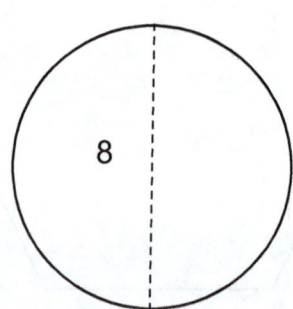

Area of Square, Rectangle, and Parallelograms

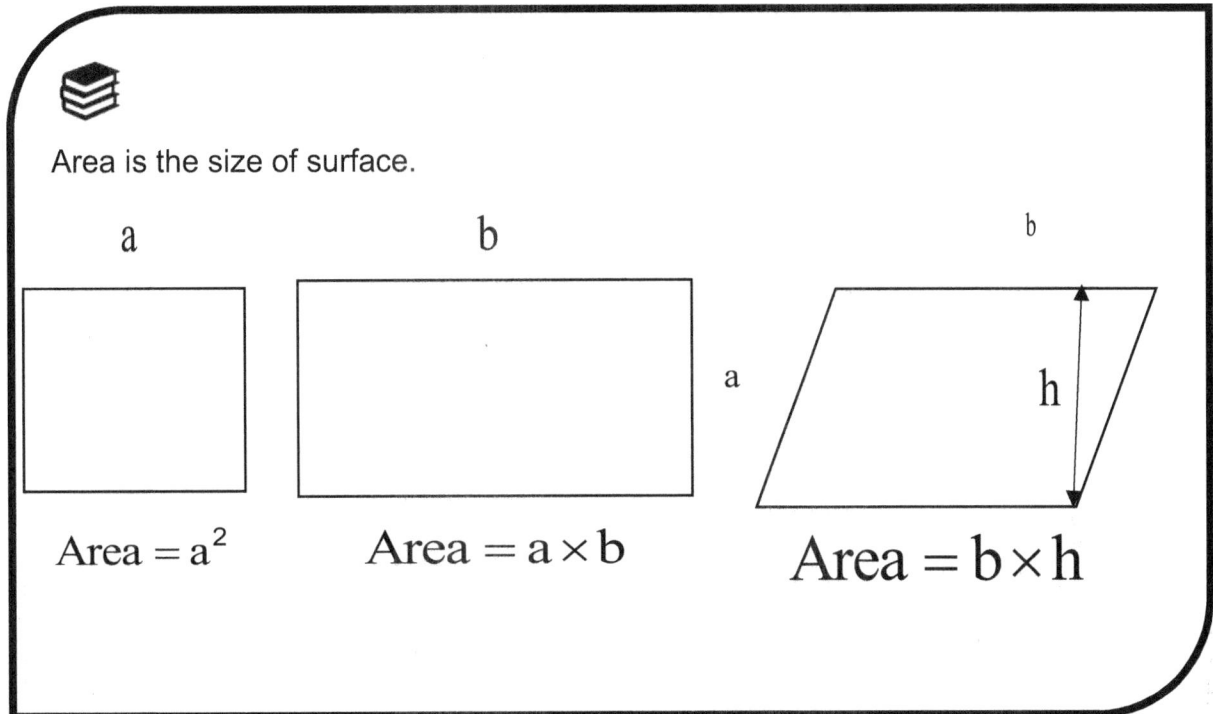

Area is the size of surface.

Area = a^2

Area = $a \times b$

Area = $b \times h$

1- Find the area of below shapes.

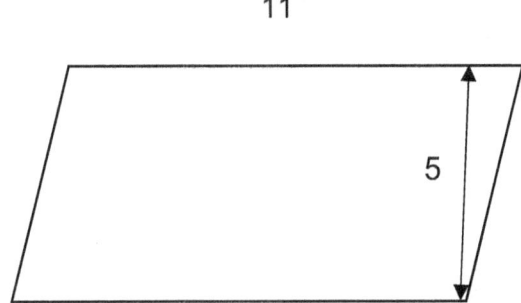

2- Sam has some colorful pencils. He wants to make a square with them.
Each pencil has 3.5 cm length. What is the area of square?

3- The area of a parallelogram is 24 square centimeters and the base is 4 centimeters. Find the height.

4- Sara draws a rectangle picture which it has 4.8 cm length and 2.6 cm width. What is the area of picture?

5- Find the area of a parallelogram with a base of 14 centimeters and a height of 8 centimeters.

Area of Trapezoids

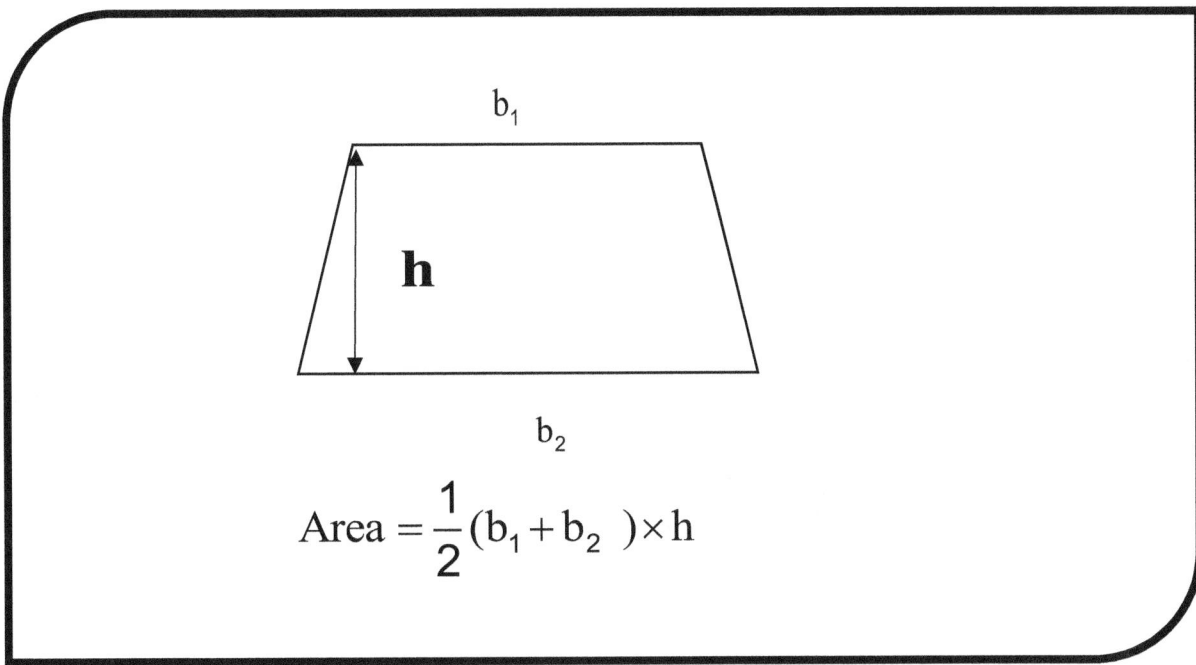

$$\text{Area} = \frac{1}{2}(b_1 + b_2) \times h$$

1- Find the area of a trapezoid with bases of 11 inches and 16 inches, and a height of 5 inches.

2- The area of a trapezoid is 52 square inches and the bases are 11 inches and 15 inches. Find the height.

Answers of Worksheets – Chapter 15

The Pythagorean Theorem

1. X=9 , x=3
2. 12
3. 1494

4. X=4.8   x=3.6   x=15

Area of Triangles

1.
36   35   3.41   4.67

Perimeter of Polygon

1.
76   35   3.11   4.16
5.78   6.80

Area and Circumference of Circles

1. 18.84
2. 2.52
3. 3.379
4. 25.12, 50.24

Area of Square, Rectangle, and Parallelograms

1.

54 55 49

2. 12.25
3. 6
4. 12.48
5. 112

Area of Trapezoids

1. 67.5
2. 4

Extra Note for Chapter 15:

Chapter 16: Solid Figures

Volume of Cubes

Volume of Rectangle Prisms

Surface Area of Cubes

Surface of a Rectangle prisms

Volume of Cylinder

Surface Area of Cylinder

Answers of Worksheets – Chapter 16

MathePathics

MathePathics

Volume of Cubes

A cube is a geometrical shape that all of its lengths have the same size.

To calculate volume of a cube:

V (volume) = $a \times a \times a = a^3$

Unit of volume is cm^3 or m^3.

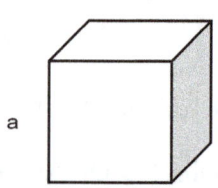

1. Count the cubes and write the volume of each shape. Use the measure cube unit.

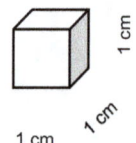

1.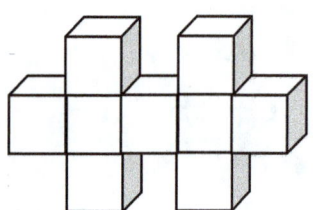

    Volume =

2.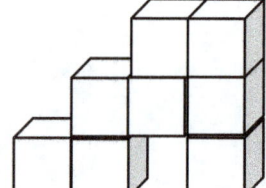

    Volume =

3.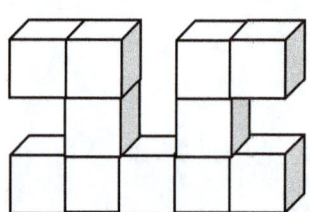

    Volume =

4.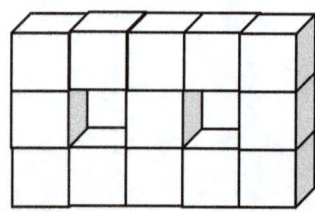

    Volume =

247

5.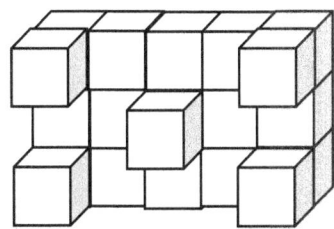

Volume =

6.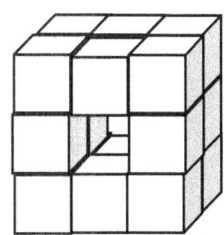

Volume =

7.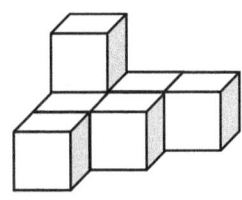

Volume =

8.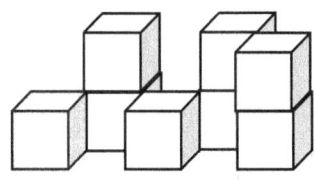

Volume =

Volume of Rectangle Prisms

A rectangle prime has three sides with different sizes.

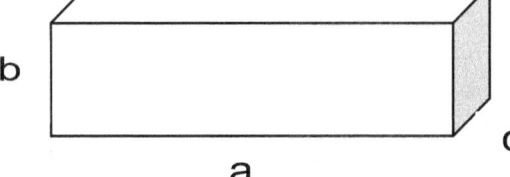

a = length
b = height
c = width

$V = a \times b \times c \, (cm^3 \text{ or } m^3)$

2. Count the cubes and find the volume of each rectangular prism.

1. 0.5 cm
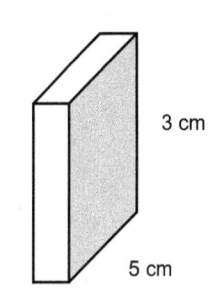
Volume = _____

2. 10 cm
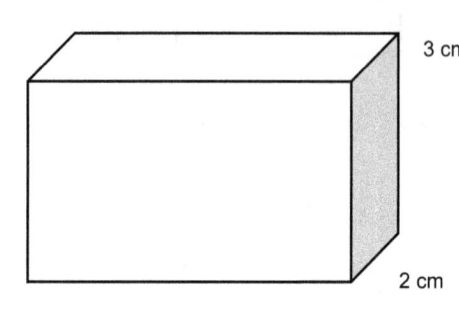
Volume = _____

3.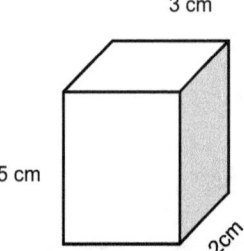
Volume = _____

4.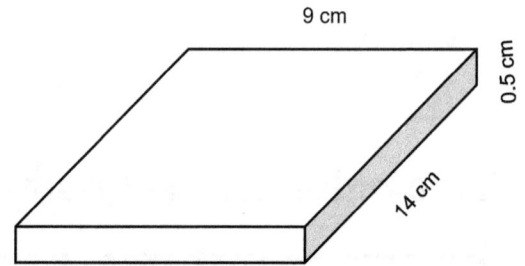
Volume = _____

5.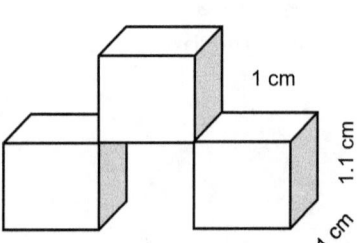
Volume = _____

6.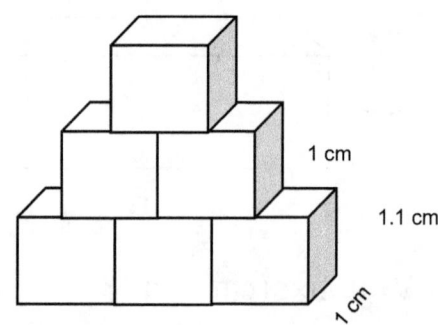
Volume = _____

7.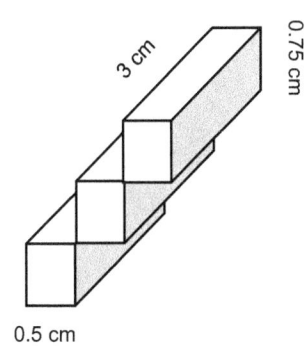

Volume = _____

8.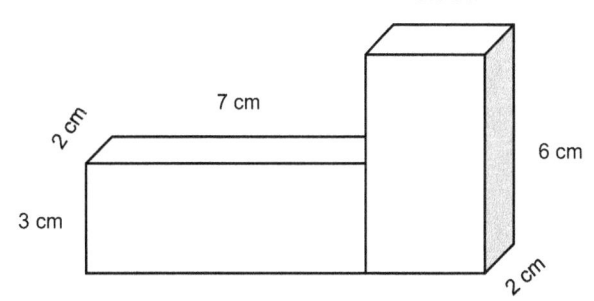

Volume = _____

9.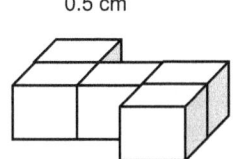

Volume = _____

10.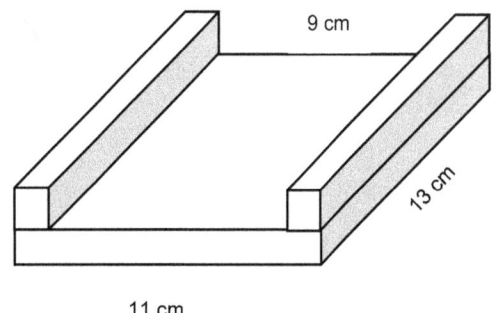

Volume = _____

11.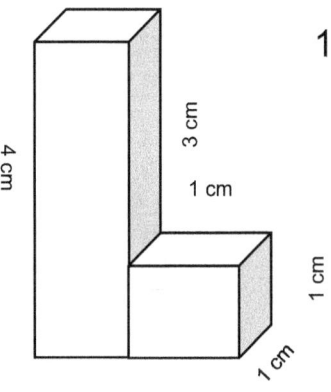

Volume = _____

12.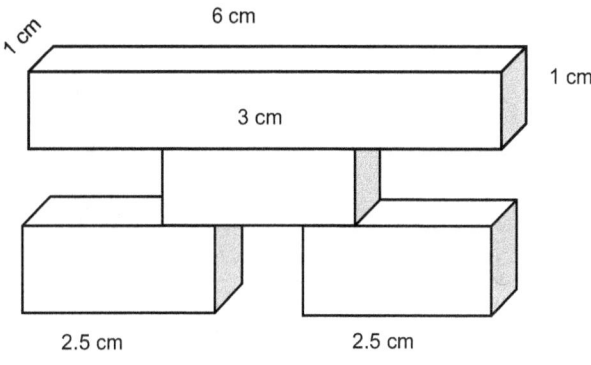

Volume = _____

250

3. Find the volume of each rectangular prism from the given parameters.

1. Width = 12 In
    Length = 21 In
    Height = 30 In

4. Length = 20 π
    Width = 9 π
    Height = 27 π

2. Length = 4 m
    Height = 20 m
    Width = 10 m

5. Length = 45 cm
    Height = 50 cm
    Width = 6.5 cm

3. Length = 14π
    Width = 12 π
    Height = 100 π

6. Length = 1 m
    Width = 3.5 m
    Height = 5 m

4. Find "x".

1.
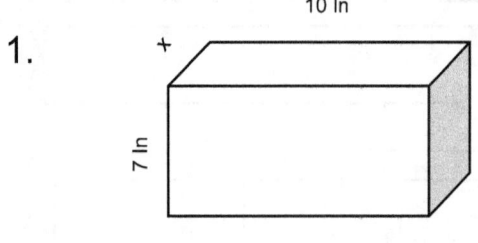

Volume = 840 In^3

X = _____

3.
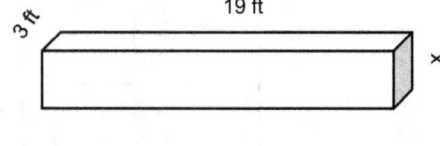

Volume = 156 ft^3

X = _____

MathePathics

Surface Area of Cubes

A cube has 6 surfaces. The area of each surface is a^2.

So, surface area of a cube is $6a^2$.

The total surface area = $6a^2$

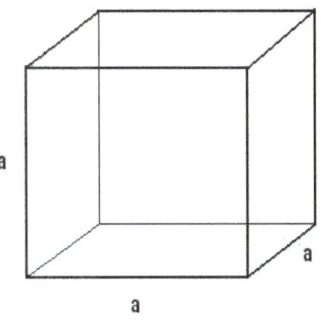

5. Find the surface area of each cube.

1.
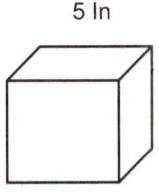
5 In

Surface area =

2.
8 cm
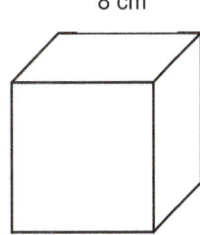

Surface area =

Surface of a Rectangle prisms

A rectangle prime has 6 surfaces that opposite surfaces are equal.

To calculate surface of a rectangle prism,

- Firstly, you must find each three areas of surface.
- Then multiply each surface's area by 2.
- Finally add all of them.

Area of surface 1 = ab
Area of surface 2 = ac
Area of surface 3 = bc
Total surface area = 2ab + 2ac + 2bc

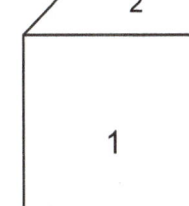

252

6. A gift box in the shape of a rectangular prism has 40 Inch length, 15 Inch width and 10 height. How much paper they will need to wrap the box?

7. Find the surface area of each rectangular prism.

1.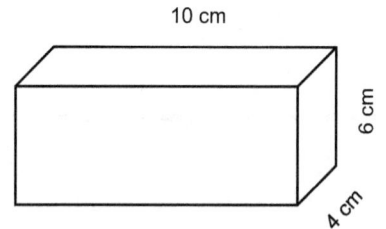

Surface area =

2.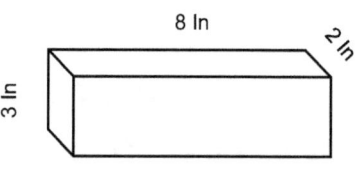

Surface area =

3.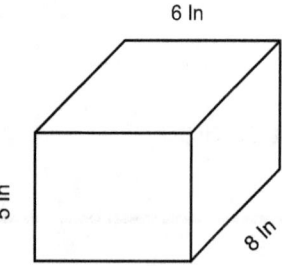

Surface area =

4.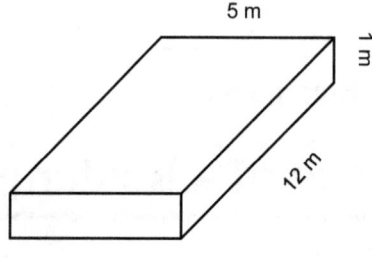

Surface area =

5.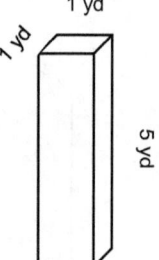

Surface area =

6.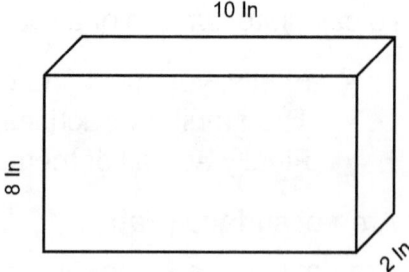

Surface area =

Volume of Cylinder

A cylinder is a closed solid that has two parallel bases connected by a curved surface.

$$V = \pi r^2 h$$

r = radius
h = distance between center to center two surfaces
$\pi = 3.14$

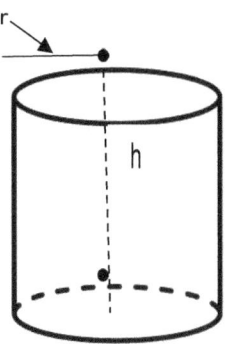

8. Calculate the volume of each cylinder.

1. r = 28 ft
   h = 27.4 ft
   Volume = _____

2. r = 10 m
   h = 18 m
   Volume = _____

3. d = 26 m
    h = 15 m
    Volume =_____

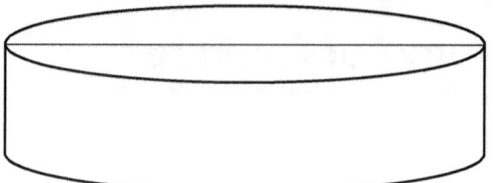

4. r = 30 ft
    h = 10 ft
    Volume =_____

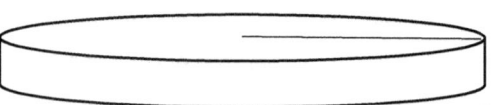

9. The cross-section of a pipe has a width of 10 centimeter and height of 15 centimeter. Calculate the volume of the pipe.

10. Find the volume of space between the two pipes below.

   (Inner pipe radius = 3, Outer pipe radius = 5, Height = 15)

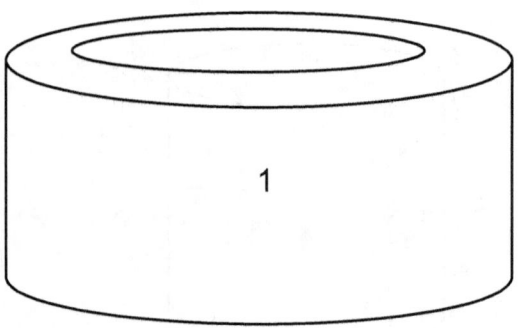

MathePathics

Surface Area of Cylinder

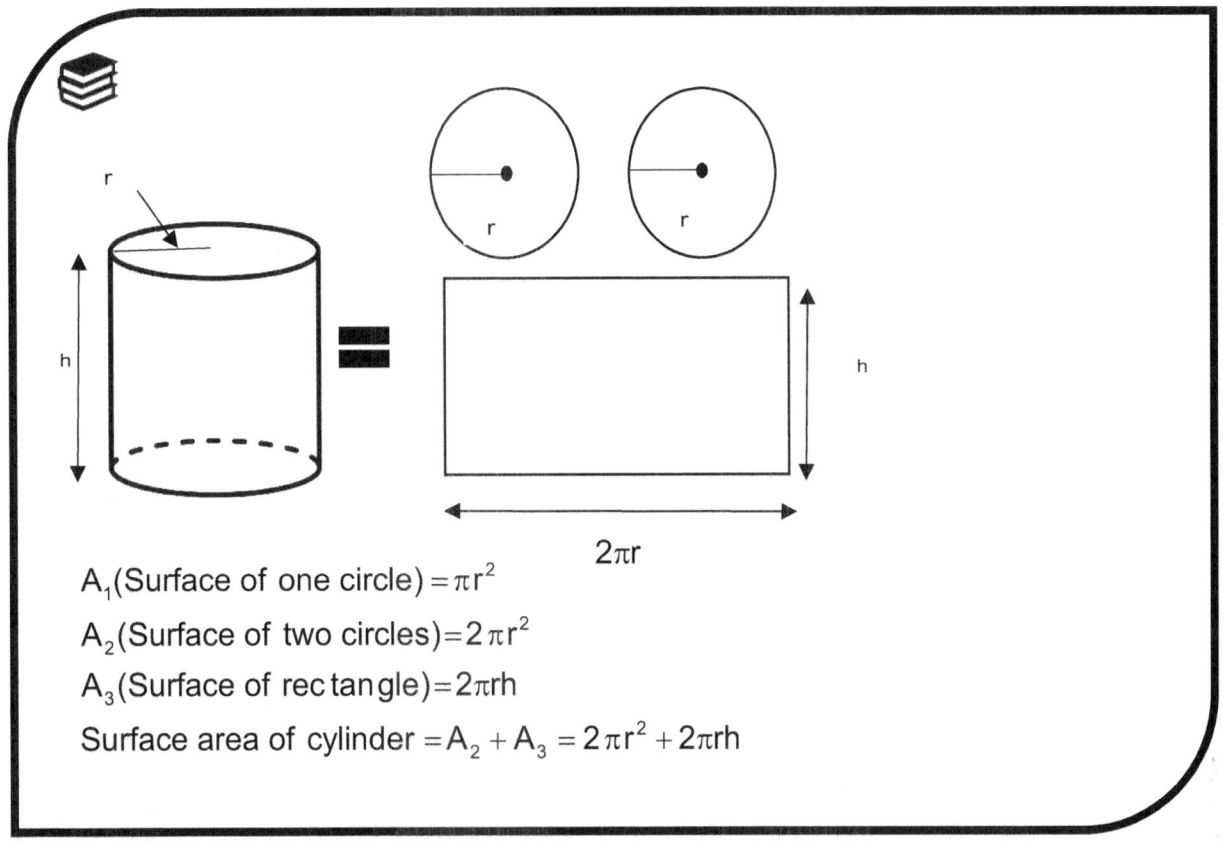

A_1(Surface of one circle) $= \pi r^2$
A_2(Surface of two circles) $= 2\pi r^2$
A_3(Surface of rectangle) $= 2\pi rh$
Surface area of cylinder $= A_2 + A_3 = 2\pi r^2 + 2\pi rh$

11- Calculate surface area of each cylinder.

1) h=12cm, r=4cm

2) h=6cm, r=5cm

3) h=3cm, r=7cm

256

12- Surface area of a cylinder is 552.64 cm² and cylinder's radius is 8 cm. How much height does it have?

13 – Adam's father is repairing a rotten pipe of kitchen. He wants to replace a new one. If new pipe has 6.5-meter height and 1.5 cm width, calculate the surface area of pipe.

14- Find unknown parameters.

1)

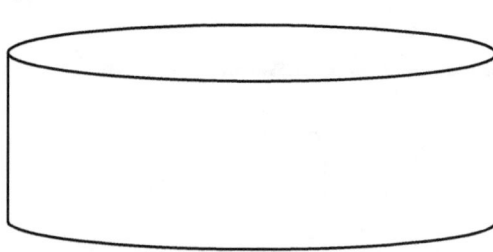

A = 568.6 cm²

r = 5 cm

h =?

2)

h = 11.5 cm

r = 4.5 cm

A =?

MathePathics

Answers of Worksheets -Chapter 16

Volume of Cubes

1.

1) $9a^3 = 9(1)^3 = 9$ 2) $8a^3 = 8(1)^3 = 8$ 3) $11a^3 = 11(1)^3 = 11$

4) $12a^3 = 12(1)^3 = 12$ 5) $13a^3 = 13(1)^3 = 13$ 6) $10a^3 = 10(1)^3 = 10$

7) $7a^3 = 7(1)^3 = 7$ 8) $6a^3 = 6(1)^3 = 6$ 9) $7a^3 = 7(1)^3 = 7$

10) $8a^3 = 8(1)^3 = 8$

Volume of Rectangle Prisms

2.

1) $1.5 \times 3 \times 0.5 = 7.5 \text{ cm}^3$ 2) $10 \times 3 \times 2 = 60 \text{ cm}^3$

3) $2 \times 5 \times 3 = 30 \text{ cm}^3$ 4) $14 \times 9 \times 0.5 = 63 \text{ cm}^3$

5) $3(1 \times 1 \times 1.1) = 3.3 \text{ cm}^3$ 6) $6(1 \times 1 \times 1.1) = 6.6 \text{ cm}^3$

7) $3(0.5 \times 7.5 \times 3) = 33.75 \text{ cm}^3$ 8) $(7 \times 12 \times 3) + (2 \times 6 \times 2.5) = 72 \text{ cm}^3$

9) $5(0.5)^2 = 1.25 \text{ cm}^3$ 10) $(11 \times 13 \times 1) + 2(13 \times 1 \times 1) = 169 \text{ cm}^3$

11) $(4 \times 3 \times 1) + (1 \times 1 \times 1) = 13 \text{ cm}^3$ 12) $(6 \times 1 \times 1) + 2(2.5 \times 1 \times 1) = 11 \text{ cm}^3$

3.

1) $12 \times 21 \times 30 = 7560$ 2) $4 \times 20 \times 10 = 800$

MathePathics

3) $14 \times 12 \times 100 = 16800$

4) $27 \times 9 \times 27 = 4860$

5) $45 \times 50 \times 6.5 = 14625$

6) $1 \times 3.5 \times 5 = 17.5$

4.

1) $7 \times 10 \times (x) = 840 \rightarrow x = \dfrac{840}{70} = 12$ in

2) $3 \times 19 \times (x) = 156 \rightarrow x = \dfrac{156}{19} = 57$ ft

Surface Area of Cubes

5.

1) $V = 6(5)^2 = 150$

2) $V = 6(8)^2 = 512 \text{cm}^3$

Surface of a Rectangle prisms

6.

$V = 2(40 \times 15) + 2(40 \times 10) + 2(15 \times 10) = 1200 + 800 + 300 = 2300$

7.

1) $2(10 \times 4) + 2(10 \times 6) + 2(4 \times 6) = 80 + 120 + 48 = 248$

2) $2(8 \times 2) + 2(8 \times 3) + 2(2 \times 3) = 32 + 48 + 12 = 92$

3) $2(6 \times 8) + 2(5 \times 6) + 2(8 \times 5) = 96 + 60 + 80 = 236$

4) $2(5 \times 1) + 2(5 \times 12) + 2(12 \times 1) = 10 + 120 + 24 = 154$

5) $2(1 \times 1) + 2(1 \times 5) + 2(5 \times 1) = 2 + 10 + 10 = 22$

6) $2(8 \times 10) + 2(8 \times 2) + 2(2 \times 10) = 160 + 32 + 40 = 232$

MathePathics

Volume of Cylinder

8.

1) $V = \pi r^2 h = \pi (28)^2 (27.4) = 67452.2$

2) $V = \pi r^2 h = \pi (10)^2 (18) = 5652$

3) $d = 2r \rightarrow r = \dfrac{d}{2} = \dfrac{26}{2} = 13 \rightarrow V = \pi r^2 h = \pi (13)^2 (15) = 7959.9$

4) $V = \pi r^2 h = \pi (30)^2 (10) = 28280$

9.

$d = 2r \rightarrow r = \dfrac{d}{2} = \dfrac{10}{2} = 5 \rightarrow V = \pi r^2 h = \pi (5)^2 (15) = 1177.5$

10.

V_1(Volume of inner pipe) $= \pi (3)^2 (15) = 423.9$

V_2(Volume of outer pipe) $= \pi (5)^2 (15) = 1177.5$

V_3(Volume of space between two pipes) $= V_2 - V_1 = 1177.5 - 423.9 = 753.6$

Surface Area of Cylinder

11.

1) $A = 2\pi rh + 2\pi r^2 = 2\pi (4)(12) + 2\pi (4)^2 = 401.92 \text{ cm}^2$

2) $A = 2\pi rh + 2\pi r^2 = 2\pi (5)(6) + 2\pi (5)^2 = 345.4 \text{ cm}^2$

3) $A = 2\pi rh + 2\pi r^2 = 2\pi (7)(3) + 2\pi (7)^2 = 439.6 \text{ cm}^2$

12.

$A = 2\pi r^2 + 2\pi rh \longrightarrow 552.64 = 2(3.14)(8)h + 2(3.14)(8)^2 \Rightarrow h = 3\,cm$

13.

$A = 2\pi r^2 + 2\pi rh \longrightarrow A = 2(3.14)(0.75)^2 + 2(3.14)(0.75)(650) = 3065.03\,cm^2$

$d = 2r \rightarrow r = \dfrac{d}{2} = \dfrac{1.5}{2} = 0.75\,cm$, $h = 6.5\,cm \xrightarrow{\times 100} 650\,cm$

14.

1) $A = 2\pi r^2 + 2\pi rh \longrightarrow 568.6 = 2(3.14)(5)^2 + 2(3.14)(5)h \longrightarrow h = 13.10\,cm$

2) $A = 2\pi r^2 + 2\pi rh \longrightarrow A = 2(3.14)(4.5)^2 + 2(3.14)(4.5)(11.5) = 452.16\,cm^2$

Extra Note for Chapter 16:

Chapter 17:
Logarithms

Rewriting Logarithms

Evaluating Logarithms

Properties of Logarithms

Natural Logarithms

Solving Exponential Equations Requiring Logarithms

Solving Logarithmic Equations

Answers of Worksheets – Chapter 17

Rewriting Logarithms

Logarithms are the "opposite" of exponentials, just as subtraction is the opposite of addition and division is the opposite of multiplication.

$$y = b^x \qquad \log_b y = x$$

$$25 = 5^2 \qquad \log_5 25 = 2$$

Notice we are dealing with three numbers:

- The **base**: the number we are multiplying. ("5" in the example above)
- How many times to use it in a multiplication. (3 times, which is the logarithm)
- The number we want to get. ("25")

 If a logarithm is written without a base, it means that the base is 10.

1- Write the following logarithms in exponentials forms.

A. $\log_2 8 = 3$

B. $\log_9 81 = 2$

C. $\log_4 64 = 3$

D. $\log_3 6561 = 8$

E. $\log_5 125 = 3$

F. $\log 1000 = 2$

G. $\log_6 1296 = 4$

H. $\log_{11} 161051 = 5$

I. $\log_8 64 = 2$

2- Rewrite in logarithmic form.

A. $7^2 = 49$

B. $3^4 = 81$

C. $11^2 = 121$

D. $30^2 = 900$ E. $12^3 = 1728$ F. $1.5^2 = 2.25$

G. $10^2 = 100$ H. $20^3 = 800$ I. $9^3 = 729$

J. $40^3 = 64000$ K. $2.5^4 = 39.0625$ L. $6^5 = 7776$

3- Find x.

A. $\log_4(x) = 2$ B. $\log_6 36 = x$ C. $\log_x(343) = 3$

D. $\log_{13}(x) = 3$ E. $\log_5 625 = x$ F. $\log_x 81 = 2$

G. $\log_{12}(x) = 2$ H. $\log_{14} 194 = x$ I. $\log_x 400 = 2$

J. $\log_{\sqrt{3}}(x) = 2$ K. $\log_{\frac{1}{5}} 0.04 = x$ L. $\log_x 8 = 6$

Evaluating Logarithms

How to evaluate a logarithm of the form $y = \log_b(x)$?

1. Rewrite the argument "x" as a power of "b": $b^y=x$.

2. Find a number that y power to it, equals to b.

Example:

$y = \log_7(49) \qquad 7^y = 49 \qquad y = 2$

1- Evaluate following logarithms.

A. $y = \log_2(4)$

B. $y = \log_2(8)$

C. $y = \log_{10}(100)$

D. $y = \log_5(625)$

E. $y = \log_2(256)$

F. $y = \log_4(1024)$

2- Adam and his friend want to solve $y = \log_3(729)$. Adam's answer is 5 and his friend's answer is 3. Which of them find correct answer?

3- Rosy does not know how to solve $y = \log_{\frac{1}{5}}(0.04)$. Help her to find answer.

Properties of Logarithms

$$\log_x 1 = 0 \qquad \log_x x = 1 \qquad \log_x (x)^n = n$$

$$\log_x A = \log_x B \to A = B \qquad \log_x A^n = n \log_x A$$

$$\log_x (AB) = \log_x A + \log_x B \quad (x \neq 1) \qquad \log_x \left(\frac{A}{B}\right) = \log_x A - \log_x B \quad (x \neq 1)$$

1- Use the logarithm's properties to rewrite following logarithm.

A. $\log_3 \left(\frac{b}{6}\right)$

B. $\log_3 (8a)$

C. $\log_2 a^5$

D. $\log 2x + \log 6y$

E. $\log 3a - \log 9b$

F. $6\log(7y)$

2- Use the logarithm's properties to solve following logarithms.

A. $\log 2xy = \ldots\ldots + \log y$

B. $\log \frac{7}{c} = \log 7 - \ldots\ldots$

C. $\log x^5 = \ldots\ldots \log x$

D. $\log_a \ldots\ldots = \log_a \ldots\ldots \to 3b = 3b$

E. $\log_2 \ldots\ldots = 0$

F. $\log_{2x+1} \ldots\ldots = 1$

267

Natural Logarithms

The number e frequently occurs in mathematics (especially calculus) and is an irrational constant. Its value is $e = 2.718281828...$

If we have logarithms to base e, these are called natural logarithms.

We usually write natural logarithms using ln.

- $\ln x$ means $\log_e x$ (that is log x to the base e)

1- Find the natural logarithms.

A. 2.56

B. 3.876

C. 6.2

D. 8.145

E. 7.23

F. 4.670

G. 52

H. 6

I. 100

2- Rosy wrote a solution for finding natural logarithm of 5.61. But she isn't sure it's true. Check her answer.

$\log_e 5.61 = \ln 5.61 = 1.37$

3- Brown wants to find natural logarithm of 7.816. But he doesn't know how to solve it. Help him to solve.

Solving Exponential Equations Requiring Logarithms

Sometimes we cannot manipulate the exponential equation to have the same or common base on both sides of the equation, so we solve exponential equations **requiring the use of logarithms**.

Steps to Solve Exponential Equations using Logarithms

1) Keep the exponential expression by itself on one side of the equation.

2) Get the logarithms of both sides of the equation. You can use any bases for logs.

3) Solve for the variable. Keep the answer exact or give decimal approximations.

1-Solve the exponential equations.

A. $3^{2X} = 21$

B. $5^{7X} = 112$

C. $2^X = 4$

D. $3^{X+1} = 28$

E. $(\frac{1}{2})^{2x+1} = 34$

F. $4^{3X-1} = 100$

2- Is the following solution for finding x is true?

$5^{6x+2} = 39$

$\ln(5^{6x+2}) = \ln 39$ $(6x+2)\ln 5 = \ln 39$

$6x + 2 = \dfrac{\ln 39}{\ln 5}$ $6x + 2 = 2.276$

$6x = 2.276 - 2$ $6x = 0.276$

$x = \dfrac{0.276}{6}$ $x = 0.46$

Solving Logarithmic Equations

- To solve a logarithmic equation, rewrite the equation in exponential form and solve for the variable.

- Remember properties logarithms.

1-Solve each of the following equations.

A. $y = 4\log_2 3x - 16$

B. $\ln(2x+3)^4 = 9$

C. $y = \log_3(2x-3)$

D. $\log_2(x-3) = 2 + \log_2(x-4)$

E. $\log 5x = 7 - 2\log(3x)$

F. $\log_5 2x - 3 = \log_5 x + 1$

2. Which solution for the following equation is true?

$\log(2x+3) = \log(7-8x)$

A.
$2x + 3 = 7 - 8x$
$2x + 8x = 7 - 3$
$10x = 4$
$x = 2.5$

B.
$(2x+3)(8x-7) = 0$
$16x^2 - 14x + 24x - 21 = 0$
$16x^2 + 10x - 21 = 0$
$x = 3.2$

MathePathics

Answers of Worksheets - Chapter 17

Rewriting Logarithms

1.

A. $2^3 = 8$

B. $9^2 = 81$

C. $4^3 = 64$

D. $8^3 = 6561$

E. $5^3 = 125$

F. $10^3 = 1000$

G. $6^4 = 1296$

H. $11^5 = 161051$

I. $8^2 = 64$

2.

A. $\log_7 49 = 2$

B. $\log_3 81 = 4$

C. $\log_{11} 121 = 2$

D. $\log_{30} 900 = 2$

E. $\log_{12} 1728 = 3$

F. $\log_{1.5} 2.25 = 2$

G. $\log 100 = 2$

H. $\log_{20} 800 = 3$

I. $\log_9 729 = 3$

J. $\log_4 64000 = 3$

K. $\log_{2.4} 39.0625 = 4$

L. $\log_6 7776 = 5$

3.

A. $x = 8$

B. $x = 2$

C. $x = 7$

D. $x = 2197$

E. $x = 4$

F. $x = 9$

G. $x = 144$

H. $x = 4$

I. $x = 20$

J. x = 3   K. x = 2   L. x = $\sqrt{2}$

Evaluating Logarithms

1.

A. y = 2   B. y = 3   C. y = 2

D. y = 4   E. y = 8   F. y = 5

2.   3.

His friend $(\frac{1}{5})^y = 0.04$ y = 2

Properties of Logarithms

1.

A. $\log_3 b - \log_3 6$ B. $\log_3 8 + \log_3 a$ C. $5\log_2 a$

D. $\log 12xy$ E. $\log \frac{ab}{3}$ F. $\log(7y)^6$

2.

A. $\log 2x$ B. $\log c$ C. 5

D. $\log 3b$ E. 1   F. $2x + 1$

Natural Logarithms

1.

A. 0.94   B. 1.354   C. 1.824

D. 2.097	E. 1.978	F. 1.541
G. 3.951	H. 1.791	I. 4.605

2.

- ln 5.61=1.724

3.

-ln 7.816=2.056

Solving Exponential Equations Requiring Logarithms

1.

A. X=1.38	B. X=0.418	C. X=5.754
D. X=2.033	E. X=-3.043	F. X=1.440

2.

Yes

Solving Logarithmic Equations

1.

A. X=5.33	B. X=-1.43	C. X=937.7
D. X=4.3	E. X=8.5	F. X=-3

2.

A

Extra Note for Chapter 17:

Chapter 18:
Matrices

Adding and subtracting Matrices

Matrix Multiplication

Finding Determinants of a Matrix

Matrix Equations

Answers of Worksheets – Chapter 18

Adding and Subtracting Matrices

Matrix addition is simple. You should add the pairs of entries, and then simplify for the final answer

$$\begin{bmatrix} a & b \\ c & d \end{bmatrix} + \begin{bmatrix} e & f \\ g & h \end{bmatrix} = \begin{bmatrix} a+e & c+f \\ b+g & d+h \end{bmatrix}$$

Matrix subtracting is simple too. You should subtract the numbers in the matching positions.

$$\begin{bmatrix} a & b \\ c & d \end{bmatrix} - \begin{bmatrix} e & f \\ g & h \end{bmatrix} = \begin{bmatrix} a-e & c-f \\ b-g & d-h \end{bmatrix}$$

For adding and subtracting matrices, they must be the same size i.e. the rows must match in size, and the columns must match in size.

1- Add and subtract following matrices.

A. $\begin{bmatrix} 2 & 5 \\ 6 & 7 \end{bmatrix} + \begin{bmatrix} 3 & 9 \\ 1 & 0 \end{bmatrix}$

B. $\begin{bmatrix} 2 \\ 11 \\ 0 \end{bmatrix} - \begin{bmatrix} 5 \\ 6 \\ 7 \end{bmatrix}$

C. $\begin{bmatrix} 0 & 10 \\ 25 & 30 \end{bmatrix} - \begin{bmatrix} 14 & 3 \\ 12 & 1 \end{bmatrix}$

D. $\begin{bmatrix} 100 & 50 & 20 \\ 30 & 90 & 80 \\ 200 & 10 & 0 \end{bmatrix} + \begin{bmatrix} 9 & 4 & 8 \\ 6 & 3 & 2 \\ 5 & 0 & 1 \end{bmatrix}$

E. $\begin{bmatrix} 55 & 39 & 28 \\ 17 & 31 & 45 \end{bmatrix} - \begin{bmatrix} 24 & 93 & 51 \\ 78 & 42 & 68 \end{bmatrix}$

F. $\begin{bmatrix} 1000 & 5000 \\ 6000 & 7000 \end{bmatrix} + \begin{bmatrix} 3000 & 0 \\ 9000 & 4000 \end{bmatrix}$

2- Three matrices are given. Find A+B, C-A.

A. $\begin{bmatrix} 13 & 4 \\ -8 & 25 \end{bmatrix}$
B. $\begin{bmatrix} 31 & 5 \\ 11 & 20 \end{bmatrix}$
C. $\begin{bmatrix} 42 & 5 \\ 60 & 4 \end{bmatrix}$

3- According to matrices, which function can't be done?

A. $\begin{bmatrix} 12 & 5 & 6 \\ 14 & 8 & 9 \end{bmatrix}$
B. $\begin{bmatrix} 12 \\ 14 \\ 0 \end{bmatrix}$
C. $\begin{bmatrix} 10 & 5 & 8 \\ 42 & 0 & 3 \end{bmatrix}$

A-C   B-C   A+C   A-B

4- Fill the blank with a correct number.

A. $\begin{bmatrix} 5 & \ldots & 6 \\ 14 & 5 & 1 \\ 3 & 7 & 8 \end{bmatrix} + \begin{bmatrix} 10 & 3 & \ldots \\ \ldots & 4 & 1 \\ 5 & 4 & 2 \end{bmatrix} = \begin{bmatrix} \ldots & 7 & 13 \\ 14 & \ldots & 2 \\ 8 & 11 & 10 \end{bmatrix}$

B. $\begin{bmatrix} \ldots \\ 12 \\ 94 \end{bmatrix} - \begin{bmatrix} 6 \\ \ldots \\ 18 \end{bmatrix} = \begin{bmatrix} 55 \\ 3 \\ \ldots \end{bmatrix}$

Matrix Multiplication

There are two kinds of matrix multiplication.

- Multiply a matrix by a single number.

$$e \cdot \begin{bmatrix} a & b \\ c & d \end{bmatrix} = \begin{bmatrix} e.a & e.b \\ e.c & e.d \end{bmatrix}$$

- Multiply a matrix by another matrix. We need to do the "dot product" of rows and columns.

When we do multiplication:

- The number of columns of the first matrix must equal the number of rows of the second matrix.
- And the result will have the same number of rows as the first matrix, and the same number of columns as the second matrix

$$\begin{bmatrix} a & b & c \\ d & e & f \end{bmatrix} \times \begin{bmatrix} g & h \\ i & j \\ k & l \end{bmatrix} = \begin{bmatrix} a.g+b.i+c.j & a.h+b.j+c.l \\ d.g+e.i+f.k & d.h+e.j+f.l \end{bmatrix}$$

1- Multiply following matrices.

A. $2 \cdot \begin{bmatrix} 5 & 6 \\ 0 & 1 \end{bmatrix}$

B. $\begin{bmatrix} 3 & 2 \\ 4 & 5 \\ -1 & 8 \end{bmatrix} \times \begin{bmatrix} 10 & 11 & 1 \\ 0 & 6 & 7 \end{bmatrix}$

C. $10 \cdot \begin{bmatrix} 12 & -8 & 0 \\ 14 & 3 & 1 \\ 2 & 15 & 4 \end{bmatrix}$

D. $\begin{bmatrix} 100 & 350 & 400 \end{bmatrix} \times \begin{bmatrix} -8 \\ 0 \\ -2 \end{bmatrix}$

2- According to below matrices, perform function.

$A = \begin{bmatrix} 5 & 8 \\ 9 & -4 \end{bmatrix}$ $\qquad B = \begin{bmatrix} 3 & -8 \\ 0 & 5 \end{bmatrix}$

a. 2A $\qquad\qquad$ b. B×A $\qquad\qquad$ c. 3A+B

3- Which of the following function cannot be done?

$A = \begin{bmatrix} 5 & 6 & 8 \\ 9 & -3 & 11 \end{bmatrix}$ $\qquad B = \begin{bmatrix} 12 & 14 & 2 \\ 5 & 8 & 10 \\ 4 & 3 & 0 \end{bmatrix}$ $\qquad C = \begin{bmatrix} 12 & 2 \\ 4 & 5 \\ 2 & 8 \end{bmatrix}$

A×C $\qquad\qquad$ B×A $\qquad\qquad$ C×B $\qquad\qquad$ B×C

4- Tim wants to find B×C. B is a 4×5 matrix and C is a 4×3 matrix. In your opinion, can he perform this function? Why?

5- Fill the blanks with correct numbers.

$\begin{bmatrix} 12 \\ 0 \\ 5 \end{bmatrix} \times \begin{bmatrix} 0 & 2 & 9 \\ 8 & 5 & 1 \\ 10 & 5 & 6 \\ 1 & 9 & 8 \end{bmatrix} = \begin{bmatrix} \ldots & 252 & 288 \\ 0 & 0 & \ldots \\ 95 & \ldots & 120 \end{bmatrix}$

Finding Determinants of a Matrix

The determinant of a matrix is a special number that can be calculated from a square matrix.

The symbol for determinant is two vertical lines either side. |A|

Calculating the Determinant:

For a 2×2 Matrix.

$$A = \begin{bmatrix} a & b \\ c & d \end{bmatrix} \qquad |A| = a.d - c.b$$

For a 3×3 Matrix.

$$A = \begin{bmatrix} a & b & c \\ d & e & f \\ g & h & i \end{bmatrix} \qquad |A| = a(ei - fh) - b(di - fg) + c(dh - eg)$$

1- Find determinants of matrices.

$$A = \begin{bmatrix} 5 & 7 \\ 8 & 6 \end{bmatrix} \qquad B = \begin{bmatrix} 0 & 2 & -1 \\ 2 & 5 & 8 \\ 3 & 4 & 9 \end{bmatrix} \qquad C = \begin{bmatrix} \sqrt{3} & \sqrt{9} \\ \sqrt{4} & \sqrt{27} \end{bmatrix}$$

2- According to matrices, perform functions.

$$A = \begin{bmatrix} -1 & 4 \\ 0 & 9 \end{bmatrix} \qquad B = \begin{bmatrix} 100 & 0 & 900 \\ 200 & 1 & 400 \\ 50 & 2 & 0 \end{bmatrix} \qquad C = \begin{bmatrix} 5 & 2 \\ -8 & 1 \end{bmatrix}$$

$|A| \times |B| \qquad |B| + |C| \qquad |A| - |B| \qquad |C| - |A|$

Finding Inverse of a Matrix

For matrices, there is no such thing as division. You can add, subtract, and multiply matrices, but you cannot divide them. There is a related concept, though, which is called "inversion".

$$A \xrightleftharpoons[\text{Inverse}]{\text{Inverse}} A^{-1}$$

When we multiply a matrix by its inverse, we get the Identity Matrix (which is like "1" for matrices) $A \times A^{-1} = -1$

How can we calculate the inverse of matrix?

$$A = \begin{bmatrix} a & b \\ c & d \end{bmatrix} \quad A^{-1} = \begin{bmatrix} a & b \\ c & d \end{bmatrix}^{-1} = \frac{1}{ad-bc} \begin{bmatrix} d & -b \\ -c & a \end{bmatrix}$$

Determinant

1- Find the inverse of the following matrices.

$$X = \begin{bmatrix} 2 & 4 \\ 5 & 3 \end{bmatrix} \qquad Y = \begin{bmatrix} 8 & 5 \\ 3 & 2 \end{bmatrix} \qquad Z = \begin{bmatrix} 2 & 3 \\ 4 & 7 \end{bmatrix}$$

2- If $A = \begin{bmatrix} 0 & 6 \\ 4 & 1 \end{bmatrix}$ and $B = \begin{bmatrix} -2 & 4 \\ 7 & 3 \end{bmatrix}$, what is $A^{-1} + 2B$?

Matrix Equations

A matrix equation is an equation in which a variable is a matrix. Using your knowledge of equal matrices and algebraic properties of addition and subtraction, you can find the value of this unknown matrix.

$$A.X = B \rightarrow X = A^{-1}.B$$

1- Solve matrix equations.

A. $\begin{cases} 4x + 9y = 1 \\ 3x - 7y = 2 \end{cases}$

B. $\begin{cases} 5x + 7y = 0 \\ 3x + 4y = -8 \end{cases}$

C. $\begin{bmatrix} -1 & 2 & 5 \\ y & 6 & 0 \\ 8 & 10 & -3 \end{bmatrix} + \begin{bmatrix} x & 7 & 8 \\ -2 & 15 & 0 \\ 11 & 13 & 4 \end{bmatrix} = \begin{bmatrix} 4 & 14 & 13 \\ 8 & 21 & 0 \\ 19 & 23 & z \end{bmatrix}$

D. $100 \begin{bmatrix} x & 5 \\ 2 & 0 \\ 8 & 12 \end{bmatrix} = \begin{bmatrix} 600 & y \\ 200 & 0 \\ z & 1200 \end{bmatrix}$

2- According to matrices from different below functions find matrix D. ($D = \begin{bmatrix} a & b \\ c & d \end{bmatrix}$)

$A = \begin{bmatrix} 0 & 1 \\ 2 & 5 \end{bmatrix}$ $B = \begin{bmatrix} 6 & 7 \\ 8 & 9 \end{bmatrix}$ $C = \begin{bmatrix} -1 & 0 \\ 10 & 0 \end{bmatrix}$

- a. 2A + D = C
- b. 3C - B = D
- c. B - A = D
- d. D - C = B

3- Adam wrote below solution for finding "x" and "y". Is his solution true? Check it.

$$\begin{cases} x - 3y = 1 \\ 2x - y = 0 \end{cases}$$

$$\begin{bmatrix} 1 & -3 \\ 2 & -1 \end{bmatrix} \begin{bmatrix} x \\ y \end{bmatrix} = \begin{bmatrix} 1 \\ 0 \end{bmatrix}$$

$$\begin{bmatrix} x \\ y \end{bmatrix} = \begin{bmatrix} 1 & -3 \\ 2 & -1 \end{bmatrix}^{-1} \begin{bmatrix} 1 \\ 0 \end{bmatrix} = \frac{1}{-1+6} \begin{bmatrix} 1 & 3 \\ -2 & -1 \end{bmatrix} \begin{bmatrix} 1 \\ 0 \end{bmatrix} = \frac{1}{5} \begin{bmatrix} 1 & 3 \\ -2 & -1 \end{bmatrix} \begin{bmatrix} 1 \\ 0 \end{bmatrix}$$

$$\begin{bmatrix} \frac{1}{5} & \frac{3}{5} \\ -\frac{2}{5} & -\frac{1}{5} \end{bmatrix} \begin{bmatrix} 1 \\ 0 \end{bmatrix} = \begin{bmatrix} \frac{4}{5} \\ -\frac{2}{5} \end{bmatrix}$$

MathePathics

Answers of Worksheets – Chapter 18

Adding and Subtracting Matrices

1.

A. $\begin{bmatrix} 5 & 14 \\ 7 & 7 \end{bmatrix}$
B. $\begin{bmatrix} -3 \\ 5 \\ -7 \end{bmatrix}$
C. $\begin{bmatrix} -14 & 7 \\ 13 & 29 \end{bmatrix}$

D. $\begin{bmatrix} 109 & 54 & 28 \\ 36 & 93 & 82 \\ 205 & 10 & 1 \end{bmatrix}$
E. $\begin{bmatrix} 31 & -54 & -23 \\ -61 & -11 & -23 \end{bmatrix}$

F. $\begin{bmatrix} 4000 & 5000 \\ 15000 & 11000 \end{bmatrix}$

2.

$A + B = \begin{bmatrix} 44 & 9 \\ 3 & 45 \end{bmatrix}$
$C - A = \begin{bmatrix} 29 & 1 \\ 68 & -21 \end{bmatrix}$

3.

B-C, A-B

4.

A. 4 – 7 – 15 – 0 – 9   B. 61 – 8 – 76

Matrix Multiplication

1.

A. $\begin{bmatrix} 10 & 12 \\ 0 & 2 \end{bmatrix}$
B. $\begin{bmatrix} 10+0 & 33+18 & 3+14 \\ 40+0 & -11+48 & 4+35 \\ -10+0 & -11+48 & -1+56 \end{bmatrix} = \begin{bmatrix} 10 & 51 & 17 \\ 40 & 74 & 39 \\ -10 & 37 & -55 \end{bmatrix}$

C. $\begin{bmatrix} 120 & -80 & 0 \\ 140 & 30 & 10 \\ 20 & 150 & 40 \end{bmatrix}$
D. $\begin{bmatrix} -800 & 0 & -800 \end{bmatrix}$

2.

a. $2A = 2\begin{bmatrix} 5 & 8 \\ 9 & -4 \end{bmatrix} = \begin{bmatrix} 10 & 16 \\ 18 & -8 \end{bmatrix}$

b. $B \times A = \begin{bmatrix} 3 & -8 \\ 0 & 5 \end{bmatrix} \times \begin{bmatrix} 5 & 8 \\ 9 & -4 \end{bmatrix} = \begin{bmatrix} 15-72 & 24+32 \\ 0+45 & 0-20 \end{bmatrix} = \begin{bmatrix} -57 & 56 \\ 45 & -20 \end{bmatrix}$

c. $3A + B = 3\begin{bmatrix} 5 & 8 \\ 9 & -4 \end{bmatrix} \times \begin{bmatrix} 3 & -8 \\ 0 & 5 \end{bmatrix} = \begin{bmatrix} 15 & 24 \\ 27 & -12 \end{bmatrix} \times \begin{bmatrix} 3 & -8 \\ 0 & 5 \end{bmatrix} = \begin{bmatrix} 45 & 240 \\ 81 & 276 \end{bmatrix}$

3.

$A \times C$

4.

No. Because matrix A has 3 columns and matrix B has 4 rows, so the number of columns in matrix A isn't equal with the number of rows in matrix B.

5.

288 – 0 – 105

Finding Determinants of a Matrix

1.

$|A| = (5 \times 6) - (7 \times 8) = 30 - 56 = -26$

$|B| = 0(45 - 32) - 2(18 - 24) + (-1)(8 - 15) = 0 + 12 + 7 = 19$

$|C| = (\sqrt{3} \times \sqrt{27}) - (\sqrt{4} \times \sqrt{9}) = \sqrt{81} - \sqrt{36} = 9 - 6 = 3$

2.

$|A| \times |B| = -9 \times -307000 = 2763000$ $|B| + |C| = -307000 + 21 = -306979$

$|A| - |B| = -9 - 307000 = -307009$ $|C| - |A| = 21 - (-9) = 30$

Finding Inverse of a Matrix

1.

$$X^{-1} = \begin{bmatrix} 2 & 4 \\ 5 & 3 \end{bmatrix}^{-1} = \frac{1}{6-20}\begin{bmatrix} 3 & -4 \\ -5 & 2 \end{bmatrix} = \begin{bmatrix} -\frac{3}{14} & \frac{4}{14} \\ \frac{5}{14} & -\frac{2}{14} \end{bmatrix}$$

$$Y^{-1} = \begin{bmatrix} 8 & 5 \\ 3 & 2 \end{bmatrix}^{-1} = \frac{1}{16-15}\begin{bmatrix} 2 & -5 \\ -3 & 8 \end{bmatrix} = \begin{bmatrix} 2 & -5 \\ -3 & 8 \end{bmatrix}$$

$$Z^{-1} = \begin{bmatrix} 2 & 3 \\ 4 & 7 \end{bmatrix}^{-1} = \frac{1}{14-12}\begin{bmatrix} 7 & -3 \\ -4 & 2 \end{bmatrix} = \begin{bmatrix} \frac{7}{2} & -\frac{3}{2} \\ -2 & 1 \end{bmatrix}$$

2.

$$A^{-1} + 2B = \frac{1}{0-24}\begin{bmatrix} 1 & -6 \\ -4 & 0 \end{bmatrix} + \begin{bmatrix} -4 & 8 \\ 14 & 6 \end{bmatrix} = \begin{bmatrix} -\frac{97}{24} & \frac{33}{4} \\ \frac{85}{6} & 6 \end{bmatrix}$$

Matrix Equations

1.

A) $A.X = B \rightarrow X = A^{-1}.B = \dfrac{1}{28-27}\begin{bmatrix} 7 & -9 \\ -3 & 4 \end{bmatrix}\begin{bmatrix} 1 \\ 2 \end{bmatrix} = \begin{bmatrix} 7-18 \\ -3+8 \end{bmatrix} = \begin{bmatrix} -9 \\ 5 \end{bmatrix}$ $x = -9$ $y = 5$

B) $X = A^{-1}.B = \dfrac{1}{20-21}\begin{bmatrix} 4 & -7 \\ -3 & 5 \end{bmatrix}\begin{bmatrix} 0 \\ 8 \end{bmatrix} = \begin{bmatrix} 56 \\ -40 \end{bmatrix}$ $x = 56$ $y = -40$

C) $-1+x = 4 \rightarrow x = 5$ $y-2 = 8 \rightarrow y = 10$ $-3+4 = z \rightarrow z = 1$

D) $x = \dfrac{600}{100} = 6$ $y = 100 \times 5 = 500$ $z = 100 \times 8 = 800$

2.

a) $\begin{bmatrix} 0 & 2 \\ 4 & 5 \end{bmatrix} + \begin{bmatrix} a & b \\ c & d \end{bmatrix} = \begin{bmatrix} -1 & 0 \\ 10 & 0 \end{bmatrix}$ $D = \begin{bmatrix} -1 & -2 \\ -6 & -5 \end{bmatrix}$

b) $\begin{bmatrix} -3 & 0 \\ 30 & 0 \end{bmatrix} - \begin{bmatrix} 6 & 7 \\ 8 & 9 \end{bmatrix} = \begin{bmatrix} a & b \\ c & d \end{bmatrix}$ $D = \begin{bmatrix} -9 & -7 \\ 22 & -9 \end{bmatrix}$

c) $\begin{bmatrix} 6 & 7 \\ 8 & 9 \end{bmatrix} - \begin{bmatrix} 0 & 1 \\ 2 & 5 \end{bmatrix} = \begin{bmatrix} a & b \\ c & d \end{bmatrix}$ $D = \begin{bmatrix} 6 & 6 \\ 6 & 4 \end{bmatrix}$

d) $\begin{bmatrix} a & b \\ c & d \end{bmatrix} - \begin{bmatrix} -1 & 0 \\ 10 & 0 \end{bmatrix} = \begin{bmatrix} 6 & 7 \\ 8 & 9 \end{bmatrix}$ $D = \begin{bmatrix} 5 & 7 \\ 18 & 9 \end{bmatrix}$

3.

Yes.

Extra Note for Chapter 18:

Chapter 19: Functions Operations

Function Notation

Adding and Subtracting Functions

Multiplying and Dividing Functions

Composition of Functions

Answers of Worksheets – Chapter 19

Function Natation

Function notation is the way a function is written.

The most popular function notation is **f (x)** which is read "f of x".

The **f (x)** notation is another way of representing the y-value in a function, $y = f(x)$.

$$f(x) = \underbrace{4x - 1}_{\text{Output value}}$$

↓
input value

1- Some functions are given. Find requested items.

A. $f(x) = 5x - 2$ $f(-1)$ B. $g(x) = 3x^2 - x^4 + 1$ $g(2)$

C. $f(x) = -\dfrac{x^2 - 1}{4 - x}$ $f(0)$ D. $g(x) = \sqrt{\dfrac{2 + 3x}{4}}$ $g(8)$

2- If $g(x) = 7 - 9x$, find $g(1 - a)$.

3- If $f(x) = x^2 + 10x + 25$ and $f(m) = 49$, what is the value of "m"?

Adding and Subtracting Functions

We can add and subtract functions. The result is a new function.

Addition $\quad (f+g)(x) = f(x) + g(x)$

Subtraction $\quad (f-g)(x) = f(x) - g(x)$

1- Add and subtract following equations.

a. $f(x) = 2x + 3 \qquad g(x) = x - 5 \qquad (f+g)(x)$

b. $f(x) = \dfrac{1}{2}x^2 - x \qquad g(x) = 2x - \dfrac{5}{6}x^2 \qquad (f-g)(x)$

c. $f(x) = 2 - 4x \qquad g(x) = 3x - 10 \qquad h(x) = -x + 1 \qquad (f+g+h)(x)$

d. $f(x) = \dfrac{x+3}{1} \qquad g(x) = 1 - \dfrac{2-x}{2} \qquad (f+g)(x)$

2- Rosy is a typist. She wrote an equation that shows the relationship between number of pages that she can type in one hour.

How many pages can she type in 3 hours?

$f(x) = 4x^2 + 1$

3- According to functions, find the requested items.

a. $f(x) = 1 - x^2$ $g(x) = 4 - x$ $(f+g)(3)$

b. $f(x) = 2 + \sqrt{x}$ $g(x) = 3 - x^2$ $(f-g)(9)$

c. $f(x) = \dfrac{x-5}{2}$ $g(x) = \dfrac{1+2x}{4}$ $(f+g)(0)$

d. $f(x) = (x+3)^2$ $g(x) = x + 10$ $(f-g)(8)$

4- Tim wrote below solution for finding $(f+g)(a+b)$. If a=2 and b=0, what is $(f+g)(a+b)$?

$f(x) = 5x + 2$ $g(x) = -11 + x^2 + 2x$

$(f+g)(x) = 5x + 2 - 11 + x^2 + 2x$

$(f+g)(x) = x^2 + 7x - 10$

$(f+g)(a+b) = (a+b)^2 + 7(a+b) - 10$

5- Complete the blanks.

a. $f(x) = x + 5$ $g(x) = 2x + 7$ $(f-g)(x) = \ldots\ldots + 11$

b. $f(x) = \dfrac{x-4}{x^2}$ $g(x) = \dfrac{6x-1}{x^2}$ $(f+g)(x) = \dfrac{7x - \ldots\ldots}{\ldots\ldots}$

Multiplying and Dividing Functions

We can multiply and divide functions. The result is a new function.

Multiplicition $\quad (f.g)(x) = f(x).g(x)$

Division $\quad (\dfrac{f}{g})(x) = \dfrac{f(x)}{g(x)}$

1- Multiply and divide below functions.

a. $f(x) = 3x + 2$ $\qquad g(x) = 5x^2 \qquad (f \cdot g)(x)$

b. $f(x) = x^2 \qquad g(x) = \dfrac{1}{2x+5} \qquad (\dfrac{f}{g})(x)$

c. $f(x) = \dfrac{1}{2}x + 7 \qquad g(x) = 3x^2 - 1 \qquad (f \cdot g)(x)$

d. $f(x) = x - 1 \qquad g(x) = (x-1)^2(x+3) \qquad (\dfrac{g}{f})(x)$

2- According to functions, find requested items.

a. $f(x) = x - 2 \qquad g(x) = 2(x-2)^2 + 1 \qquad (\dfrac{f}{g})(3)$

b. $f(x) = \dfrac{1}{6}x + 5$ $g(x) = 36x$ $(f \cdot g)(1)$

c. $f(x) = \sqrt{x} + 1$ $g(x) = (\sqrt{x} + 1)(2x - 1)$ $(g/f)(4)$

d. $f(x) = 7 - 4x^3$ $g(x) = -1 + x$ $(g \cdot f)(0)$

3- Adam and Tim want to use two functions to find a new function. They write four methods. Which of them is correct?

$f(x) = x + 1$ $g(x) = 4x$

a. $(f + g)(x) = 5x + 1$

b. $(f/g)(x) = \dfrac{4x}{x+1}$

c. $(g - f)(x) = -3x + 1$

d. $(g \circ f)(x) = 4x(x + 1)$

Composition of Functions

"Function Composition" is applying one function to the results of another.

$$\longrightarrow \boxed{f()} \longrightarrow \boxed{g()} \longrightarrow$$

The result of f () is sent through g (). It is written: $(g \circ f)(x)$

Which means: $g(f(x))$

a. $f(x) = 2x$ $g(x) = x - 1$ $(f \circ g)(x)$

b. $f(x) = \sqrt{x+2}$ $g(x) = 4 - x^2$ $(g \circ f)(x)$

c. $f(x) = \dfrac{1}{2}x + 3$ $g(x) = 2x^6$ $(f \circ g)(x)$

2- According to function, find requested items.

a. $f(x) = 1 + 4x$ $g(x) = \sqrt{x}$ $(g \circ f)(2)$

b. $f(x) = \dfrac{x+1}{4}$ $g(x) = 2x - 3$ $(f \circ g)(3)$

MathePathics

Answers of Worksheets – Chapter 19

Function Natation

1.

A. $f(-1) = 7(-1) - 5 = -7 - 5 = -12$

B. $g(2) = 3(2)^2 - (2)^4 + 1 = 12 - 16 + 1 = -3$

C. $f(0) = -\dfrac{0-1}{4-0} = \dfrac{1}{4}$

D. $g(8) = \sqrt{\dfrac{2+3(8)}{4}} = \sqrt{\dfrac{24}{6}} = \sqrt{6.5}$

2.

$g(1-a) = 7 - 9(1-a) = 7 - 9 + 9a = -2 - 9a$

3.

$f(m) = m^2 + 10m + 25 = 49 \quad m^2 + 10m + 25 = 49 \rightarrow (m+5)^2 = 49 \rightarrow m+5 = 7 \rightarrow m = 2$

Adding and Subtracting Functions

1.

a. $(f+g)(x) = 2x + 3 + x - 5 = 5x - 2$

b. $(f-g)(x) = \dfrac{1}{2}x^2 - x + 2x - \dfrac{5}{6}x^2 = \dfrac{1}{3}x^2 + x$

c. $(f+g+h)(x) = 2 - 4x + 3x - 10 - x + 1 = -2x - 7$

d. $(f+g)(x) = \dfrac{x+1}{3} + 1 - \dfrac{2-x}{2} = \dfrac{2x+2+6-6+3x}{6} = \dfrac{5x+2}{6}$

2.

$f(3) = 4(3)^2 + 1 = 27 + 1 = 28$

3.

a. $(f+g)(x) = 1 - x^2 + 4 - x = -x^2 - x + 5 \quad \rightarrow \quad (f+g)(3) = 11$

b. $(f-g)(x) = 2 + \sqrt{x} - 3 + x^2 \quad \rightarrow \quad (f-g)(9) = 83$

c. $(f+g)(x) = \dfrac{x-5}{2} + \dfrac{1+2x}{4} = \dfrac{4x-9}{4}$ → $(f+g)(0) = -\dfrac{9}{4}$

d. $(f-g)(x) = (x+3)^2 - x + 10$ → $(f-g)(8) = 123$

4.

$(f+g)(2+0) = (2+0)^2 + 7(2+0) - 10 = 8$

5.

a. $3x$ b. $-5, x^2$

Composition of Functions

1.

a. $(f \circ g)(x) = (3x+2)(5x^2)$

b. $\left(\dfrac{f}{g}\right)(x) = \dfrac{x^2}{2x+5}$

c. $(f \circ g)(x) = (\dfrac{1}{2}x + 7)(3x^2 - 1) = \dfrac{3}{2}x^3 - \dfrac{1}{2}x + 21x^2 - 7$

d. $\left(\dfrac{g}{f}\right)(x) = \dfrac{(x-1)^2(x+3)}{x-1} = (x-1)(x+3)$

2.

a. $\left(\dfrac{f}{g}\right)(x) = \dfrac{x-2}{2(x-2)^2 + 1}$ → $\left(\dfrac{f}{g}\right)(3) = \dfrac{1}{3}$

b. $(f \circ g)(x) = 6x^2 + 180x$ → $(f \circ g)(1) = 186$

c. $\left(\dfrac{g}{f}\right)(x) = \dfrac{(\sqrt{x}+1)(2x-1)}{\sqrt{x}+1} = 2x-1$ → $\left(\dfrac{g}{f}\right)(4) = 7$

d. $(g \circ f)(x) = (-1+x)(7-4x^3)$ → $(g \circ f)(0) = 7$

4.

- a and c.

Composition of Function

1.

a. $(f \circ g)(x) = f(g(x)) = 2(x-1) = 2x - 2$

b. $(g \circ f)(x) = g(f(x)) = 4 - (\sqrt{x+2})^2 = 4 - x + 2 = 6 - x$

c. $(f \circ g)(x) = f(g(x)) = \frac{1}{2}(2x^6) + 3 = x^6 + 3$

2.

a. $(g \circ f)(x) = g(f(x)) = \sqrt{1 + 4x} \quad \rightarrow \quad (g \circ f)(2) = 3$

b. $(f \circ g)(x) = f(g(x)) = \frac{2x - 3 + 1}{4} = \frac{2x - 2}{4} \quad \rightarrow \quad (f \circ g)(3) = 1$

Extra Note for Chapter 19:

MathePathics

Chapter 20:
Trigonometric Functions

Trig ratios of General Angles

Sketch Each Angle in standard Position

Finding Co-terminal Angles and References Angles

Writing Each Measure in Radians

Writing Each Measure in Degrees

Evaluating Each Trigonometric Function

Missing Sides and Angles of a Right Triangle

Arc Length and Sector Area

Answers of Worksheets – Chapter 20

Trig ratios of General Angles

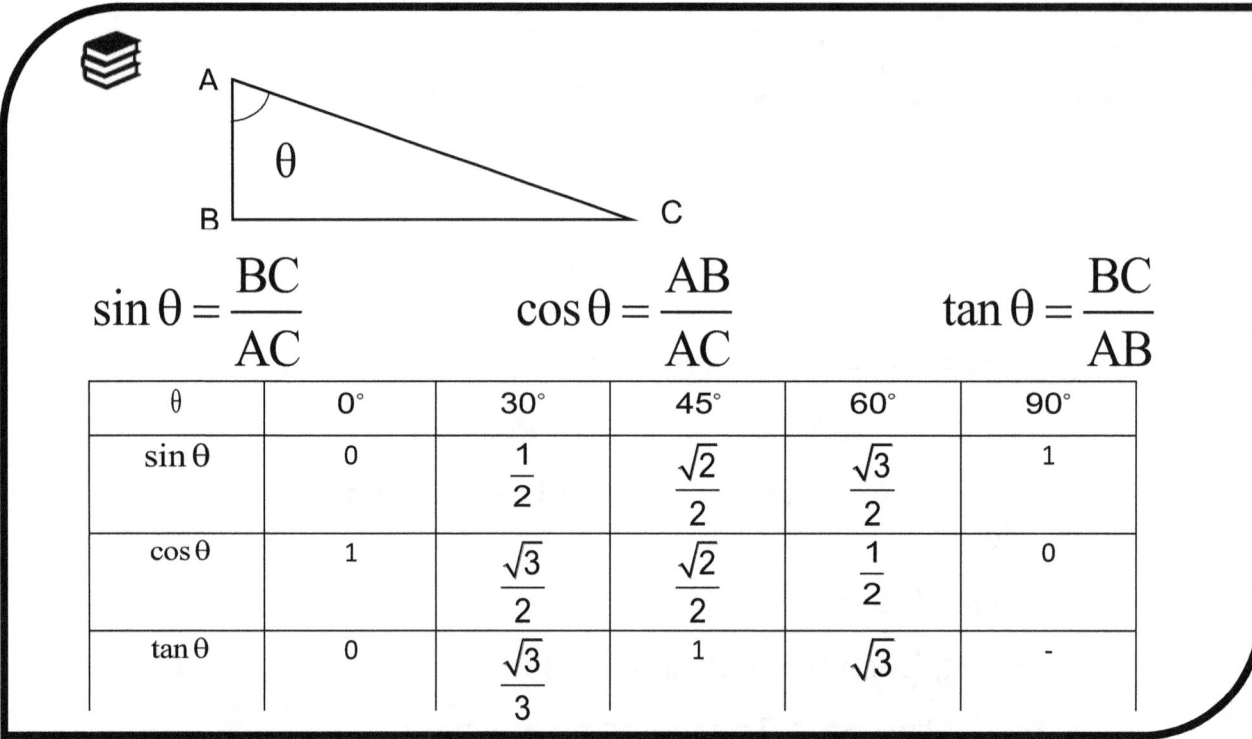

1- Find the value of each trigonometric function.

a. $\cos\dfrac{2\pi}{3}$

b. $\tan\dfrac{3\pi}{4}$

c. $\sin\dfrac{5\pi}{6}$

d. $\sin(-\dfrac{\pi}{4})$

e. $\cos(3\pi)$

f. $\tan(4\pi)$

g. $\cos(3\pi)+\sin(-\dfrac{\pi}{4})$

h. $\tan\dfrac{3\pi}{4}-\tan(4\pi)$

i. $\cos\dfrac{\pi}{4}+\sin\dfrac{\pi}{4}$

2- According to below triangles, find the requested items.

MathePathics

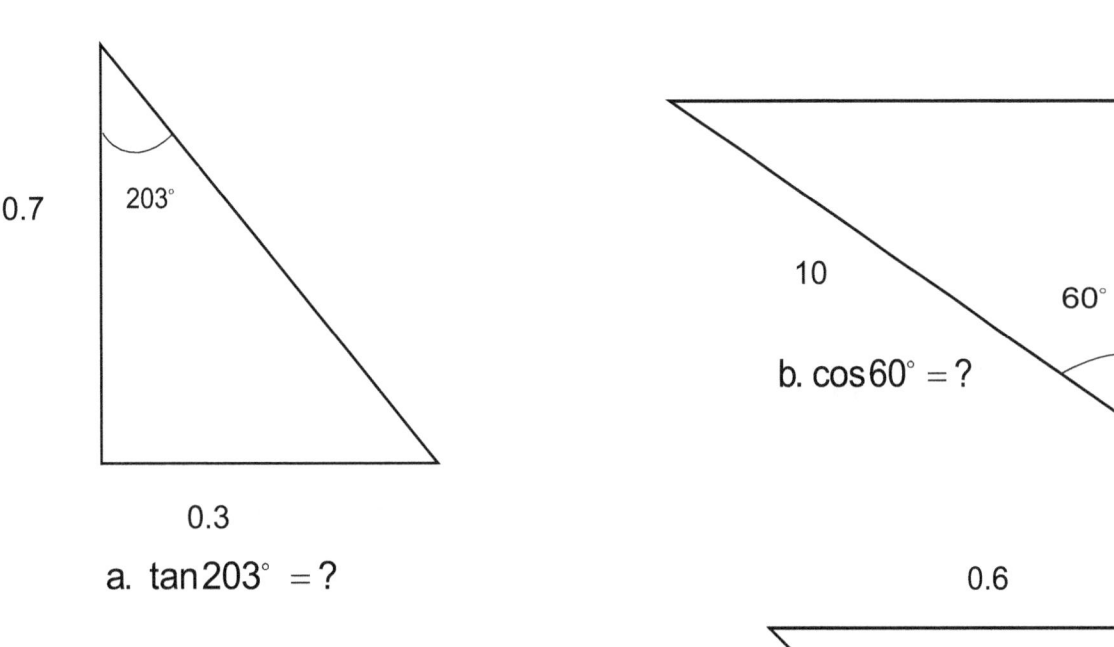

a. $\tan 203° = ?$

b. $\cos 60° = ?$

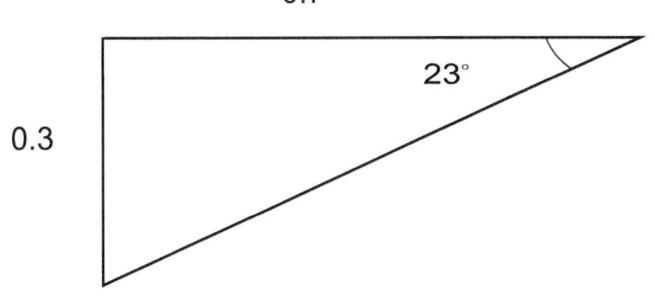

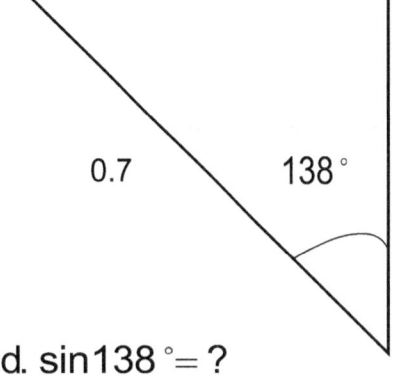

c. $\tan 23° = ?$

d. $\sin 138° = ?$

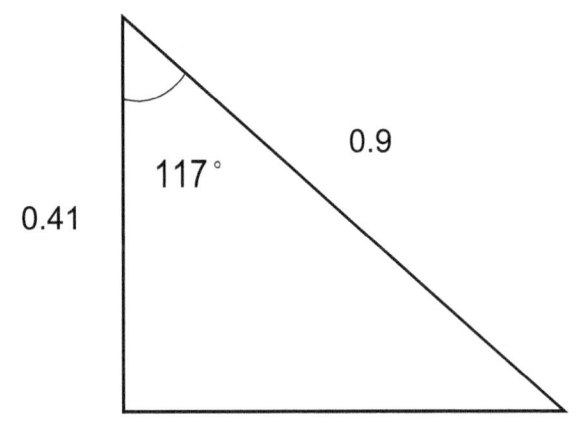

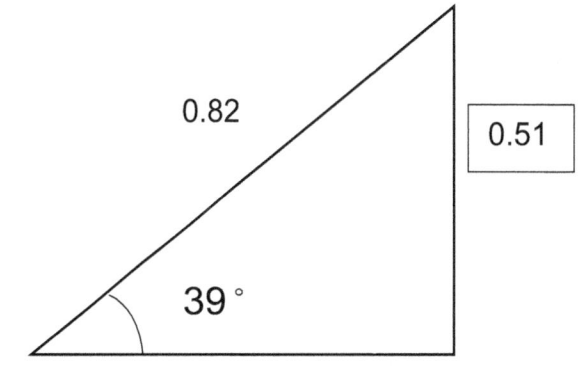

e. $\cos 117° = ?$

f. $\sin 39° = ?$

Sketch Each Angle in Standard Position

An angle consists of two parts, initial side, and terminal side. The ray on the x-axis is called the initial side and the other ray is called the terminal side.

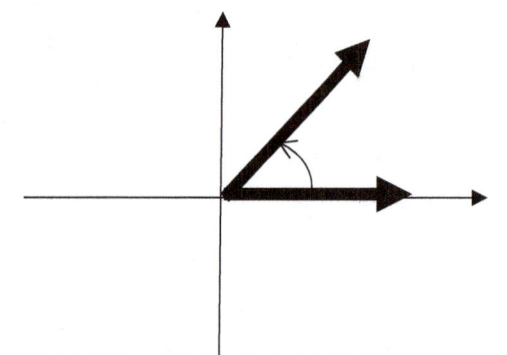

Positive angles in standard position

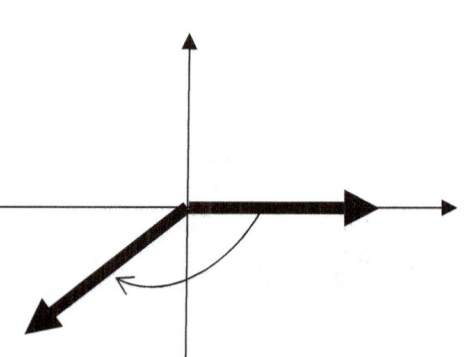

Negative angles in standard position

1- Which of the following picture shows $80°$?

1)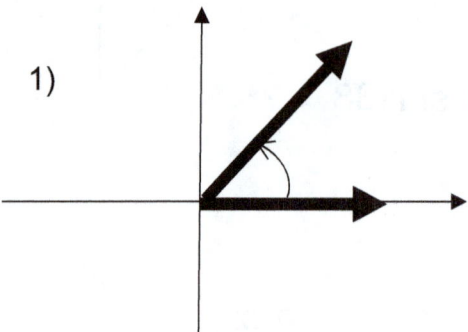

2)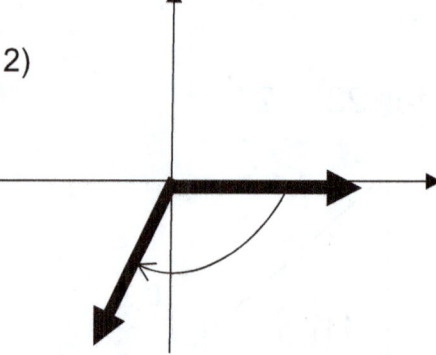

3)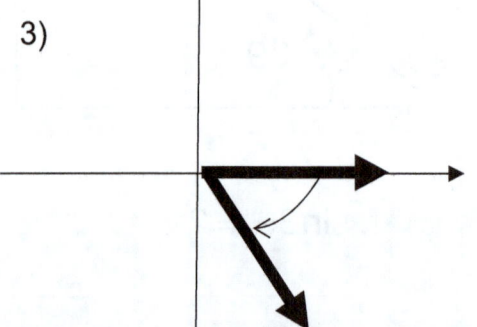

4)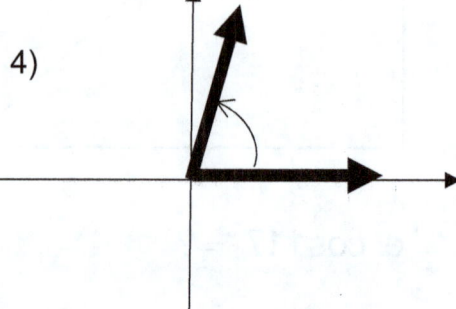

MathePathics

2- Jack runs around a circular pool. After 10 minutes he gets tired and stops. When he stops, he is in position of $\frac{2\pi}{3}$ pool.

Sketch his position on the pool.

3- Sketch the below angles in standard position.

a. $45°$ b. $120°$ c. $-30°$

4- Which of the following picture shows $-\frac{\pi}{6}$?

1)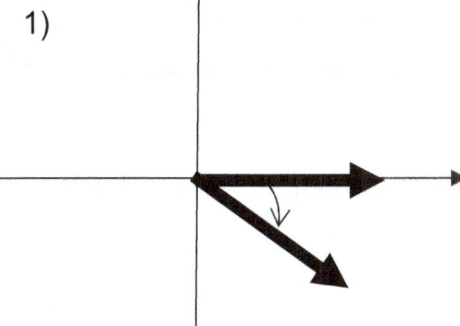

2)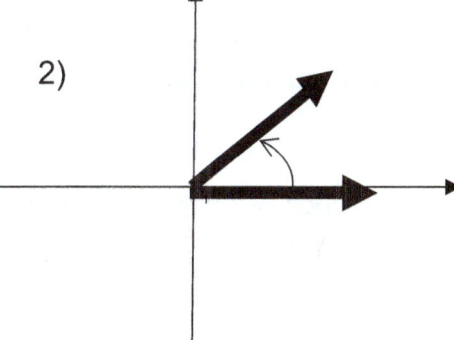

3)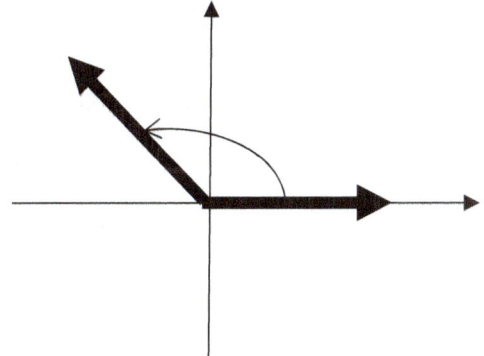

4)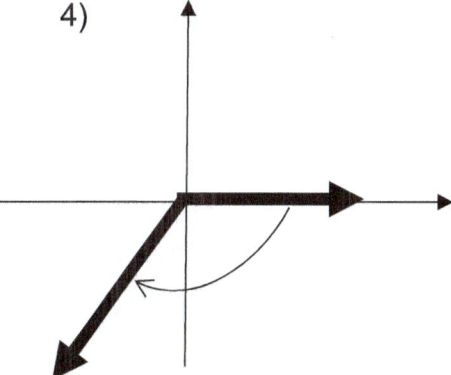

Finding Co-terminal Angles and Reference Angles

If two angles in standard position have the same terminal side, they are called co-terminal angles.

The reference angle is the **acute angle** (the smallest angle) formed by the terminal side of the given angle and the *x*-axis. Reference angles may appear in all four quadrants.

A reference angle is always positive, and it is always less than 90°.

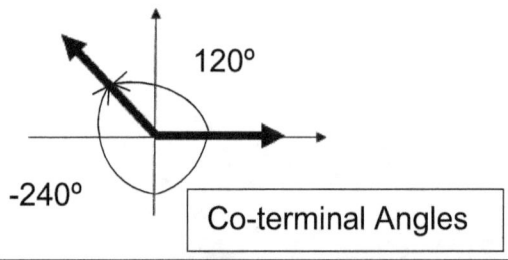

Co-terminal Angles

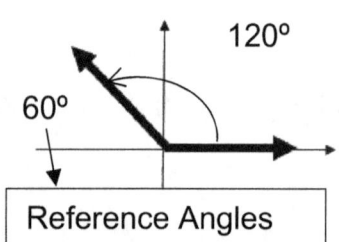

Reference Angles

1- Find the reference of below angles and find the quadrant which the terminal sides lay.

a. 600°

b. −200°

c. 780°

d. −202°

e. 235°

f. −306°

g. 1101°

h. −510°

i. −460°

2- Find two co-terminal following angles. (One positive and one negative)

a. 128°

b. 320°

c. 150°

d. 47°

e. 32°

f. 201°

g. 1101°

h. −510°

i. −460°

3- Which picture shows negative co-terminal angles of 215° ?

1)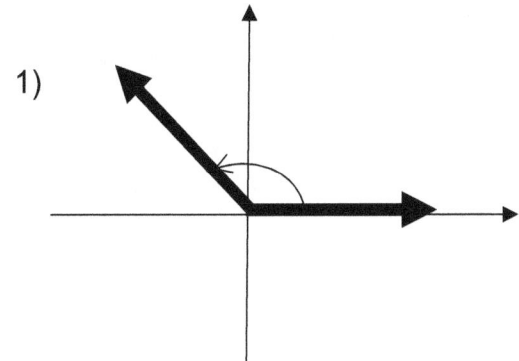

2)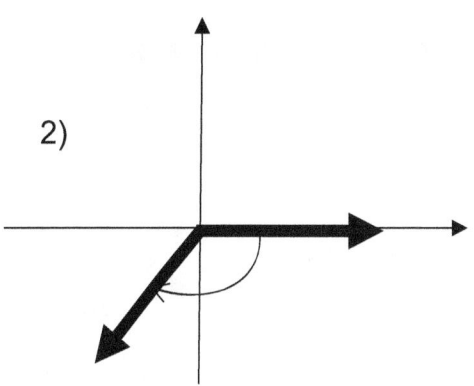

3)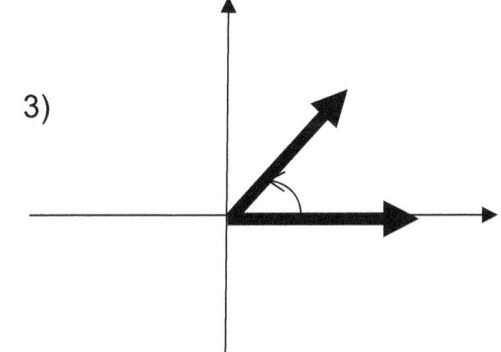

4)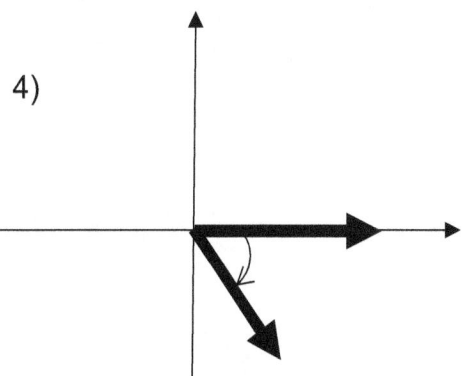

Writing Each Measure in Radians

The radian measure of an angle drawn in standard position in the plane is equal to the length of arc on the unit circle subtended by that angle.

Radians $\times \dfrac{180}{\pi}$ → Degrees

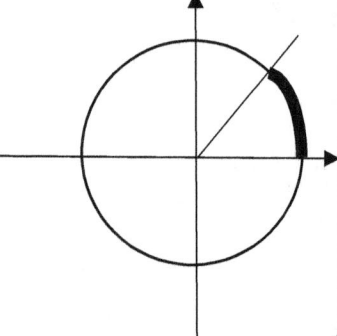

1- Convert each radian measures into degree.

a. $\dfrac{5\pi}{7}$　　　　　b. $\dfrac{2\pi}{9}$　　　　　c. $\dfrac{3\pi}{6}$

d. $\dfrac{4\pi}{5}$　　　　　e. $\dfrac{7\pi}{8}$　　　　　f. $\dfrac{12\pi}{2}$

g. $\dfrac{3\pi}{8}$　　　　　h. $\dfrac{9\pi}{8}$　　　　　i. $\dfrac{4\pi}{5}$

Writing Each Measure in Degrees

A degree is a measurement of a plane angle, a full rotation is 360 degrees.

The degree symbol is (°).

Convert degree to radians

Degrees $\times \dfrac{\pi}{180}$ ⟶ Radians

1- Convert each degree measure into radian.

a. 450°

b. 27°

c. 98°

d. 317°

e. 900°

f. 210°

g. 801°

h. 641°

i. 1010°

Evaluating Each Trigonometric Function

How to evaluate trigonometric functions using reference angles?

1. Find the reference angle of the given angle.

2. Rewrite the original trigonometric function with the reference angle.

3. Affix the appropriate sign to the trigonometric function (+ or -), depending which quadrant the angle terminates in.

4. Evaluate the trigonometric function

1- Find the exact value of each trigonometric function.

a. $\cos 325°$

b. $\sin 210°$

c. $\tan 600°$

d. $\sin 850°$

e. $\cos 1150°$

f. $\tan 690°$

g. $\cos \dfrac{6\pi}{7}$

h. $\sin \dfrac{5\pi}{6}$

i. $\tan \dfrac{3\pi}{4}$

j. $\cos\dfrac{5\pi}{4}$ k. $\sin\dfrac{7\pi}{6}$ l. $\tan\dfrac{2\pi}{3}$

2- Tim and Brown found exact value of $\cos 570°$. Who found the correct answer?

Tim's soultion

$\cos 570° = \cos(500 + 70)$ $\cos 500° = \cos(500 - 360)$

$\cos(500 - 360) = \cos 140$ $\cos 140° = \cos(180 - 140)$

$\cos(180 - 140) = \cos 40 = 0.76$

Brown's soultion

Finding reference angle

$570 - 360 = 210$ 210 is in second quadrant so cos is negative.

$210 - 180 = 30$ $210 - 180 = 30$ Reference angle: $30°$

$\cos 570° = -\cos 30° = -0.8$

Missing Sides and Angles of a Right Triangle

A right-angled triangle is a triangle which has a right angle (90°).

It's possible that we find an unknown side in a right-angled triangle when we know:

- One length and one angle.
- Two lengths.

We can find an unknown angle in a right-angled triangle, as long as we know the lengths of two of its sides.

1- Tim wants to climb a wall. He puts a 4-meter ladder on the ground.

The distance between the ladder and the wall is 2 meters.

Find the angle between the ladder and the ground.

2- A triangle has a 2 cm height and a $\sqrt{2}$ cm base.

What is the angle between the height and the hypotenuse?

MathePathics

3- Find the size of angle x in the following right-angle triangles.

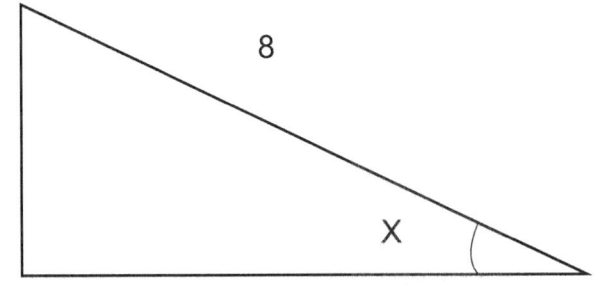

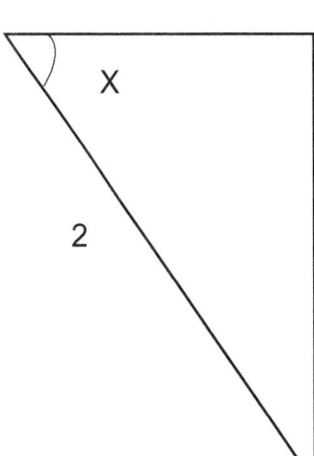

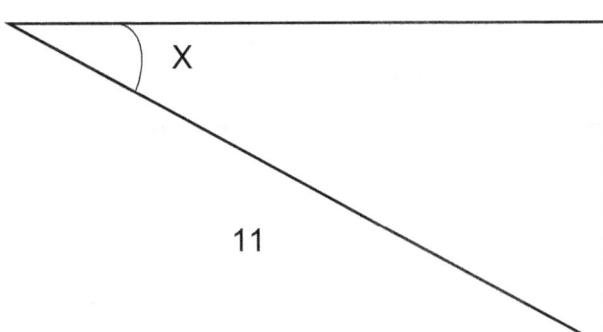

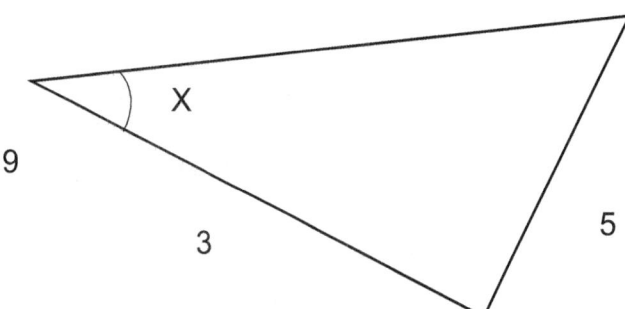

4- Max wants to make a triangle with his pens, first he puts a 20 cm red pen.
Then he puts a 17 cm blue pen, finally he puts a brown.
What is the angle between the red pen and the brown pen?

Arc Length and Sector Area

There are two arcs in a circle.

Minor Arc

It is an arc smaller than a semicircle. A central angle which is subtended by a minor arc that has a measure less than $180°$.

Major Arc

It is an arc larger than a semicircle. A central angle which is subtended by a major arc that has a measure larger than $180°$.

Arc Length: $r\theta$

Sector Area: $\frac{1}{2}r^2\theta$

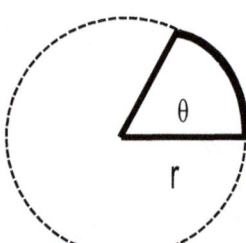

1- Circulate the length of the arc AB in the below circles.

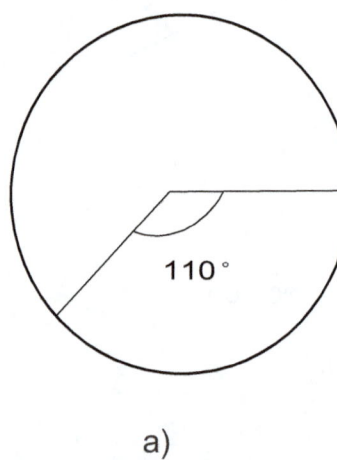

a)

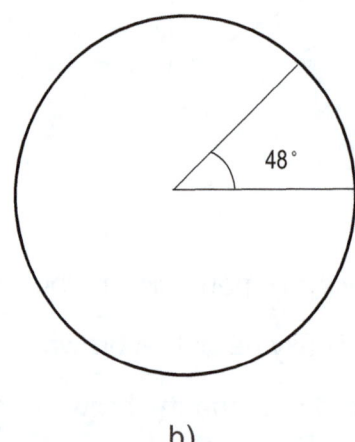

b)

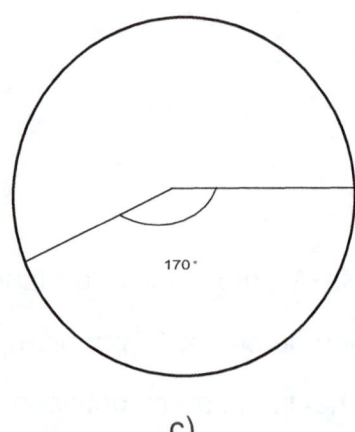

c)

2- A swimming pool that has a semicircle shape with 65 cm diameter.

What is the area of the swimming pool?

3- Circulate the area of the sector POQ.

a)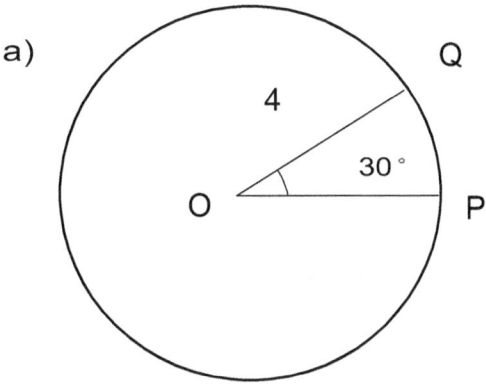

b)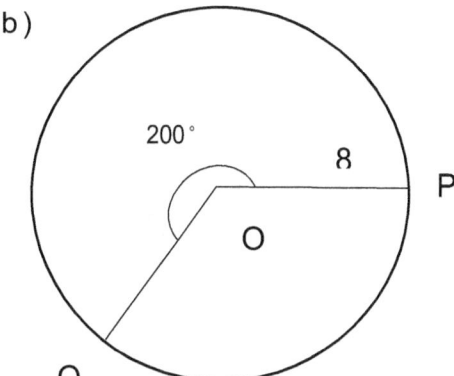

c)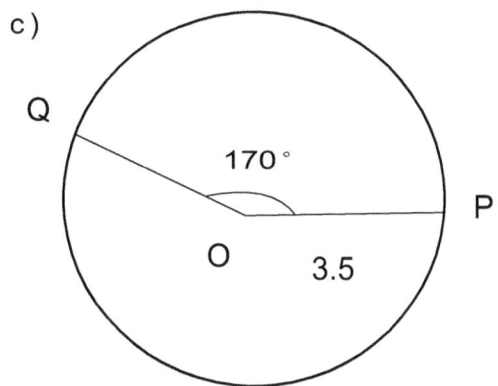

d)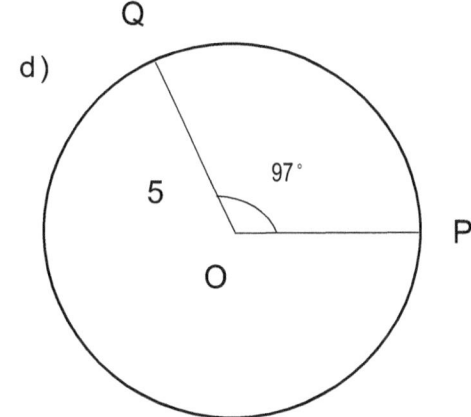

Answers of Worksheets – Chapter 20

Trig ratios of General Angles

1.

a. $\cos\dfrac{2\pi}{3} = \cos(\pi - \dfrac{\pi}{3}) = -\cos\dfrac{\pi}{3} = -\dfrac{1}{2}$

b. $\tan\dfrac{3\pi}{4} = \tan(\pi - \dfrac{\pi}{4}) = \tan(-\dfrac{\pi}{4}) = -\tan\dfrac{\pi}{4} = -\dfrac{\sqrt{2}}{2}$

c. $\sin\dfrac{5\pi}{6} = \sin(\pi - \dfrac{\pi}{6}) = \sin(\dfrac{\pi}{6}) = \dfrac{1}{2}$

d. $\sin(-\dfrac{\pi}{4}) = -\sin\dfrac{\pi}{4} = -\dfrac{\sqrt{2}}{2}$

e. $\cos(3\pi) = \cos(\pi + 2\pi) = \cos\pi = -1$

f. $\tan(4\pi) = \tan(2\pi + 2\pi) = \tan 2\pi = 1$

g. $\cos(3\pi) + \sin(-\dfrac{\pi}{4}) = -1 - \dfrac{\sqrt{2}}{2}$

h. $\tan\dfrac{3\pi}{4} - \tan(4\pi) = -\dfrac{\sqrt{2}}{2} - 1$

i. $\cos\dfrac{\pi}{4} + \sin\dfrac{\pi}{4} = \dfrac{\sqrt{2}}{2} + \dfrac{\sqrt{2}}{2} = \sqrt{2}$

2.

a. $\tan 203° = \dfrac{0.3}{0.7} = 0.42$

b. $\cos 60° = \dfrac{5}{10} = \dfrac{1}{2}$

c. $\tan 23° = \dfrac{0.3}{0.7} = 0.42$

d. $\sin 138° = \dfrac{0.6}{0.9} = 0.66$

e. $\cos 117° = \dfrac{0.41}{0.9} = 0.45$

f. $\sin 39° = \dfrac{0.51}{0.82} = 0.62$

MathePathics

Sketch Each Angle in Standard Position

1.

80 < 90 → 4

2.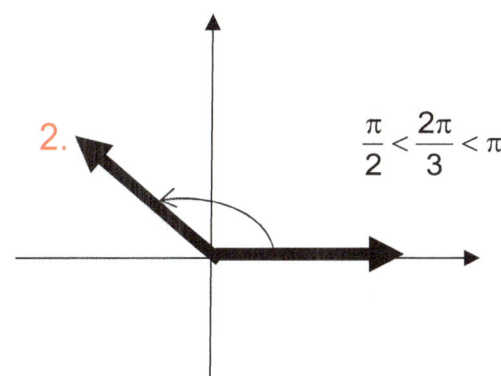

$\frac{\pi}{2} < \frac{2\pi}{3} < \pi$

3.

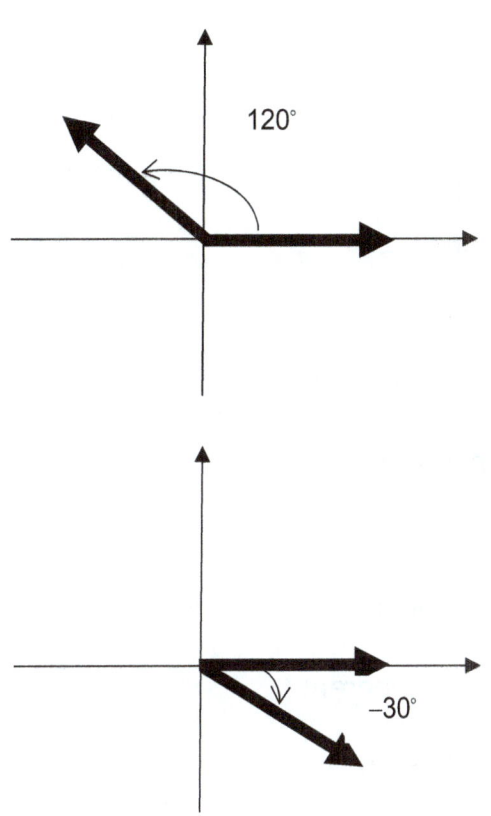

4.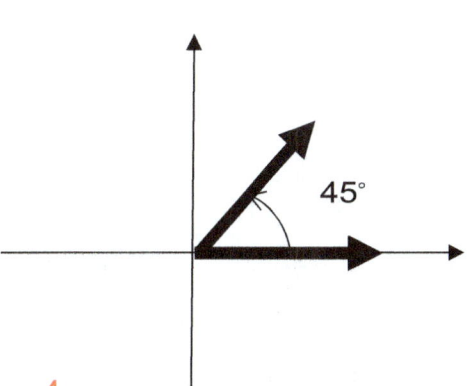

$\frac{\pi}{6} < \frac{\pi}{2} \rightarrow -\frac{\pi}{6} > -\frac{\pi}{2} \quad \rightarrow 1$

316

Finding Co-terminal Angles and Reference Angles

1.

a. $600° - 360° = 60°$ — Lies in the first quadrant.

b. $-200° + 360° = 160°$ — Lies in the second quadrant.
$180° - 160° = 20°$ — Reference angle= $20°$

c. $780° - 360° = 420°$ — Lies in the first quadrant.
$420° - 360° = 60°$ — Reference angle= $60°$

d. $-202° + 360° = 158°$ — Lies in the second quadrant.
$180° - 158° = 22°$ — Reference angle= $22°$

e. $360° - 235° = 135°$ — Lies in the second quadrant.
$180° - 135° = 45°$ — Reference angle= $45°$

f. $-306° + 360° = 54°$ — Lies in the first quadrant.

h. $-510° + 360° = 150°$ — Lies in the second quadrant.
$180° - 150° = 30°$ — Reference angle= $30°$

i. $-460° + 360° = -100°$ — Lies in the third quadrant.
$180° - 100° = 80°$ — Reference angle= $80°$

2.

a. $128° - 360° = -232°$ $128° + 360° = 488°$

b. $320° - 360° = -40°$ $320° + 360° = 980°$

c. $150° - 360° = -210°$ $150° + 360° = 510°$

d. $47° - 360° = 313°$ $47° + 360° = 407°$

e. $32° - 360° = -328°$ $32° + 360° = 392°$

f. $201° - 360° = -150°$ $201° + 360° = 561°$

g. $300° - 360° = -60°$ $300° + 360° = 960$

h. $-710° - 360° = -1070°$ $-710° + 360° = -350°$

i. $-610° - 360° = -970°$ $-610° + 360° = -250°$

3.

2

Writing Each Measure in Radians

1.

a. $\dfrac{5\pi}{7} \times \dfrac{180}{\pi} = 128.5°$ b. $\dfrac{2\pi}{9} \times \dfrac{180}{\pi} = 40°$

c. $\dfrac{3\pi}{6} \times \dfrac{180}{\pi} = 90°$ d. $\dfrac{4\pi}{5} \times \dfrac{180}{\pi} = 144°$

e. $\dfrac{7\pi}{8} \times \dfrac{180}{\pi} = 157.5°$ f. $\dfrac{12\pi}{2} \times \dfrac{180}{\pi} = 1080°$

g. $\dfrac{3\pi}{8} \times \dfrac{180}{\pi} = 67.5°$

h. $\dfrac{9\pi}{8} \times \dfrac{180}{\pi} = 202.5°$

i. $\dfrac{4\pi}{5} \times \dfrac{180}{\pi} = 194°$

Writing Each Measure in Degrees

1.

a. $450° \times \dfrac{\pi}{180} = 7.85$

b. $27° \times \dfrac{\pi}{180} = 0.41$

c. $98° \times \dfrac{\pi}{180} = 1.70$

d. $317° \times \dfrac{\pi}{180} = 5.25$

e. $900° \times \dfrac{\pi}{180} = 15.7$

f. $210° \times \dfrac{\pi}{180} = 3.66$

g. $801° \times \dfrac{\pi}{180} = 13.97$

h. $641° \times \dfrac{\pi}{180} = 15.7$

i. $1010° \times \dfrac{\pi}{180} = 17.61$

Evaluating Each Trigonometric Function

1.

a. $360 - 325 = 35$ first quadrant $(+) \to \cos 35° = +0.81$

b. second quadrant $(-) \to 210 - 180 = 30 \to \sin 30° = -0.5$

c. $600 - 360 = 240$ second quadrant $(+) \to 240 - 180 = 60 \to \tan 60° = +1.73$

d. $850 - 360 = 490$ $490 - 360 = 130$ second quadrant $(+)$
$180 - 130 = 50 \to \sin 50 = +0.7$

e. $1150 - 360 = 790$ $790 - 360 = 430$ $430 - 360 = 70$

first quadrant$(+) \rightarrow \cos 70 = +0.34$

f. $690 - 360 = 330$ fourth quadrant$(-)$ $360 - 330 = 30 \rightarrow \tan 30° = -0.57$

g. $\cos\dfrac{6\pi}{7} = \cos(\pi - \dfrac{\pi}{7}) = -\cos\dfrac{\pi}{7} = -0.4$ h. $\sin\dfrac{5\pi}{6} = \sin(\pi - \dfrac{\pi}{6}) = +\sin\dfrac{\pi}{6} = 0.52$

i. $\tan\dfrac{3\pi}{4} = \tan(\pi + \dfrac{\pi}{4}) = +\tan\dfrac{\pi}{4} = 0.01$ j. $\cos\dfrac{5\pi}{4} = \cos(\pi + \dfrac{\pi}{4}) = -\cos\dfrac{\pi}{4} = -0.7$

k. $\sin\dfrac{7\pi}{6} = \sin(\pi + \dfrac{\pi}{6}) = -\sin\dfrac{\pi}{6}$ l. $\tan\dfrac{2\pi}{3} = \tan(\pi - \dfrac{\pi}{3}) = -\tan\dfrac{\pi}{3} = -0.01$

2.

Brown

Missing Sides and Angles a Right Tringle

1.
$\cos\theta = \dfrac{1}{2} \rightarrow \theta = 60°$

2.
$\tan\theta = \dfrac{\sqrt{2}}{2} \rightarrow \theta = 45°$

3.

A) $\tan X = \dfrac{8}{5} \rightarrow X = 27.9°$ B) $\cos X = \dfrac{\sqrt{3}}{2} \rightarrow X = 30°$

C) $\sin X = \dfrac{9}{11} \rightarrow X = 54.9°$ D) $\tan X = \dfrac{5}{3} \rightarrow X = 29°$

4.

$\sin\theta = \dfrac{17}{20} \rightarrow \dfrac{17 \div 10}{20 \div 10} = \dfrac{1.7}{2}$ $(1.7 = \sqrt{3}) \rightarrow \sin\theta = \dfrac{\sqrt{3}}{2} \rightarrow \theta = 60°$

MathePathics

Arc Length and Sector Area

1.

a. $AB = (\theta \times \dfrac{\pi}{180}) \times r = (110 \times \dfrac{3.14}{180}) \times 5 = 9.5\,cm$

b. $AB = (\theta \times \dfrac{\pi}{180}) \times r = (48 \times \dfrac{3.14}{180}) \times 3 = 2.5\,cm$

c. $AB = (\theta \times \dfrac{\pi}{180}) \times r = (170 \times \dfrac{3.14}{180}) \times 7 = 20.75\,cm$

2.

$d = 65 \rightarrow r = \dfrac{d}{2} = \dfrac{65}{2} = 32.5\,cm$

Area of the pool : $A = \pi r^2 \rightarrow A = 3.14 \times (32.5)^2 = 3316$

Area of the semicircular pool $= 3316 \div 2 = 1658\,cm^2$

3.

a) $A = \dfrac{1}{2}r^2\theta = \dfrac{1}{2}(4)^2(30) = 240\,cm^2$

b) $A = \dfrac{1}{2}r^2\theta = \dfrac{1}{2}(8)^2(200) = 6400\,cm^2$

c) $A = \dfrac{1}{2}r^2\theta = \dfrac{1}{2}(3.5)^2(170) = 1041\,cm^2$

d) $A = \dfrac{1}{2}r^2\theta = \dfrac{1}{2}(5)^2(97) = 1212.5\,cm^2$

Extra Note for Chapter 20:

Chapter 21: Sequences and Series

Arithmetic Sequences

Geometric Sequences

Comparing Arithmetic and Geometric sequences

Finite Geometric Series

Infinite Geometric Series

Answers of worksheets – Chapter 21

Arithmetic Sequences

An **arithmetic sequence** is a list of numbers that has a **definite pattern**.

An arithmetic sequence is made by adding and subtracting each sequence by the previous one.

We can write an Arithmetic Sequence as a rule:

$$X_n = a + d(n-1)$$

a ⟶ First term

d ⟶ Difference between terms

1- What is the sixth term of the arithmetic sequence in $3, 7, 11, \ldots$?

2- Two terms of an arithmetic sequence are given. Find d.

$X_3 = 6$, $X_4 = 8$

3- According to following arithmetic sequence, find the rule that there is between items.

$5, 9, 13, 17, \ldots$

4- The fifth term of arithmetic sequence is 25 and difference between terms is 5.
What is the first term of sequence?

5- What is the sum of twentieth term to thirtieth term of below sequence?
1, 4, 7, ...

6- The rule between terms of an arithmetic sequence is $X_n = 2n + 1$.
Write terms of sequence.

Geometric Sequences

In a Geometric Sequence each term is found by multiplying the previous term by a constant.

We can write a Geometric Sequence as a rule:

$$X_n = a\, r^{(n-1)}$$

a ⟶ First term

r ⟶ The factor between the terms

📎 But be careful, **r** should not be 0. When r = 0, we get the below sequence which is not geometric. {a,0,0,...}

1- What is eighth term of the geometric sequence in 6,12,24,...?

2- What is the factor between terms of the geometric sequence below?

3,9,27,...

3- The eleventh term of a geometric sequence is 209715 and the factor between terms is 4.

Find the first term.

4- Adam found the rule between terms of the geometric sequence below.

But he is not sure if it's correct.

Check his solution.

$$\frac{1}{2}, \frac{1}{4}, \frac{1}{8}, \ldots$$

$a = \frac{1}{2}$ $\qquad$ $\frac{1}{2} \xrightarrow{\times \frac{1}{2}} \frac{1}{4} \xrightarrow{\times \frac{1}{2}} \frac{1}{8} \rightarrow$ $\qquad$ $r = \frac{1}{2}$

$X_n = a r^{n-1} \rightarrow X_n = \frac{1}{2}(\frac{1}{2})^{n-1}$

5- The rule of a geometric sequence is $X_n = (1 + \frac{1}{2})^n$

Write terms of sequence.

6- What is the sum of fifth term with sixth term of geometric sequence in 11 , 22 , 88 ,...

Comparing Arithmetic and Geometric Sequences

Arithmetic sequence of each term is found by subtracting the previous term.

1, 3, 5, ... $1 \xleftarrow{-2} 3 \xleftarrow{-2} 5$

In a Geometric Sequence each term is found by multiplying the previous term.

2, 4, 8, ... $2 \xrightarrow{\times 2} 4 \xrightarrow{\times 2} 8$

1- Which of the following sequence is arithmetic and which of them geometric?

a) 10, 20, 30, 40, ...

b) 2, 4, 8, 16, ...

c) −3, 6, −12, ...

d) −12, −15, −18, ...

2- For each rule of sequence, state if it is arithmetic or geometric.

a) $X_n = 4n - 123$

b) $X_n = 2(3)^{5n+1}$

c) $X_n = -12 + 5n$

d) $X_n = 5(\frac{1}{2})^{2n-1}$

Finite Geometric Series

A finite geometric series describes a set which does not have an infinite number of elements. That is a set which can have its elements counted using natural numbers.

The formula for the sum of a finite geometric series:

$$S_n = \frac{a(1-r^n)}{1-r} \quad r \neq 1 \qquad a\text{:First term} \qquad r\text{:Ratio}$$

1- Add up the first 12 terms of the following geometric sequence.

$\frac{1}{3}, \frac{1}{5}, \frac{1}{75}, ...$

2- According to the following information that is for a geometric sequence, find first term.

$S_4 = 343 \quad r = 7$

3- Find the sum of series below.

5, 25, 125 , ...

Infinite Geometric Series

An infinite geometric series is a set which is not finite. Formally, a set is infinite if it can be placed in one-to-one correspondence with a proper subset of itself.

The formula for the sum of an infinite geometric series.

$n \to \infty \quad r^n \to 0$

$$S_\infty = \frac{a}{1-r} \quad -1 < r < 1$$

1- Find the value of the following infinite geometric series.

$6, 2, \dfrac{2}{3}, \dfrac{2}{9}, ...$

2- The following series is an infinite geometric series. What is its ratio?

$5, -\dfrac{5}{3}, \dfrac{5}{27}, ...$

3- Jack and Max wrote the sum of the following infinite geometric series. Which of them wrote it correctly?

$16 + 4 + 1 + ...$

Jack's soultion

$a = 16 \quad r = \dfrac{1}{4} \quad (r<1) \quad \rightarrow S_\infty = \dfrac{a}{1-r} = \dfrac{1}{1-\dfrac{1}{4}} = \dfrac{1}{\dfrac{3}{4}} = \dfrac{4}{3} \quad \rightarrow S_\infty = \dfrac{4}{3}$

Max's soultion

$a = 16 \quad r = \dfrac{1}{2} \quad (r<1) \quad \rightarrow S_\infty = \dfrac{a}{1-r} = \dfrac{1}{1-\dfrac{1}{2}} = \dfrac{1}{\dfrac{1}{2}} = \dfrac{2}{1} \quad \rightarrow S_\infty = 2$

4- What is the sum of the infinite geometric series with a first term of 6 and a ratio of $\frac{2}{3}$?

5- The sum of an infinite geometric series is -25 and the ratio is $\frac{2}{5}$.

What is the first term?

Answers of worksheets – Chapter 21

Arithmetic Sequences

1.

$a = 3$, $d = 4$, $X_n = a + d(n-1) \to X_n = 3 + 4(n-1)$

$X_n = 4n - 1 \to X_6 = 4(6) - 1 = 24 - 1 = 23$

2.

$d = X_4 - X_3 = 8 - 6 = 2$

3.

$a = 5$, $d = 4$, $X_n = a + d(n-1) \to X_n = 5 + 4(n-1)$ $X_n = 4n + 1$

4.

$X_5 = 25$, $d = 5$, $X_n = a + d(n-1) \to X_5 = a + 5(5-1) = 25$

$a + 20 = 25 \to a = 25 - 20 = 5$

5.

$a = 1$, $d = 3$, $X_n = a + d(n-1) \to X_n = 1 + 3(n-1)$

$X_n = 3n - 2$

$X_{20} = 3(20) - 2 = 60 - 2 = 58$ $X_{30} = 3(30) - 2 = 90 - 2 = 88$

$X_{20} + X_{30} = 58 + 88 = 146$

6.

$X_1 = 2(1) + 1 = 3$ $X_2 = 2(2) + 1 = 5$ $X_3 = 2(3) + 1 = 7$ 3, 5, 7,...

Geometric Sequences

1.

$X_n = a\,r^{n-1} \to X_n = 6(2)^{n-1} \to X_8 = 6(2)^{8-1} = 6(2)^7 = 768$

2.

$$3 \xrightarrow{\times 3} 9 \xrightarrow{\times 3} 27 \quad r = 3$$

3.

$$X_n = a\, r^{n-1}, \quad r = 4, \quad X_{11} = a\, 4^{(11-1)} = 209715.5 \rightarrow a = \frac{209715.5}{4^{10}} = 0.2$$

4.

$$a = \frac{1}{2} \qquad \frac{1}{2} \xrightarrow{\times \frac{1}{2}} \frac{1}{4} \xrightarrow{\times \frac{1}{2}} \frac{1}{8} \rightarrow r = \frac{1}{2}$$

$$X_n = a\, r^{n-1} \rightarrow X_n = \frac{1}{2}\left(\frac{1}{2}\right)^{n-1}$$

5.

$$X_n = \left(1+\frac{1}{2}\right)^n \quad X_1 = \left(1+\frac{1}{2}\right) = \frac{3}{2} \qquad X_2 = \left(1+\frac{1}{2}\right)^2 = \frac{9}{4} \qquad X_3 = \left(1+\frac{1}{2}\right)^3 = \frac{27}{8}$$

$$\frac{3}{2}, \frac{9}{4}, \frac{27}{8}, \ldots$$

6.

$$a = 11, \quad r = 2 \quad X_n = a\, r^{n-1} \rightarrow X_n = 11\,(2)^{n-1}$$

$$X_{15} = 11\,(2)^{15-1} = 11(2)^{14} \qquad X_{16} = 11\,(2)^{16-1} = 11(2)^{15}$$

$$X_{15} + X_{16} = 11(2)^{14} + 11(2)^{15} = 11(2^{14} + 2^{15})$$

Comparing Arithmetic and Geometric Sequences

1.

a) Arithmetic   b) Geometric   c) Geometric

d) Arithmetic

MathePathics

2.

a) Arithmetic   b) Geometric   c) Geometric

d) Arithmetic

Finite Geometric Series

1.

$$a = \frac{1}{3} \quad r = \frac{1}{5} \quad n = 12$$

$$S_n = \frac{a(1-r^n)}{1-r} \rightarrow S_{12} = \frac{\frac{1}{3}\left(1-\frac{1}{5}^{12}\right)}{1-\frac{1}{5}} = \frac{0.3(1-0.2^{12})}{0.8} = 0.21$$

2.

$$S_n = \frac{a(1-r^n)}{1-r} \rightarrow S_4 = \frac{a(1-7^4)}{1-7} = 343 \rightarrow -2400a = -2058$$

$$a = 0.85 \approx 1$$

3.

$$a = 5 \quad r = 5 \quad S_n = \frac{a(1-r^n)}{1-r} \rightarrow S_n = \frac{5(1-5^n)}{1-5} = \frac{5}{4}(1-5^n)$$

Infinite Geometric Series

1.

$$a = 6 \quad r = \frac{1}{3} \quad (r<1) \rightarrow S_\infty = \frac{a}{1-r} \qquad S_\infty = \frac{6}{1-\frac{1}{3}} = \frac{6}{\frac{2}{3}} = 9$$

2.

$$5, -\frac{5}{3}, \frac{5}{27}, \ldots \quad 5 \xrightarrow{\times(-\frac{1}{3})} -\frac{5}{3} \xrightarrow{\times(-\frac{1}{3})} \frac{5}{27} \Rightarrow r = -\frac{1}{3}$$

3.

Jack's solution is correct.

4.

$a = 6 \quad r = \dfrac{2}{3} \quad (r<1) \quad \rightarrow \quad S_\infty = \dfrac{a}{1-r} = \dfrac{6}{1-\dfrac{2}{3}} = \dfrac{6}{\dfrac{1}{3}} = 18 \quad \rightarrow \quad S_\infty = 18$

5.

$S_\infty = -25 \;,\; r = \dfrac{2}{5} \quad (r<1) \quad \rightarrow \quad S_\infty = \dfrac{a}{1-r} \quad \rightarrow \quad -25 = \dfrac{a}{1-\dfrac{2}{5}} \quad \rightarrow \quad a = -15$

Extra Note for Chapter 21:

MathePathics

Samples:

Review & Check

Sample Number One

Sample Number Two

Sample Number Three

Sample Number Four

1

If -4z – 9 = 14z, what is the value of 3z – 2?

1. $\frac{7}{2}$
2. $\frac{2}{7}$
3. $-\frac{2}{7}$
4. $-\frac{7}{2}$

2

The variables x and y are directly proportional and f(4) = 5. What is the value of f(12)?

A. 11
B. 12
C. 13
D. 15

3

In below x y-plane, if point B (2, 9), what is the equation of AB?

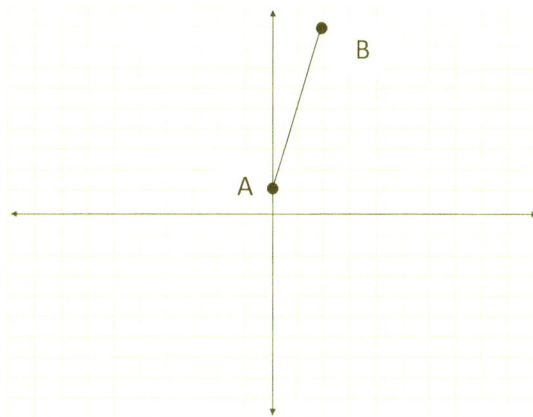

1. 4x – 1
2. -4x – 1
3. 4x + 1
4. -4x + 1

4

There are 2x – 5 flowers planted in each row of a rectangular garden. If there are a total of 16x – 13 flowers planted in the garden, how many rows of flowers are there in the garden?

1. 14x + 18
2. 14x – 8
3. -14x +1
4. -8x +14

5

Max with 13 of his friends go to a restaurant for dinner and order salad and hamburger. The hamburger cost $8.5 each and the salad $3.10. If the total cost of all 14 dinners is $95.80, how many salads are ordered?

1. 4
2. 5
3. 3
4. 11

6

Which of the following equation has both 2 and -5 as solutions?

1. $-x^2 - 3x - 15$
2. $x^2 - 3x - 15$
3. $x^2 + 3x - 15$
4. $x^2 + 3x + 15$

7

In the x y- plane, the y- intercept of the equation y = 4 (x − 5) (x + 1) is:

1. 10
2. -10
3. 20
4. -20

8

The equation $x^2 - 16$ is equal to:

1. $4x(x - 4)$
2. $(x - 16)(x + 16)$
3. $(x - 4)(x + 4)$
4. $4x(x - 4)^2$

9

What is the answer of $(2x^2y + 6x^2y)^3$?

1. $128x^6y^2$
2. $128x^6y$
3. $18x^6y^2$
4. $8x^6y^2$

10

What is the value of x in the below equation?

$$\sqrt{2+x} = 5\sqrt{x}$$

1. 0.2
2. 0.3
3. 0.4
4. 0.5

11

If $\dfrac{x-2}{x+1} = 3$, then $2x+1$ is:

1. 4
2. $-\dfrac{5}{2}$
3. -4
4. 6

12

A ball was felt down from a wall that has 15 meters height. The amount of ball's height each time is calculated from the equation $h(t) = 20 + 15t^2 - 35t$.

When did the ball hit the ground?

1. 2
2. 3
3. 4
4. 1

13

There is a circular field next to the Sara's house. With 4.5 m radius. She wants to plant tree around the field. How many meters of the field can she plant?

1. 26.28 m
2. 28.26 m
3. 45.21 m
4. 21.36 m

14

Number	Grade
1	X
2	82
3	76
4	53
5	93

The table above shows the grades of 5 students. If the median of grades is 76, which of the following items could NOT be the grade for student number 1?

1. 45
2. 37
3. 81
4. 70

15

There are 30 students that 14 of them are girls and 5 girls have ball. 12 boys don't have ball. If a student is chosen at random, what is the probability that the student <u>doesn't have</u> a colorful ball?

1. $\dfrac{23}{30}$

2. $\dfrac{11}{30}$

3. $\dfrac{12}{30}$

4. $\dfrac{1}{23}$

16

What is answer of 0.58 + 42.924 + 1.028 + 0.00081?

1. 20.45678
2. 789.341
3. 44.53281
4. 985.324

17

$0.57 \div 3 =$

1. 0.019
2. 1
3. 0.19
4. 1.9

18

$2(18 \div 6) \times 4(40 \div 8) =$

1. 23
2. 24
3. 25
4. 26

19

$1.21 \div 2.42 =$

1. 0.005
2. 0.5
3. 5.1
4. 5.01

20

What is the answer of (-851) + (432) – (201)?

1. -620
2. -419
3. 620
4. 419

21

39% equals

1. 0.00039
2. 0.0039
3. 0.039
4. 0.39

22

What kind of sequence is this?

5, 10, 15, 20, 25, 30

1. Descending geometric sequence
2. Ascending geometric sequence
3. Descending arithmetic sequence
4. Ascending arithmetic sequence

23

Which of the following items is a whole number followed by its square?

1. 4.8
2. 9.81
3. 3.6
4. 5.15

24

There are 15 melons less than kiwis in the basket of 45 melons and kiwis.

How many melons are there in the basket?

1. 30
2. 15
3. 45
4. 12

25

Which of the following items correctly identifies 4 consecutive even integers where the sum of the middle two integers is equal to 32?

1. 4, 6, 8, 10
2. 8, 10, 14, 18
3. 10, 14, 18, 22
4. 18, 20, 22, 24

26

What is before the number 192?

3, 12, ..., 192

1. 36
2. 191
3. 24
4. 48

27

Which of the following numbers could be described in the following way: an integer that is positive.

1. 5.2
2. -3
3. 10
4. 0

28

What is the correct answer for the blank?

0.5, 3.5, 6.5, ...

1. 12
2. 11.5
3. 7.5
4. 9.5

29

Which of the following fractions is equivalent to $\frac{5}{6}$?

1. $\frac{4}{12}$
2. $\frac{20}{24}$
3. $\frac{10}{4}$
4. $\frac{2}{36}$

30

What is the answer of 0.45 + 0.78?

1. $\frac{4}{5}$
2. $\frac{2}{3}$
3. $\frac{3}{2}$
4. $\frac{5}{4}$

31

Find the square of $\frac{4}{10}$.

1. $\frac{16}{100}$
2. $\frac{8}{20}$
3. $\frac{10}{16}$
4. $\frac{20}{16}$

32

There are 100 centimeters in one meter. How many centimeters are there in 54 meters?

1. 4500
2. 0.54
3. 5400
4. 0.45

33

Which of the following fractions is equivalent to %0.2?

1. $\frac{1}{5}$
2. $\frac{2}{500}$
3. $\frac{1}{500}$
4. $\frac{5}{500}$

34

Which of the following numbers is a factor of 42?

1. 84
2. 43
3. 5
4. 6

35

If the average person drinks five 5 oz glasses of water per day, 2 people who drink 42.5 oz of water after noon exercise have consumed what fraction of daily average?

1. 2.4

2. 5.4

3. 6.3

4. 3.4

Answer Sheet of Test #1

1.

4

$-4z - 9 = 14z \longrightarrow -4z - 14z = 9$

$\longrightarrow -18z = 9 \longrightarrow z = -\dfrac{1}{2}$

$3z - 2 \xrightarrow{z=-\frac{1}{2}} 3\left(-\dfrac{1}{2}\right) - 2$

$= -\dfrac{3}{2} - 2 = \dfrac{-3-4}{2} = -\dfrac{7}{2}$

2.

4.

$f(4) = 5$

$4 \times 3 = 12, \quad 5 \times 3 = 15$

$\longrightarrow f(12) = 15$

3.

3.

$A(0,1) \quad B(2,9)$

$m = \dfrac{9-1}{2-0} = \dfrac{8}{2} = 4$

$y - 1 = 4(x - 0)$

$y = 4x + 1$

4.

2.

$16x - 13 - (2x - 5) =$

$16x - 13 - 2x + 5 = 14x - 8$

5.

3.

Hamburger's price = $8.5 x$

Salad's price = $3.10 y$

Max + 13 friends = 14

$\begin{cases} 8.5x + 3.10y = 95.80 \\ x + y = 14 \end{cases}$

$x + y = 14 \rightarrow x = 14 - y$

$\xrightarrow{x=14-y} 8.5x + 3.10y = 95.80$

$8.5(14 - y) + 3.10y = 95.80$

$112 - 8.5y + 3.10y = 95.80$

$-5.4y = -16.2$

$y = 3$

6.

3.

$x^2 + 3x - 15 = (x - 2)(x + 5)$

$x - 2 = 0 \rightarrow x = 2$

$x + 5 = 0 \rightarrow x = -5$

7.
4.

$y = 4(x-5)(x+1) = 4x - 20(x+1) =$

$4x^2 + 4x - 20x - 20 = 4x^2 - 16x - 20$

8.
3.

$x^2 - y^2 = (x-y)(x+y)$

$\longrightarrow x^2 - 16 = (x-4)(x+4)$

9.
1.

$(2x^2y + 6x^2y)^3 = (8x^2y)^3 = 128x^6y^2$

10.
4.

$\sqrt{2+x} = 5\sqrt{x} \xrightarrow{(\,)^2} 2 + x = 25x$

$x - 25x = -2 \longrightarrow -24x = -2$

$x = \dfrac{1}{2} = 0.5$

11.
3.

$\dfrac{x-2}{x+1} = 3 \longrightarrow x - 2 = 3(x+1)$

$\longrightarrow x - 2 = 3x + 3 \longrightarrow x - 3x = 3 + 2$

$\longrightarrow -2x = 5 \longrightarrow x = -\dfrac{5}{2}$

$2x + 1 \xrightarrow{x = -\frac{5}{2}} 2\left(-\dfrac{5}{2}\right) + 1 = -5 + 1 = -4$

$2x + 1 = -4$

12.
4.

$+15t^2 - 35t + 20 = 0 \xrightarrow{\div 5} +3t^2 - 7t + 4 = 0$

$\Delta = (-7)^2 - 4(3)(4) = 49 - 48 = 1$

$t_1 = \dfrac{-(-7)+\sqrt{1}}{2(3)} = \dfrac{7+1}{6} = \dfrac{8}{6} = \dfrac{4}{3}$

$t_2 = \dfrac{-(-7)-\sqrt{1}}{2(3)} = \dfrac{7-1}{6} = \dfrac{6}{6} = 1$

MathePathics

13.
2.

$2\pi r = 2(3.14)(4.5) = 28.26 m$

14.
3.

Because median is the middle number and the number must be bigger than the median.

$45 < 76$ ×

$37 < 76$ ×

$70 < 76$ ×

$76 < 81$

15.
1.

30 students = 14girls + 16boys

5 girls have ball and 11 girls don't have ball.

4 boys have ball and 12 boys don't have ball.

Students don't have ball = 11 + 12 = 23

$\rightarrow \dfrac{23}{30}$

16.
3.

$0.58 + 42.942 + 1.028 + 0.00081 = 44.53281$

17.
3.

$\dfrac{57}{100} \div 3 = \dfrac{57}{100} \times \dfrac{1}{3} = \dfrac{19}{100} = 0.19$

18.
4.

$2(18 \div 6) \times 4(40 \div 8) =$
$2(3) + 4(5) = 6 + 20 = 26$

19.
2.

$1.21 \div 2.42 = \dfrac{121}{10} \div \dfrac{242}{10} =$

$\dfrac{121}{10} \times \dfrac{10}{242} = \dfrac{121}{242} = \dfrac{1}{2} = 0.5$

20.
1.

$-851 + 432 = -(851 - 432) = -419$

$(-419) - (201) = -(419 + 201) = -620$

348

MathePathics

21.

4.

$\dfrac{39}{100} = 0.39$

22.

4.

$5 \xrightarrow{+5} 10 \xrightarrow{+5} 15 \xrightarrow{+5} 20$

23.

2.

Area of square $= a^2 \longrightarrow 9^2 = 81$

24.

2.

melon $= x$, kiwi $= y$, $x + y = 45$

$x = y - 15 \longrightarrow y - 15 + y = 45$

$2y - 15 = 45 \longrightarrow 2y = 60$

$\longrightarrow y = 30$

$x = 30 - 15 = 15$

25.

3.

1. $6 + 8 = 14$ ×
2. $10 + 14 = 24$ ×
3. $14 + 18 = 32$

26.

4.

$3 \xrightarrow{\times 4} 12 \xrightarrow{\times 4} 48 \xrightarrow{\times 4} 192$

27.

3.

Integer: $..., -2, -1, 0, 1, 2, ...$

Positive integer: $1, 2, ...$

28.

4.

$0.5 \xrightarrow{+3} 3.5 \xrightarrow{+3} 6.5$

$\xrightarrow{+3} 9.5 \xrightarrow{+3} 12.5$

29.

2.

$\dfrac{5 \times 4}{6 \times 4} = \dfrac{20}{24}$

349

MathePathics

30.

4.

$$\frac{47}{100}+\frac{78}{100}=\frac{125}{100}=\frac{5}{4}$$

31.

1.

$$\left(\frac{4}{10}\right)^2=\frac{16}{100}=4$$

32.

3.

100 cm   1 m
  x cm   54 m

$$x=\frac{100\times 54}{1}=5400\text{ cm}$$

33.

3.

$$\frac{0.2}{100}=\frac{\frac{2}{10}}{100}=\frac{2}{10}\times\frac{1}{100}=\frac{2}{1000}=\frac{1}{500}$$

34.

4.

Factors of 42: 1, 2, 3, 6, 7, 14, 21

35.

4.

$$\frac{2\left(\frac{425}{10}\right)}{25}=3.4$$

MathePathics

1

You need $\frac{6}{5}$ cups of milk for recipe. You accidently put $\frac{2}{3}$ cup into the mixing bowl with dry ingredient. How much more milk in cups do you need to add?

1. $\frac{7}{15}$
2. $\frac{6}{15}$
3. $\frac{1}{3}$
4. $\frac{4}{5}$

2

$\frac{7}{8} - \frac{10}{4}$ equals to:

1. $\frac{8}{13}$
2. $-\frac{8}{13}$
3. $-\frac{13}{8}$
4. $-\frac{5}{13}$

3

89.3 − 42.7 =

1. 43.6
2. 44.5
3. 41.7
4. 41.8

4

Joe wants to buy a car that is $2500.

But the car's price has increased by 10%.

If Joe earns $2 everyday, after how many days can he buy the car?

1. 125 days
2. 25 days
3. 56 days
4. 32 days

5

If Ted can write two pages in q minutes, what piece of the page could he do in 8 minutes?

1. 16 + q
2. 16 − q
3. $\frac{q}{16}$
4. $\frac{16}{q}$

6

If Rosy can paint a tree in 40 minutes and Jack can paint the same tree in a quarter of the time that Rosy can.

How long will it take for Jack to paint the tree?

1. 30 minutes
2. 10 minutes
3. 45 minutes
4. 25 minutes

7

Ted wants to buy a T-shirt that has 12% off. He has $310. After buying, how much money will be left for him?

(The first price of T-shirt is $56.)

1. $653.15
2. $257.64
3. $563.12
4. $260.72

8

The sale price of a motorcycle is $4567 which is 70% of the original price. What is the original price?

1. $370.1
2. $4567
3. $6524.28
4. $5891

9

What is the value of B in equation $2\frac{B+1}{5}=3B-7$?

1. $\frac{37}{13}$
2. $-\frac{37}{13}$
3. $\frac{13}{37}$
4. $-\frac{13}{37}$

10

If Max is 8 years older than his brother, Adam, and Alfred is 3 years older than Max, and the total of their ages is 25, then how old is Alfred?

1. 13
2. 10
3. 8
4. 2

11

Mike wants to invest $5500 at 7% interest for 3 years. How much interest will he receive?

1. $260
2. $11550
3. $2205
4. $4978

12

Alex is able to sell some special cloths for $850 which was 45% profit over his cost. How much did he the clothes cost him?

1. 986.45
2. 574.32
3. 493.10
4. 981.32

13

If $m = 2n + 1$ and $n = 4c - 1$, then $m =$

1. $8c - 1$
2. $4c - 1$
3. $8c + 1$
4. $4c + 1$

14

If $2x - 4x + 3(x - 5) = 45$, then $2x - 9 =$

1. 50
2. 64
3. 15
4. 51

15

$0.6985 + 0.5897 - 0.1253 =$

1. 0.2356
2. 0.2589
3. 1.1629
4. 1.2365

16

Sam has $250. He wants to buy a cap that costs $42 and a coat that is $125. The coat has 12% off. How much money will be left for him?

1. $152
2. $256
3. $98
4. $89

17

If q = 3p – 4 and 2p = 8, then q =

1. 5
2. 6
3. 7
4. 8

18

If 5 jelly powders cost you x dollars, how many jelly powders can you purchase for 30 cents at the same rate?

1. $\frac{3}{2}x$
2. $\frac{2}{3}x$
3. $\frac{3}{2x}$
4. $\frac{2}{3x}$

19

Jason worked 20 hours this week and made $128. If he works 12 hours next week at the same pay rate, how much will he make?

1. $ 45.9
2. $ 76.8
3. $ 53.4
4. $ 91.3

20

If 2 (x + 5) – 4x + 7x = 15, then 3 – 4x

1. -1
2. 1
3. 5
4. -5

21

Lee wants to buy a history book that costs $60.00 and the sale tax where he is purchasing the book is 7.70%. She has $120. How much change will she receive back?

1. $64.62
2. $75.30
3. $ 55.38
4. $ 27.19

22

Rex sold 360 pencils and 18 pens. Pencils are sold in sets of 12 for $3.15 per pack. Pens are sold in sets of 2 for $2.50. How much would it cost to purchase these products?

1. $94.5
2. $22.5
3. $72
4. $117

23

If $x = 2$, then $x^2 \left(\dfrac{x^3}{5}\right)$

1. $\dfrac{5}{32}$
2. $\dfrac{32}{5}$
3. $\dfrac{2}{32}$
4. $\dfrac{5}{33}$

24

$4.869 \times 5.342 =$

1. 15.26
2. 26.15
3. 4.78
4. 9.32

25

What is the missing number?

(2, 18), (4, …)

1. 37
2. 38
3. 36
4. 50

26

What is the answer of $15 \div \dfrac{5}{9} =$

1. 21
2. 22
3. 23
4. 24

27

7.9 + 8.1 − 2.3 + 4.2 =

1. 14.1
2. 15.3
3. 17.9
4. 8.10

28

What is the percentage form of $\frac{30}{100}$?

1. 30%
2. 0.3%
3. 0.03%
4. 0.003%

29

0.0005 × 42300 =

1. 22.7
2. 21.15
3. 61.5
4. 23.5

30

What is 38% of 250?

1. 85
2. 95
3. 45
4. 53

31

If 7.8231 rounds to nearest hundredth, it's

1. 782.31×10^{-2}
2. 782.31×10^{2}
3. 7823.1×10^{-3}
4. 78.231×10^{-2}

32

3a − 5b + 2a + 8a − 3b =

1. 13a − 8b
2. 8b − 13a
3. 8a + 13b
4. 8a − 13b

33

What is the value of x in the equation below?

$5(x + 3) = 14x - 7$

1. 1
2. 2
3. 3
4. 4

34

Simplify $\dfrac{35a^3 b^6}{7a^2 b}$

1. $5ab^3$
2. $2ab^5$
3. $5ab^{-5}$
4. $5ab^5$

35

34% + 56% - 45% =

1. 45%
2. 78%
3. 12%
4. 65

Answer Sheet of Test #2

1.

2.

$$\frac{6}{5} - \frac{2}{3} = \frac{18-10}{15} = \frac{6}{15}$$

2.

3.

$$\frac{7}{8} - \frac{10}{4} = \frac{7-20}{8} = -\frac{13}{8}$$

3.

1.

$$\frac{863}{10} - \frac{427}{10} = \frac{436}{10} = 43.6$$

4.

1.

Initail car's price : $2500

Car's price after 10% increasing $\Rightarrow$

$2500 + 10\% \times $2500

$2500 + \dfrac{10}{100} \times 2500 = 2750

$2750 - 2500 = 250$

He earns $2 evrey day $= 250 \div 2 = 125$

125 days

5.

4.

2 pages — q minute

x — 8 minutes

$$x = \frac{2 \times 8}{q} = \frac{16}{q}$$

6.

2.

Quarter $= \dfrac{1}{4}$

$40 \times \dfrac{1}{4} = 10$ minutes

7.

4.

$100\% - 12\% = 88\%$

$56 \times 88\% = 56 \times \dfrac{88}{100} = 49.28

Price of T−shirt with 12% off $= 49.28

$310 - $49.28 = 260.72

8.

3.

$x	100
$4567	(100−30)

$$x = \frac{4567 \times 100}{70} = \frac{456700}{70} = \$6524.28$$

Original Price = $6524.28

9.

1.

$$2\frac{B+1}{5} = 3B-7 \longrightarrow 2B+2 = 5(3B-7)$$

$$2B+2 = 15B-35 \longrightarrow 2B-15B = -35-2$$

$$-13B = -37 \longrightarrow B = \frac{37}{13}$$

10.

1.

Max's age = x

Adam's age = y

Alfred's age = z

$x = y+8$, $z = x+3$

$x+y+z = 25$

$x+x-8+x+3 = 25$

$3x-5 = 25 \rightarrow 3x = 30$

$\rightarrow x = 10$

$x = y+8 \xrightarrow{x=10} y = 10-8 = 2$

$\rightarrow y = 2$

$z = x+3 \xrightarrow{x=10} z = 10+3 = 13$

$\rightarrow z = 13$

11.

2.

1 year = 12 month

3 years = 12 × 3 = 36 months

$$\frac{55000}{12} \times \frac{7}{100} = 320.83$$

$320.83 \times 36 = \$11550$

12.

2.

$x + 48\% \, x = 850$

$\to 1.48x = 850 \to x = 574.32$

13.

1.

$m = 2n+1, \, n = 4c-1$

$m = 2(4c-1)+1 = 8c-2+1$

$m = 8c-1$

14.

4.

$2x - 4x + 3(x-5) = 45$

$2x - 4x + 3x - 15 = 45$

$x - 15 = 45 \to x = 45 - 15 = 30$

$x = 30$

$2x - 9 \xrightarrow{x=30} 2(30) - 9 = 60 - 9 = 51$

15.

3.

$0.6985 + 0.5897 - 0.1253 = 1.1629$

16.

3.

Cap's price = $42

Coat's price

$100\% - 12\% = 88\%$

Coat's price $= 125 \times \dfrac{88}{100} = \$110$

$\$42 + \$100 = \$152$

$\$250 - \$152 = \$98$

17.

4.

$q = 3p - 4 \, , \, 2p = 8 \to p = 4$

$q = 3(4) - 4 = 12 - 4 = 8$

18.

3.

| 5 | $x = C(cent)100 |
| y | C 30 |

$y = \dfrac{5 \times 30}{100x} = \dfrac{15}{10x} = \dfrac{3}{2x}$

MathePathics

19.

2.

20 hours $128
12 hours   x

$x = \dfrac{128 \times 12}{20} = \$76.8$

20.

1.

$2(x+5) - 4x + 7x = 15$

$2x + 10 - 4x + 7x = 15$

$5x = 15 - 10$

$5x = 5 \rightarrow x = 1$

$3 - 4x \xrightarrow{x=1} 3 - 4(1) = -1$

21.

1.

Price of book $= \$60.00 + 7.70\%\,(\$60.00)$

$60 + \dfrac{7.70}{100}(60) = \$64.62$

$\$120 - \$64.62 = \$55.38$

22.

4.

360 pencils $\rightarrow 360 \div 12 = 30$

$30 \times \$3.15 = \$94.5$

18 pens $\rightarrow 18 \div 2 = 9$

$9 \times \$2.50 = \$22.5$

$\$94.5 + \$22.5 = \$117$

23.

2.

$x^2\left(\dfrac{x^3}{5}\right) \xrightarrow{x=2} 2^2\left(\dfrac{2^3}{5}\right) = 4\left(\dfrac{8}{5}\right)$

$\rightarrow \dfrac{32}{5}$

24.

2.

$4.896 \times 5.342 = 26.15$

25.

3.

$2 \times 9 = 18$ $4 \times 9 = 36$ $(4, 36)$

26.

1.

$15 \div \dfrac{5}{9} = 15 \times \dfrac{9}{5} = 3 \times 9 = 21$

27.
3.
$7.9 + 8.1 - 2.3 + 4.2 = 17.9$

28.
3.
$\dfrac{30}{100} = 0.03\%$

29.
2.
$0.0005 \times 42300 = \dfrac{5}{10000} \times 42300 = 21.15$

30.
2.
$\dfrac{38}{100} \times 250 = 95$

31.
1.
$7.8231 = 782.31 \times 10^{-2}$

32.
1.
$3a - 5b + 2a + 8a - 3b$

$= (3a + 2a + 8a) + (-5b - 3b)$

$= 13a - 8b$

33.
2.
$5(x+3) = 14x - 7$

$5x + 15 = 14x - 7$

$5x - 14x = -7 - 15$

$-11x = -22 \rightarrow x = 2$

34.
4.
$\dfrac{35a^3 b^6}{7a^2 b} = 5a^{(3-2)} b^{(6-1)} = 5ab^5$

35.
1.
$34\% + 56\% - 45\% = 45\%$

1

The average of a, b, and c is 2b. If two of the numbers are 53 and 68, then what is the other number?

1. 509
2. 510
3. 76
4. 98

2

What is the value of **x** in the following equation?

$2(x-3)(x+5) = 0$

1. 3, 5
2. 3, -5
3. -3, 5
4. -3, 4

3

What is the value of **7y** in the following system of equation?

$\begin{cases} x + 3y = -5 \\ 2x - y = 0 \end{cases}$

1. 10
2. -7
3. 7
4. -10

4

In which quadrant will you find ordered pairs for which x < -4 and y > 1?

1. First quadrant
2. Second quadrant
3. Third quadrant
4. Fourth quadrant

5

What is the value of **y**?

$5y - 2 > -7$

1. y > 1
2. y < 0
3. y > -1
4. y < 1

6

What are the values of **x** for which

$x^2 - 10x = 0$?

1. 0, -10
2. -10, 1
3. -1, 0
4. 0, 10

7

What is simplified form of $2x^2y + 8xy^2$?

1. $xy(x+2y)$
2. $2xy(x+4y)$
3. $2xy(x+4y)$
4. $2x(x-4y)$

8

What is the value of m?

$\frac{m+1}{2m} = 10$

1. $\frac{10}{19}$
2. $-\frac{10}{19}$
3. $\frac{19}{10}$
4. $-\frac{19}{10}$

9

$16x^4 - y^2 =$

1. $(4x-y)(4x+y)$
2. $(4x^2-y^2)(4x^2+y^2)$
3. $(x^2-y)(x^2+y)$
4. $(4x^2-y)(4x^2+y)$

10

$-9x(10x - 4x) =$

1. $53x$
2. $54x^2$
3. $51x$
4. $58x^2$

11

If you simplify $\frac{100x^2y}{25xy^3}$, your answer is

1. $4xy^2$
2. $-4xy$
3. $\frac{4x}{y}$
4. $\frac{4x}{y^2}$

12

What is the answer to the combination of the following polynomials?

$2x(4x - 6 + 3x) - 7x(x + 2)$

1. $x(x^2 - 20)$
2. $x(x - 20)$
3. $x(20 - x)$
4. $(x - 20)$

13

If you remove the greatest common factor from $21x^3y^2 + 49xy^2 + 56xy$ the answer is:

1. $xy(3x^2y + 7y + 8)$
2. $21xy(3x^2y + 7y + 8)$
3. $xy(3x^2y + y + 8)$
4. $7xy(3x^2y + 7y + 8)$

14

If $A = 2\pi rh + \pi r^2$ then $h =$

1. $h = \dfrac{\pi r^2}{A - 2\pi r}$
2. $h = \dfrac{A - \pi r^2}{2\pi r}$
3. $h = \dfrac{A + \pi r^2}{2\pi r}$
4. $h = \dfrac{A - \pi r^2}{\pi r}$

15

What is the slope of

$7x - 4x - 2y + 3 - y = 0$

1. -1
2. -3
3. 1
4. 3

16

Which of the following xy - plane is the answer to x + 3 < 4 -2x?

1.

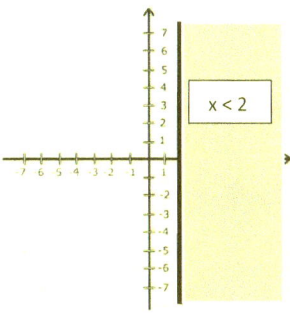

2.

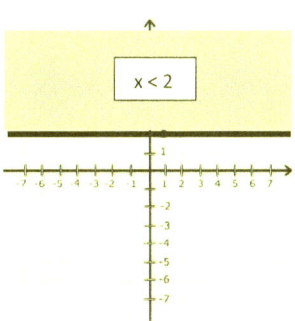

3.

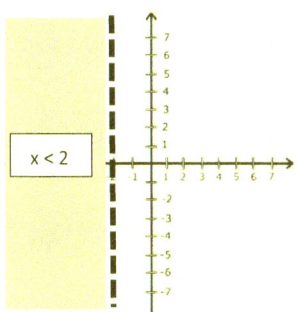

4.

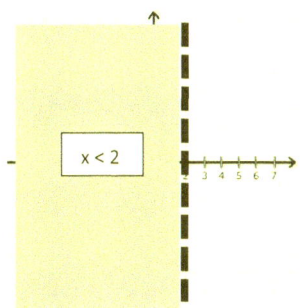

17

If A (5, 8) and B (3, 9), what is the equation of the line that passes through them?

1. $y = -\dfrac{1}{2}x + \dfrac{11}{2}$

2. $y = \dfrac{1}{2}x - \dfrac{11}{2}$

3. $y = \dfrac{1}{2}x + \dfrac{11}{2}$

4. $y = -\dfrac{1}{2}x - \dfrac{11}{2}$

18

If $f(x) = 2x^2 - 5x + 8$,

what is $f(5) - 3f(0)$?

1. 25

2. 9

3. 32

4. 5

19

If 8y = 24x + 16, m equals to:

1. 2
2. 24
3. 32
4. 16

20

$7^8 \cdot 7^5 =$

1. 7^3
2. 7^{13}
3. 49^{13}
4. 14^{13}

21

$(-3y^2)(-10y^4) =$

1. $-30y^5$
2. $30y^5$
3. $-30y^6$
4. $30y$

22

Which of the following graphs represents the answer to below inequality?

$x - 10 \geq 5$

1.
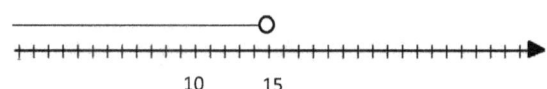

2.
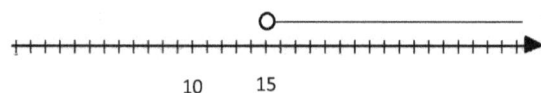

3.
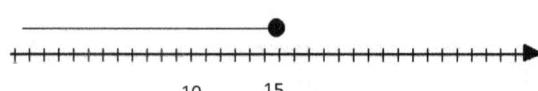

4.
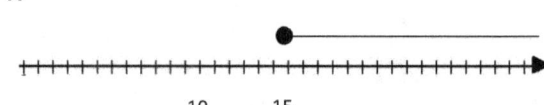

23

$3^{-4}(x-1)^{-2} =$

1. $81(x-1)^2$
2. $\dfrac{1}{9(x-1)^2}$
3. $\dfrac{81(x-1)^2}{x}$
4. $\dfrac{1}{81(x-1)^2}$

24

Which of the following is NOT a form of 13700000?

1. 13700×10^{-3}
2. 137×10^{-4}
3. 137×10^{-5}
4. 1.37×10^{-7}

25

$(5x + 3) - (2x - 10y + 7)$

1. $3x + 10y - 4$
2. $10y - 3x + 4$
3. $10y - 4 + 3x$
4. $x(16x + 1) - 4$

26

$(4x + 2)^2$

1. $16(x + 1) + 4$
2. $16x(x + 1) + 4$
3. $16x(x - 1) - 4$
4. $x(16x + 1) - 4$

27

$$\frac{2(x-1)}{(x-1)^2(x+2)}$$

1. $\dfrac{2}{(x-1)(x+2)}$
2. $\dfrac{(x-1)}{2(x+2)}$
3. $2(x-1)(x+2)$
4. $\dfrac{(x-1)}{(x+2)}$

28

$(24x^5 - 40x + 64x^3) \div 8x =$

1. $3x^4 + 8x^2 - 5$
2. $-3x^4 - 8x^2 - 5$
3. $-3x^4 + 8x^2 + 5$
4. $-3x^4 + 8x^2 - 5$

29

If $(8x^{-5})^{-3}$ is written with positive exponent, answer is

1. $\dfrac{x^5}{8}$

2. $\dfrac{-x^5}{8}$

3. $8x^5$

4. $\dfrac{1}{x^5 8}$

30

If $f(x) = 5x - 3x^2$ and $g(x) = 4x + 7$, then $2f(0) + 5g(-1)$ is

1. -12
2. 15
3. 11
4. -11

31

If $a = 2b + c$ and $b = 4c - a$, what is the value of c?

1. $c = 3a$
2. $c = 3 + a$
3. $c = \dfrac{1}{3}a$
4. $c = \dfrac{3}{a}$

32

$f(a) = \dfrac{2a+3}{5}$, $f(2) - 3f(1) =$

1. $\dfrac{8}{5}$

2. $\dfrac{5}{8}$

3. $\dfrac{8}{5}$

4. $-\dfrac{8}{5}$

33

If a circle has a 5 cm diameter, what's the half of its Area?

1. 19.625 cm²
2. 9.81 cm²
3. 78.5 cm²
4. 39.25 cm²

34

3^5=

1. 3 + 3 + 3 + 3 + 3
2. $3^{(5+5+5+5+5)}$
3. 3.3.3.3.3
4. 3×5

35

0.9856423 =

1. 9.856423×10^1
2. 9856.423×10^{-4}
3. 98564.23×10^4
4. 985642.3×10^{-6}

Answer Sheet of Test #3

1.

1.

$\dfrac{a+b+c}{3} = 210 \longrightarrow a+b+c = 630$

$a = 53$, $b = 68$, $c = ?$

$53 + 68 + c = 630 \longrightarrow c = 630 - 121 = 509$

2.

2.

$2(x^2 + 5x - 3x - 15) = 0$

$2(x^2 + 2x - 15) = 0$

$2x^2 + 4x - 30 = 0$

$\Delta = b^2 - 4ac = (4)^2 - 4(2)(-30)$

$\rightarrow 16 + 240 = 256$

$x_1 = \dfrac{-b + \sqrt{\Delta}}{2a} = \dfrac{-4 + \sqrt{256}}{2(2)} = \dfrac{-4 + 16}{4} = 3$

$x_2 = \dfrac{-b - \sqrt{\Delta}}{2a} = \dfrac{-4 - \sqrt{256}}{2(2)} = \dfrac{-4 - 16}{4} = -5$

$3, -5$

3.

4

$\begin{cases} x + 3y = -5 \\ 2x - y = 0 \longrightarrow y = 2x \end{cases}$

$x + 3y = -5 \longrightarrow x + 3(2x) = -5$

$x + 6x = -5 \longrightarrow 7x = -5$

$x = \dfrac{-5}{7}$, $y = 2x = 2(\dfrac{-5}{7}) = \dfrac{-10}{7}$

$7y = 7(\dfrac{-10}{7}) = -10$

4.

2

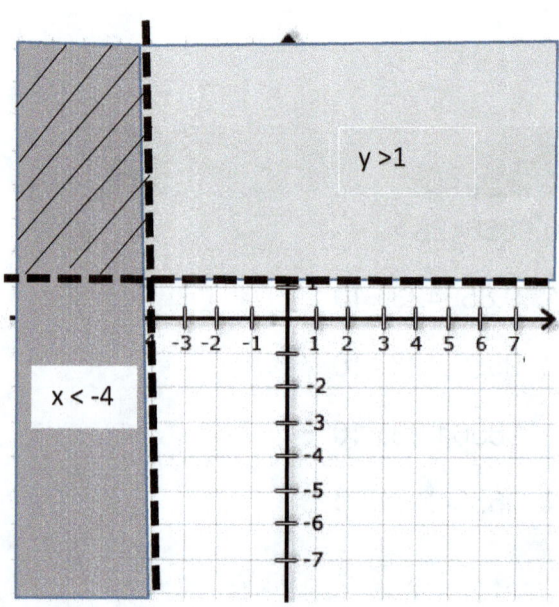

5.

3

$5y - 2 > -7 \longrightarrow 5y > -7 + 2$

$\longrightarrow 5y > -5 \xrightarrow{:5} y > -1$

6.

4

$x^2 - 10x = 0 \rightarrow x(x-10) = 0$

$\begin{cases} x = 0 \\ x - 10 = 0 \rightarrow x = 10 \end{cases}$

7.

2

$2x^2y + 8xy^2 = 2xy(x + 4y)$

8.

1

$\dfrac{m+1}{2m} = 10 \longrightarrow m + 10 = 20m$

$m - 20m = -10 \longrightarrow -19m = -10$

$m = \dfrac{10}{19}$

9.

4

$x^2 - y^2 = (x-y)(x+y)$

$16x^4 - y^2 = (4x^2 - y)(4x^2 + y)$

10.

2

$-9x(10x - 4x) = -9x(6x) = -54x^2$

11.

4

$\dfrac{100x^2y}{25xy^3} = 4x^{(2-1)}y^{(1-3)} = 4xy^{-2} = \dfrac{4x}{y^2}$

12.

2

$2x(4x - 6 + 3x) - 7x(x+2) =$

$8x^2 - 12x + 6x - 7x^2 - 14x =$

$(8x^2 - 7x^2) + (-12x + 6x - 14x)$

$x^2 - 20x = x(x - 20)$

13.

4

$21x^3y^2 + 49xy^2 + 56xy =$

$7xy(3x^2y + 7y + 8)$

14.

2

$A = 2\pi rh + \pi r^2 \longrightarrow 2\pi rh = A - \pi r^2$

$h = \dfrac{\pi r^2}{A - 2\pi r}$

15.

1

$7x - 4x - 2y + 3 - y = 0$

$-3x - 3y + 3 = 0$

$-3y = 3x - 3$

$y = mx + b$

$\xrightarrow{\div -3} y = -x + 1$

$m = -1$

16.

4

$x + 3 < 9 - 2x \longrightarrow x + 2x < 9 - 3$

$\longrightarrow 3x < 6 \longrightarrow x < 2$

17.

4

$m = \dfrac{9 - 8}{3 - 5} = \dfrac{1}{-2} = -\dfrac{1}{2}$

$(5, 8) \longrightarrow y - 8 = -\dfrac{1}{2}(x - 5)$

$y = -\dfrac{1}{2}x + \dfrac{5}{2} + 8 \longrightarrow y = -\dfrac{1}{2}x - \dfrac{11}{2}$

18.

2

$f(5) = 2(5)^2 - 5(5) + 8 = 50 - 25 + 8 = 33$

$f(0) = 2(0)^2 - 5(0) + 8 = 0 - 0 + 8 = 8$

$f(5) - 3f(0) = 33 - 3 \times 8 = 33 - 24 = 9$

19.

1

$8y = 24x + 16 \; , \; y = mx + b$

$\xrightarrow{\div 8} y = 3x + 2 \rightarrow m = 3$

20.

2

$7^8 \cdot 7^5 = 7^{(8+5)} = 7^{13}$

21.

3

$(-3y^2)(-10y^4) = -30y^{2+4} = -30y^6$

22.

4

$x - 10 \geq 5$

$x \geq 5 + 10 \longrightarrow x \geq 15$

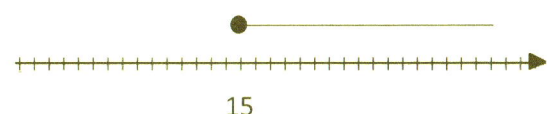
15

23.

4

$3^{-4}(x-1)^{-2} = \dfrac{1}{3^4(x-1)^2} = \dfrac{1}{81(x-1)^2}$

24.

3

$1370000 = 137 \times 10^{-5}$

$13700000 \neq 137 \times 10^5$

25.

1

$(5x+3) - (2x - 10y + 7) =$

$5x + 3 - 2x + 10y - 7 =$

$5x - 2x - 10y + 3 - 7 =$

$3x - 10y - 4$

26.

2

$(a+b)^2 = a^2 + 2ab + b^2$

$(4x + 2)^2 = (4x)^2 + 2(4x)(2) + (2)^2$

$(4x + 2)^2 = 16x^2 + 16x + 4$

$(4x + 2)^2 = 16x(x+1) + 4$

$16(x+1) + 4$

27.

1

$\dfrac{2(x-1)}{(x-1)^2(x+2)} = \dfrac{2}{(x+2)}(x-1)^{1-2}$

$= \dfrac{2}{(x+2)}(x-1)^{-1} = \dfrac{2}{(x-1)(x+2)}$

28.

4

$$\frac{-24x^5 - 40x + 64x^3}{8x} = \frac{-24x^5}{8x} - \frac{40x}{8x} + \frac{64x^3}{8x}$$

$$= -3x^{(5-1)} - 5 + 8x^{(3-1)} = -3x^4 - 5 + 8x^2 =$$

$$= -3x^4 + 8x^2 - 5$$

29.

1

$$8x^{-5} = \frac{8}{x^5} \longrightarrow \left(\frac{8}{x^5}\right)^{-3} = \frac{1}{\left(\frac{8}{x^5}\right)^3} = \frac{x^5}{8}$$

30.

2

$f(0) = 5(0) - 3(0) = 0 \quad 2f(0) = 2(0) = 0$

$g(-1) = 4(-1) + 7 = -4 + 7 = 3$

$2f(0) = 2(0) = 0$

$5g(-1) = 5(3) = 15$

$2f(0) + 5g(-1) = 0 + 15 = 15$

31.

3

$a = 2(4c - a) \longrightarrow a = 8c - 2a$

$3a = 9c \xrightarrow{\div 3} a = 3c \longrightarrow c = \frac{1}{3}a$

32.

4

$$f(a) = \frac{2a + 3}{5}$$

$$f(2) = \frac{2(2) + 3}{5} = \frac{4 + 3}{5} = \frac{7}{5}$$

$$f(1) = \frac{2(1) + 3}{5} = \frac{5}{5} = 1$$

$$f(2) - 3f(1) = \frac{7}{5} - 3(1) = \frac{7 - 15}{5} = \frac{-8}{5}$$

33.

1

$$A = \pi r^2 = \pi \left(\frac{d}{2}\right)^2 = 3.14 \left(\frac{5}{2}\right)^2 = 19.625\, cm^2$$

$$\text{half} = \frac{1}{2} \longrightarrow \frac{A}{2} = \frac{19.625}{2} = 9.81\, cm^2$$

34.

3

$3^1 \cdot 3^1 \cdot 3^1 \cdot 3^1 \cdot 3^1 = 3^{(1+1+1+1+1)} = 3^5$

35.

1

$0.9856423 = 9.856423 \times 10^1$

MathePathics

1

What is the value of x in the following equation?

$x + 23 - 10x = 2x + 1$

1. 1
2. 2
3. 3
4. 4

2

If $f(x) = \dfrac{5}{x+8}$ then $f(12) - 2f(2)$ is...

1. $\dfrac{1}{4}$
2. $\dfrac{2}{3}$
3. $-\dfrac{1}{4}$
4. $-\dfrac{3}{4}$

3

Which of the following graphs is for

$y = x + 3$?

1.

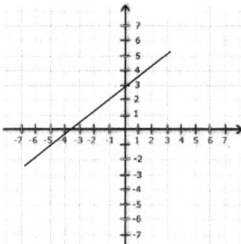

2.

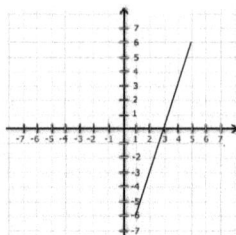

3.

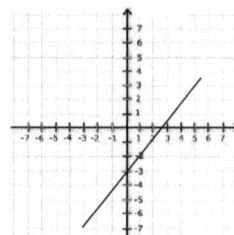

4.

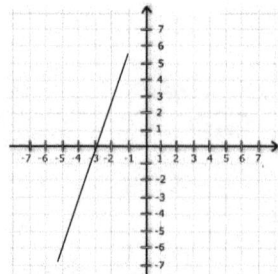

4

What is sum of 58% of 400 and 28% of 500?

1. 371
2. 372
3. 373
4. 374

5

If 85847 rounds to nearest thousands, it's …

1. 858.47×10^3
2. 8.584×10^3
3. 85.877×10^3
4. 8584.7×10^1

6

$$\frac{22a^3 + 16a^2 - 32a}{2a} =$$

1. $11a^2 + 8a - 16$
2. $11a^2 + 8a - 16a$
3. $-11a^2 + 8a - 16a$
4. $11a^3 + 8a - 16a$

7

If $m = 2a - 3$, $a = \dfrac{4b}{5}$ and $b = 10$, then m + 2 ….

1. 8
2. 13
3. 15
4. 14

8

Rosy has $500. She wants to buy a $2 book by 2% off and a $150 coat by 13% off. How much money will be left for her?

1. $11.76
2. $130.5
3. $142.76
4. $377.74

9

If $5a^{-5}+3^{-1}a^{-5}$ is written in positive exponent, the answer is ….

1. $\dfrac{15-a}{3a^6}$

2. $\dfrac{15+a}{3a^6}$

3. $\dfrac{-15+a}{3a^6}$

4. $\dfrac{15+a}{3a^4}$

10

What is the value of $\dfrac{2B+3}{5}=6B-9$?

1. $\dfrac{12}{7}$

2. $-\dfrac{12}{7}$

3. $\dfrac{7}{12}$

4. $-\dfrac{7}{12}$

11

Which graph represents the answer of below inequality?

$3y-5\geq 7$

1.

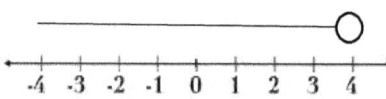

2.

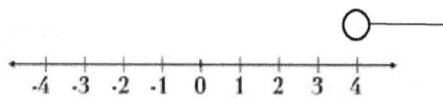

3.

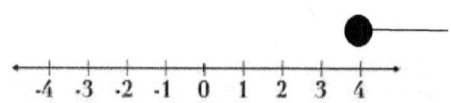

4.

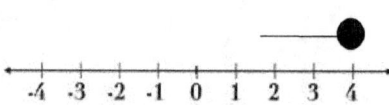

12

Alex works 8 hours a day and makes $50. If he makes $200, how many hours did he work?

1. 31
2. 32
3. 33
4. 34

13

$$\frac{4}{3} - \frac{7}{8} + \frac{5}{6} =$$

1. $\frac{30}{24}$
2. $-\frac{30}{24}$
3. $\frac{31}{24}$
4. $-\frac{31}{24}$

14

What is the square of 3 + 5?

1. 16
2. 32
3. 64
4. 36

15

$\frac{58}{1000}$ equals to:

1. 0.58
2. 0.058
3. 0.0058
4. 0.0058

16

What is the third sentence of the below sequence?

$$\frac{5}{8}, 1, \ldots\ldots, \frac{64}{5}$$

1. $\frac{5}{8}$
2. $\frac{7}{8}$
3. $\frac{4}{5}$
4. $\frac{8}{5}$

17

$2(3^2+5) \times 7(5-8) =$

1. 28
2. 21
3. 588
4. 498

18

According to the graph below, what is slope of the line?

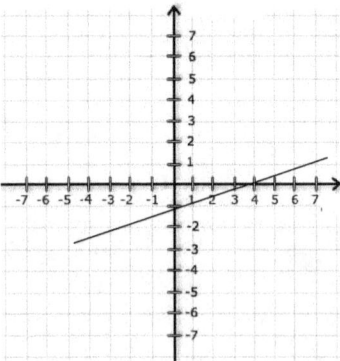

1. $\frac{1}{2}$
2. $-\frac{1}{2}$
3. 2
4. -2

19

Ted buys a circle table with a diameter of 5.4 m. What is the quarter of its area?

1. 22.89
2. 26.89
3. 5.72
4. 7.89

20

$f(x)=x^2-1$ and $g(x)=5x+2$. What is $f(-1)+g(-2)$?

1. -8
2. 8
3. 4
4. -4

21

The speed of a car is calculated from the equation below. When does it stop?

$V(t)=5t^2+3t-2$

1. 0.2
2. 0.3
3. 0.4
4. 0.5

22

If $a = \dfrac{2b+3}{4}$, then b is

1. $b = \dfrac{3-4a}{2}$
2. $b = \dfrac{4a-3}{2}$
3. $b = \dfrac{4a+3}{2}$
4. $b = \dfrac{4a-3}{-2}$

23

$(x-3)(x+5) =$

1. $x^2 - 2x + 15$
2. $x^2 + 2x + 15$
3. $x^2 - 2x - 15$
4. $x^2 + 2x - 15$

24

The price of 2 notebooks is $12. What is the price of 8 notebooks?

1. 12
2. 42
3. 48
4. 36

25

If $f(x) = 2x - 5$, $f(a) = 3$, $a - 6$ is

1. 2
2. 42
3. 48
4. 36

26

Sum of Alex and Andrew's grade is 58. Jack's grade is 10 points more than Andrew's. How much Alex's grade is less than Jack's?

1. 68 + x
2. 58 − x
3. 68 − x
4. 58 + x

27

What is the missing number in the sequence below?

8 , 11 , 14 , ... , 20

1. 16
2. 17
3. 18
4. 19

28

$$\frac{30x^2y^3}{5x^3y^7} =$$

1. $\dfrac{6}{xy^4}$
2. $-\dfrac{6}{xy^4}$
3. $\dfrac{6}{xy^3}$
4. $\dfrac{6}{xy}$

29

If A (5, 8) and B (-3, -1) lay on a line, what is the equation of the line?

1. y = x + 1
2. y = x + 2
3. y = x – 1
4. y = -x + 1

30

According to the tables below, 80 mm is

mm	cm
10	1

m	cm
1	100

1. 0.8 m
2. 0.008 m
3. 8
4. 0.08 m

31

$f(x) = x^2 + 2^x$, $f(3) =$

1. 15
2. 17
3. 16
4. 14

32

$0.58 - 0.24 + 0.37 =$

1. 0.68
2. 0.42
3. 0.39
4. 0.71

33

If $a = 4b + 2c$ and $b = c - a$, what is the value of c?

1. c = 5b
2. c = -5b
3. c = 4 b
4. c = -4 b

34

$2a + 9b - 8a - 5b + 11a =$

1. 16a – 8b
2. 15a + 5b
3. 9a + 3b
4. 17a + 4b

35

What is the mean of numbers below?

98	24
83	38

1. 25.77
2. 56.32
3. 48.78
4. 77.25

Answer Sheet of Test #4

1.

2.

$x + 23 - 10x = 2x + 1$

$x - 10x - 2x = 1 - 23$

$-11x = -22$

$x = 2$

2.

4.

$f(12) = \dfrac{5}{12+8} = \dfrac{5}{20} = \dfrac{1}{4}$

$f(2) = \dfrac{5}{2+8} = \dfrac{5}{10} = \dfrac{1}{2}$

$f(12) - 2f(2) = \dfrac{1}{4} - 2(\dfrac{1}{2}) = \dfrac{-3}{4}$

3.

1

$y = mx + b \longrightarrow y = x + 3 \longrightarrow b = 3$

4.

2

$\dfrac{58}{100} \times 400 + \dfrac{28}{100} \times 500 =$

$(58 \times 4) + (28 \times 5) = 372$

5.

3

$85847 = 85.847 \times 10^3$

6.

1

$\dfrac{22a^3 + 16a^2 - 32a}{2a} =$

$\dfrac{22a^3}{2a} + \dfrac{16a^2}{2a} - \dfrac{32a}{2a} =$

$11a^2 + 8a - 16$

7.

3

$b = 10 \longrightarrow a = \dfrac{4(10)}{5} = 8$

$m = 2(8) - 3 = 16 - 3 = 13$

$m + 2 = 13 + 2 = 15$

8.

4

The price of book : $\$12 \times (100\% - 2\%) =$

$\$12 \times \dfrac{98}{100} = \$11.76$

The price of coat : $\$150 \times (100\% - 13\%) =$

$150 \times \dfrac{87}{100} = \$130.5$

$500 - (11.76 + 130.5) =$

$500 - 142.26 = 377.74$

9.
2

$5a^{-5} + 3^{-1}a^{-5} = \dfrac{5}{a^6} + \dfrac{1}{3a^5} = \dfrac{15+a}{3a^6}$

10.
1

$\dfrac{2B+3}{5} = 6B - 9$

$2B + 3 = 5(6B - 9)$

$2B + 3 = 30B - 45$

$2B - 30B = -45 - 3$

$-28B = -48$

$B = \dfrac{-48}{-18} = \dfrac{7}{12}$

11.
3

$3y - 5 \geq 7 \longrightarrow 3y \geq 7 + 5$

$3y \geq 12 \longrightarrow y \geq 4$

12.
2

8 hours $50
x hours $200

$x = \dfrac{8 \times 200}{50} = 32$

13.
3

$\dfrac{4}{3} - \dfrac{7}{8} + \dfrac{5}{6} = \dfrac{32 - 21 + 20}{24} = \dfrac{31}{24}$

14.
3

$3 + 5 = 8 \rightarrow 8^2 = 64$

15.
2

$\dfrac{58}{1000} = 0.058$

16.
4

$\dfrac{5}{8} \xrightarrow{\times \frac{8}{5}} 1 \xrightarrow{\times \frac{8}{5}} \dfrac{8}{5} \xrightarrow{\times \frac{8}{5}} \dfrac{64}{5}$

17.

3

$2(3^2+5) \times 7(5-8) =$

$3^2 + 5 = 9 + 5 = 14$

$5 - 8 = 3$

$(2 \times 14) \times (7 \times 3) =$

$281 \times 21 = 588$

18.

1

$m = \dfrac{0-(-1)}{4-0} = \dfrac{2}{4} = \dfrac{1}{2}$

19.

3

$d = 5.4 m \longrightarrow d = 2r \longrightarrow r = \dfrac{d}{2}$

$A = \pi r^2 = 3.14(2.7)^2 = 22.89$

quarter: $\dfrac{1}{4}$

$A = 22.89 \times \dfrac{1}{4} = 5.72$

20.

1

$f(-1) = (-1)^2 - 1 = 1 - 1 = 0$

$g(-2) = 5(-2) + 2 = -10 + 2 = -8$

$f(-1) + g(-2) = 0 - 8 = -8$

21.

2

$5t^2 + 3t - 2 = 0 \longrightarrow$

$\Delta = (3)^2 - 4(5)(-5) = 9 + 25 = 36$

$t_1 = \dfrac{-3 + \sqrt{36}}{10} = \dfrac{-3+6}{10} = 0.3$

$t_2 = \dfrac{-3 - \sqrt{36}}{10} = \dfrac{-3-6}{10} = -0.9 (t > 0) \quad \otimes$

22.

2

$a = \dfrac{2b+3}{4} \longrightarrow 4a = 2b + 3$

$2b = 4a - 3 \longrightarrow b = \dfrac{4a-3}{2}$

23.
4

$(x-3)(x+5) = x^2 + 5x - 3x - 15$

$x^2 + 2x - 15$

24.
3

2 notebooks $12
8 notebooks x

$x = \dfrac{8 \times 12}{2} = 48$

25.
2

$f(a) = 3 \longrightarrow 2(a) - 5 = 3$

$\longrightarrow 2a = 3 + 5 \longrightarrow a = 4$

$a - 6 = 4 - 6 = -2$

26.
2

Alex's grade = x

Andrew's grade = y

Jack's grade = z

$x + y = 58$

$z = 10 + y$

$y = 58 - x \rightarrow z = 68 - x$

27.
2

$8 \xrightarrow{+3} 11 \xrightarrow{+3} 14 \xrightarrow{+3} 17 \xrightarrow{+3} 20$

28.
1

$\dfrac{30 x^2 y^3}{5 x^3 y^7} = 6 x^{(2-3)} y^{(3-7)}$

$= 6x^{-1} y^{-4} = \dfrac{6}{xy^4}$

29.
3

$m = \dfrac{-1 - 8}{-3 - 6} = 1$

$y - 8 = 1(x - 5)$

$y = x - 5 + 8 = x + 3$

$y = x + 3$

30.
4

$\dfrac{80}{1000} = 0.08 \, m$

31.

2

$f(x) = 3^2 + 2^3 = 9 + 8 = 17$

32.

4

$0.58 - 0.24 + 0.37 = 0.71$

33.

2

$b = c - a \longrightarrow c = b + a = b + 4b + 2c$

$\longrightarrow c = 5b + 2c \longrightarrow c - 2c = 5b$

$-c = 5b \longrightarrow c = 5b$

34.

4

$2a + 9b - 8a - 5b + 11a$

$2a - 8a + 11a + 9b - 5b =$

$17a + 4b$

35.

4

$\dfrac{98 + 24 + 104 + 83}{4} = 77.25$

www.ingramcontent.com/pod-product-compliance
Lightning Source LLC
Chambersburg PA
CBHW060243240426
43673CB00047B/1871